A HISTORY OF AMERICAN BUSINESS CYCLES

Thomas Kevin Swift

Contents

Preface and Acknowledgments 1

1 On Business Cycles 7

Introduction 7
Understanding and Defining the Business Cycle .8
Stages of the Business Cycle 10
The Role of the Entrepreneur 24
Law of Markets. 27
Internal Forces: The Cause of the Business Cycle 30
Inflation has Different Meanings 39
Credit Disturbances as a Cause of the Business Cycle 40
Other External Forces and the Business Cycle .43
Lengths and Types of Business Cycles. 46
Signs of Peaks and Troughs 52

2 On Measuring Business Activity. 57

Introduction 57
Need for a Measure of Business Activity 58
Concept of Gross Output. 63
A New Measure of Real Business Activity 66

3 Revolutionary War to Civil War 75

Introduction 75
Prelude: The American Revolution. 77

Cycle 0: Depressed Conditions and Emergence of a New Republic.....80
Cycle 1: Seaborne Commerce and the Panic of 1796-97 86
Cycle 2: Carrying Trade Prosperity, Peace of Amiens, and the
    Recession of 1801-03...92
Cycle 3: European War, Maritime Commerce, and the Embargo
    Depression of 1807-09 95
Cycle 4: European War, Restricted Carrying Trade, and the Brief
    Recession of 1812...101
Cycle 5: War of 1812, Post-War Depression, Expansion, and the
    Panic of 1819...103
Cycle 6: Era of Good Feeling (I) and the 1822-23 Recession 113
Cycle 7: Era of Good Feeling (II) and the Panic of 1825.............115
Cycle 8: Jacksonian Era and the 1833-34 Recession 118
Cycle 9: The Panic of 1837 122
Cycle 10: Brief Boom, the Panic of 1839, America's First Great
    Depression, and Debt Repudiation............................127
Cycle 11: The Mexican American War and the Mild Recession of
    1846 134
Cycle 12: Mexican-American War and Crisis in Europe.............137
Cycle 13: Post-War, Gold Rush, and Railroad Prosperity.............140
Cycle 14: Panic of 1857 144
Cycle 15: Prelude to Civil War and the Succession Recession of
    1860-61 148

4   Civil War to World War II 151

Introduction 151
Cycle 16: Civil War Prosperity and the Primary Post-War Depression ..155
Cycle 17: Recovery and Secondary Post-War Depression.............160
Cycle 18: Panic of 1873 and the Long Depression...................161
Cycle 19: Gold Resumption Prosperity and the Crisis/Depression
    of 1884...168
Cycle 20: Recovery and Railroad Prosperity I 171
Cycle 21: Railroad Prosperity II
    and the Panic of 1890.......................................173
Cycle 22: The Panic of 1893 176
Cycle 23: Revival of 1895 and the Silver Campaign Depression.......180
Cycle 24: "Splendid Little War" Prosperity and Mild Post-War
    Recession...182
Cycle 25: Merger Prosperity and the Rich Man's Panic of 1903.......184
Cycle 26: Corporate Prosperity and the Panic of 1907..............186
Cycle 27: Recovery and Mild Panic of 1910-11.....................191
Cycle 28: Progressive Era and the War Recession...................193
Cycle 29: War Prosperity and the 1918-19 Influenza Pandemic.......197

Cycle 30: The Forgotten Depression. 204
Cycle 31: Recovery, the Roaring 20s,
  and the 1923-24 Recession. 210
Cycle 32: Coolidge Prosperity and the 1926-27 Recession. 214
Cycle 33: Bull Market Boom, Stock Market Crash, and the Great
  Depression 218
Cycle 34: Slow Recovery, Experimentation, and FDR's Depression 228
Cycle 35: War Prosperity and Transition to a Consumer Economy . . .237

5   Post-World War II to the Present 245

Introduction 245
Cycle 36: Transition to Consumer Economy and Brief Recession
  of 1949 250
Cycle 37: Korean War Prosperity and Post-War Recession 254
Cycle 38: Golden Age of American Prosperity and Recession of 1958. . .257
Cycle 39: End of 1950s and Mild Recession of 1960-61 260
Cycle 40: The Go-Go 1960s, Heyday of Keynesian Economics,
  the Rise of Inflation, and Recession of 1970. .262
Cycle 41: Wage and Price Controls,
  the Decoupling from Gold, Inflation,
  Oil Price Shock, and Recession of 1973-75. 268
Cycle 42: Stagflation, Second Oil Price Shock and 1980 Recession 274
Cycle 43: Stagflation, Second Oil Price Shock, the 1980 Recession
  and Volcker, the Taming of Inflation, and the 1981-82 Recession . .279
Cycle 44: The Heyday of Supply-Side Economics, a Long Expansion,
  the Gulf War, and 1990-91 Recession 282
Cycle 45: The Great Moderation and Long Expansion of the 1990s,
  and the Internet Bubble and Bust. 288
Cycle 46: The Housing Bubble and Bust, and the Great Financial
  Crisis 294
Cycle 47: Slow, Long Economic Recovery and the COVID Recession. .301
Cycle 48: From the Pandemic: The Start of a New Cycle 312

Epilogue. 317

Bibliography. 323

About the Author. 329

Preface and Acknowledgments

The genesis for this book was during my graduate studies at Case Western Reserve University (CWRU) in the 1970s where I developed an interest in business cycles. It was possibly before that as a chart of booms and busts titled *American Business Activity Since 1790* was often published in various American high school and college American history texts. I had found the chart fascinating and would later learn that it was developed by Leonard P. Ayres (1935) and was a staple of the *Business Bulletin* published for decades by The Cleveland Trust Company.

Economics had fundamentally changed (and not in a good way) after the publication of Keynes' *General Theory of Employment, Interest and Money* (1936), and the older theories of the business cycle and the analytical approaches to assessing business cycles had long fallen out of favor by the 1970s. The Sears Library at CWRU provided a table of books taken out of circulation offered for sale at 10 to 25 cents apiece. During my graduate studies, I purchased a variety of discarded texts on business cycles. Some were classics, and some were by relatively unknown authors. All helped in some way with my economic thinking because it is the cycle (and where we are in it) that is important. I also managed to buy (and read) such texts dealing with practical foundry management and similar applied texts, which helped during my career as a business econo-mist and consultant to industry.

In my career, in addition to my focus on industry economics, I was also intrigued by the interaction of markets, industries, and the tactical and strategic responses of companies to the business cycle. While many business economists focus on analysis and fore-casts of key U.S. economic variables (real GDP and its components, interest rates, inflation, income, employment, industrial production, house prices, etc.), I concentrated on the interaction of strategy and economic developments and industry dynamics within this cyclical context. I've found the influence of the business cycle to be of greater importance, and more interesting and rewarding. Working as a consultant to industry confirmed the importance of the business cycle as a critical determinant of corporate performance in general, and profit and loss, as well as equity performance over the intermediate term.

What happens today is the result of events of yesterday, and what will happen tomorrow will be the effect of causes presently operating. That is, what happens occurs as the consequence of previous states of things, and the predetermination of economic developments is predicated on sound knowledge of existing conditions. This forms the basis of intelligent forecasting.

The purpose of this book is to examine the various business cycles since the formation of the United States in 1789. At the time of this writing, I count 47 complete business cycles. The 48th commenced in April 2020 after the short (two months) and deep recession that started in February 2020 when the advent of the coronavirus pandemic was fostered by government-mandated lock-downs of wide swaths of the economy. For convenience, I count cycles beginning at a trough in real gross output. I then define the complete cycle as from trough to trough. This makes sense since the seeds of the downswing of the cycle (recession) are often sown in the previous upswing (recovery and expansion).

This book uses a measure of economic activity — a monthly index of the volume of (or real) gross output — developed by the author to gauge business cycles. This monthly index is better than quarterly measures of GDP and in a way just as comprehensive. Although a multitude of measures is preferred, a paucity of time series exists. As is appropriate, measures of the output of leading industries are provided.

I was a history major and never took an economics course as an undergraduate. At my first job, I was at a meeting in Milwaukee and had some spare time. I wandered into a bookstore and found a copy of Samuel Hollander's *Economics of Adam Smith.* I picked it up because I had heard of this Adam Smith and thought knowing something about economics might help in a business career. I bought it, read it, and found economics to be fascinating. In 2012, I tracked Samuel Hollander down (he had retired) and thanked him. My graduate macroeconomics education was largely Keynesian, with a little monetarism thrown in. In my first job out of graduate school, I found that Keynesian economics didn't explain the real world of the early 1980s. So, I went back to the classical economists and the students of the business cycle. The approach in this book uses the framework of classical economics to examine the business cycle. There are other approaches (Keynesian, monetarist, etc.), however, that focus on demand. These are not included in this book.

My framework for understanding the economy starts with this production side of the economy: the entrepreneur (in the original sense of the word) and the law of markets. I view recessions as a failure in the structure of supply and demand and credit imbalances. Downswings are fostered by entrepreneurs miscalculating what consumers wish to buy, thus causing unsold goods to pile up (i.e., inventories), production to be cut, employment and incomes to fall, and finally consumer spending to drop. These failures in the structure of supply and demand are usually fostered by "loose" money and credit creation.

This book is meant to supplement popular texts on American history and will also prove useful to business leaders, practicing business economists, investors, public policymakers, and others. "All happy families are alike; each unhappy family is unhappy in its own way" is the opening sentence of Tolstoy's classic novel *Anna Karenina*. Like unhappy families, no two business cycles are the same.[1] There are many ways for industry and market level imbalances to arise and for money and credit inflation to foster boom and bust episodes. That said, there are many similarities among cycles, and a study of past cycles can inform the present and provide a better assessment of the future. In my view if you don't see the big picture, you won't see the next cycle. Our knowledge is often based on what we experience, a small chapter in the sweeping history of America, which guides our view of the world, and a reason we often miss the tides and timing of economic movements. Studying business cycle history makes business leaders, investors, and others better prepared to weather cyclical vicissitudes. My specialty is in business economics, and I have always viewed that as the integration of economic theory with business practice to facilitate decision-making, problem-solving, and planning by management. In addition to integrating corporate culture with strategy, assessing changing market dynamics/industry structure and turns in the business cycle are the major tasks of outstanding business leadership that determine success. Understanding the past is essential to preparing for the future.

A knowledge of past cycles proved fruitful when the coronavirus pandemic and associated lockdowns fostered a recession in early 2020. I was quickly able to assess what happened during the 1918-19 influenza epidemic and the short seven-month recession associated with that episode. Lessons drawn provided insight for

---

[1] I likely came up with the idea to use this quote from Ed Yardeni, a brilliant business economist, and president of Yardeni Research, Inc., a provider of global investment strategy and asset allocation analyses and recommendations.

potential scenarios in 2020. Knowledge of the past supports good forecasting and decision making.

The current research does not pretend to develop new knowledge or explore theory, but to provide a clear, concise, and readable history of business cycles in the United States. I write this book so that it will be accessible to a broad readership. For this reason, I avoid discussion of previous scholarship and employ limited footnotes and no other academic conventions. Academic and technical terms are avoided as much as possible, and this book is not meant to be scholarly research. I do draw upon some of the great economic historians and business cycle scholars. I "plough no new fields" and claim no original thought, but rather harvest the work of others listed under Bibliography in the back of the book. The cycles since 1970, however, do reflect the records and recollections of this participant in history. My hope is that the current research will inspire others to reconsider the past. I am inspired by two quotations, one ancient and one modern:

> "...and there is nothing new under the sun."
> —*Ecclesiastes 1:9*

> "A knowledge of the past prepares us for the crisis
> of the present and the challenge of the future."
> —*President John F. Kennedy*

Chapter 1 presents a review of business cycles; what they are, what happens during the cycle, and a summary of orthodox theory explaining the cycle. Chapter 2 presents a review of gross output and a short summary of the data sources and methodology. Chapters 3 through 5 provide a short history of the business cycles during the post-Revolutionary War through the end of the Civil War, from the Civil War through the end of World War II, and in the post-World War II period until the present. Each chapter will include sub-chapters on each cycle, as illustrated by the index of the volume of real gross output and other relevant data, as well as a succinct history of events and distinctive characteristics of each.

My economic thinking is influenced by Adam Smith, David Ricardo, Jean Baptiste Say, Francis Wayland, Arthur Latham Perry, Alfred Marshall, Joseph Shield Nicholson, Henry Clay, and most recently, Milton Friedman, Arthur Laffer, Thomas Sowell, and Steven Kates, and, of course, Chauncey Gardiner. I am forever indebted to the business cycle research of Arthur B. Adams, Leonard P. Ayres, Gottfried Haberler, Edward C. Harwood, Clement Juglar, Philip A. Klein, Frederick Lavington, Wesley C. Mitchell, Geoffrey H. Moore, Joseph A. Schumpeter, and Carl Snyder. And Lakshman Achuthan of the Economic Cycle Research Institute (ECRI), who showed me that the business cycle approach to forecasting turning points was still relevant.

I am grateful to Susan Hoffer McMillan, my editor and renown author and historian. I am particularly grateful to Emma Ruth Nantz (my best student ever) who reviewed the draft and provided essential final editing. I'm equally indebted to Anne Malarich for her advice on publishing. I also want to thank Jenna Swift for reviewing an early draft of several chapters. My biggest thanks are due to my wife Sherry, for her patience throughout this project. Finally, I'm thankful for everyone who reads this book.

CHAPTER 1

On Business Cycles

Introduction

Many forces are constantly operating in the world of commerce, industry, trade, and finance that comprise business.[2] Business conditions are never static. They are constantly undergoing change. Changes occur in some branches of business which do not align with corresponding changes in other branches. Forces determining the demand for a given good operate independently of forces determining supply, with the result that the market for the good is disrupted until a change in prices can bring it back into balance. This is the essence of price discovery, which is essential for economic efficiency. Both supply and demand provide for this price discovery within markets.

---

[2] When I refer to business, I am referring to all industries and aspects of commerce, industry, trade and finance. In constructing the index of the volume of gross output that is used in the research, for example, I've used data from 156 distinct industries covering the spectrum of economic sectors, from agriculture to services.

Forecasting is seeing in advance or anticipating the direction of these forces, these future conditions, and trends. Success is knowing what is going to happen to business conditions in advance of others. The purpose of this volume is to better understand and analyze these forces so that an intelligent opinion may be framed to their effect.

Understanding and Defining the Business Cycle

Known as alternative periods of prosperity and decline — of business activity and dullness — business cycles are not new. Genesis 41 records the seven fat years and seven lean years of Pharaoh's dream, which Joseph interpreted. This was perhaps the first record of boom and bust, prosperity and decline. Boom-and-bust cycles (and financial panics and crises) occurred in the ancient, medieval, and into our modern era. These cycles can foster powerful social consequences, in addition to the usual economic outcomes.

The occurrence of these cycles has been noted for centuries, and the underlying causes have attracted the attention of leading economists, from Petty to Smith, to Ricardo, Mill, Mitchell, Keynes, and others. The birth of the business cycle can be located in England soon after the Glorious Revolution of the closing decades of the seventeenth century. Sir William Petty (1623-1687) had referred to them as successions of "dearth and plenty." A wide variance of opinion exists as to the cause of these fluctuations in business activity an even greater diversity of opinion exists on whether or how these cycles can be controlled.

The modern concept of the business cycle emerged in the early twentieth century and was largely completed mid-century by Wesley C. Mitchell and Arthur F. Burns. They took the indicator approach that uses cyclical economic indicators to explore patterns of economic fluctuations. Their definition:

"Business cycles are a type of fluctuation found in the aggregate economic activity of nations that organize their work mainly in business enterprises: a cycle consists of expansions occurring at about the same time in many economic activities, followed by similarly general recessions, contractions, and revivals which merge into the expansion phase of the next cycle; this sequence of changes is recurrent but not periodic; in duration business cycles vary from more than one year to ten or twelve years; they are not divisible into shorter cycles of similar character with amplitudes approximating their own." Burns and Mitchell, 1946

The "two quarters of declining GDP" is not an adequate definition, nor a proper criterion for a recession. In fact, the 2001 recession was not marked by two successive declines in quarterly GDP. Rather, the historical dates of U.S. business cycle peaks and troughs are based on the consensus of the dates of the peaks and troughs in the broad measures of GDP, as well as industrial output, employment, real (i.e., inflation-adjusted) personal income (less transfer payments), and real business sales, among other metrics. These properly mark the start- and end-dates of recessions. That is, the peaks and troughs. The Dating Committee of the National Bureau of Economic Research (NBER) is the arbiter of peaks and troughs, and maintains an up-to-date list of business cycle dates, which is available at www.nber.org. I have used NBER's dating of business cycles (peaks and troughs) back to 1854. I also calculate the changes in real gross output using the NBER dates. For cycles prior to 1854, I suggest my own business cycle dates.

Referred to as trade cycles in the United Kingdom and economic cycles more broadly, business cycles are fluctuations in the movement in aggregate economic activity as measured by the gross domestic product (GDP) and other indicators (measures). Cycles refer to a series of stages in economic activity as it expands and contracts. They are intervals of expansion followed by contraction in economic activity. The idea that there is any regularity to these cycles is not true. In this sense, there is no such thing as a business cycle, as there is no circle of events through which business must pass. There are, however, similarities among different periods of expansion and contraction through time and also among different industries and sectors.

Stages of the Business Cycle

With a knowledge of the stage and characteristics of business cycles, a means of assessing the current situation and the likely future is possible. Commerce, industry, trade, and finance (i.e., business) at any point in time is either in one of two stages – a period of expanding activity or a period of declining activity. In the 19th and early 20th centuries, these were referred to as 1) prosperity and 2) depression. I employ the terms upswing and downswing and prefer the simplicity of a two-stage rather than four- or even six-stage cycles suggested by some business cycle theorists and practitioners.[3] Moreover, at any given time, different industries will be in different stages of a cycle, but in the aggregate, they will tend to correlate with each other. That is, to follow each other. The terms upturn and downturn, as well as expansion and contraction, are used interchangeably with upswing and downswing.

Sometimes business is in a period of transition between the two stages. In the transition between expanding and declining activity, this transition period is referred to as a business cycle **peak**. In the transition between declining and expanding business activity, this transition period is referred to as a business cycle **trough**.

---

[3] Some business cycle theorists and practitioners prefer to divide the upswing stage into three periods: 1) early-cycle; 2) mid-cycle; and 3) late-cycle. Some divide the downswing into two periods, and some refer to the transition peaks and troughs as separate periods, stages, or phases.

A crisis (or panic) often marks the transition from the upswing to the downswing and, as a result, enables the two stages to be easily differentiated. It is often harder to distinguish, however, between the end of a downswing and the beginning of the upswing or expanding activity. Panics and crises are not regarded as separate stages. This is because the transition from expanding to declining business activity often transpires without their occurrence, and in many ways, they can be regarded as the final phase of upswing period. It is often difficult to precisely date the start of a crisis. On the other hand, panics may be dated with more assurance.

A **crisis** is the state of business conditions when it becomes apparent that, for one or more reasons, business cannot be conducted further in the same manner as in the immediate past and, as a result, a readjustment is needed because of the instability (or maladjustment) of production. That happens when a larger proportion of businesses than usual finds that they are producing goods or services that cannot be sold at prices that cover production costs, or credit availability is exhausted. Financial panics are often preceded by credit booms. A crisis often comes out of the blue, and it appears that things are falling apart. In actuality, the challenges had been brewing for a while beneath the surface. No single spectacular event occurring on the eve of a crisis is the cause of the crisis. In nearly all cases, the seeds had already been sown, often years before. Attention must be given to the conditions which precede, rather than to those which accompany the crisis. The causes are very numerous and complex. A financial crisis reveals large, widespread miscalculation of economic values. The extent of these miscalculations has to be worked out before the economy can begin to function normally again. The ending of a crisis is marked by cessation of large demand for prompt liquidation. Early crises were largely credit contractions brought on by monetary manipulation. They were quite common during the 19th century but with the creation of the Federal Reserve, and more importantly deposit insurance, America didn't have any major crises between 1934 and 2007.

A **panic** is a state of business conditions when fear and apprehension that preceding conditions of expanding business activity are about to end suddenly and change radically, thus suddenly fostering a spirit of extreme pessimism on the part of business leaders (i.e., entrepreneurs). It often results from previous economic exchange (or asset valuations) occurring without proper regard for underlying values. Panics often occur at or near business cycle peaks. Often, the realization that a downswing was underway was the catalyst.

A panic is usually of short duration, while a crisis is lengthier, as it includes the final stages of the period of expanding activity, as well as the early stages of the period of declining activity. Panics are often marked by an acute shortage of loanable capital, very high interest rates, an inability for many businesses to obtain credit, and often a preponderance of business failures. Panics (and crises) have been associated with recessions in the United States.

In many cases, productive activity peaked before the crisis or panic occurred. In 1929, for example, the recession had already started in August, three months prior to the Great Crash in October. In the Great Financial Crisis (GFC) of 2007-09, production (and other indicators used by the NBER to date cycle turns) peaked in December 2007, nine months before the collapse of Lehman Brothers. In a similar manner, the index of real gross output used in this book peaked in October 2007. In November 2019, real gross output peaked, setting a weak foundation for the Covid-recession, or "lockdown recession" of 2020, as state and local governments sought to contain the coronavirus pandemic.

A peak is the state of business conditions when activity is extremely high, while a trough is the state of conditions when business activity is abnormally low. These transitions between the alternative periods of expanding and contracting business activity are regarded apart from the conditions into which they lead.

Complete movement of business conditions tends to return to a previous status and is regarded as a complete business cycle. For practical purposes in this book, I date cycles from trough to trough, with the peak in between. Classical economist James Stuart Mill (1806-1873) noted that the seeds of each boom are sown in the preceding crisis. This presents a good framework. The following are rough summaries of the characteristics of both stages of the business cycle and are based on over 230 years of American economic history. That is, what typically happens during the cycle.

The following provides some common characteristics of downswings and upswings. The discussion is meant to be descriptive of broad trends and developments within both phases of the business cycle. No two cycles are exactly alike, although all have similar characteristics.

Characteristics of the Downswing – This is a period of contraction beginning with the last month of expansion (i.e., peak of the business cycle) and ending with the trough (or end) of contraction. It was referred to as depression in earlier times and is currently referred to as recession. Marx and other 19th century economists sometimes referred to these as crises or commercial crises. We know that these downswings usually follow periods of rapid increase in output, accompanied by speculation, and expansion of credit.

Downswings are periods of maladjustment between supply and demand for goods, between cost and availability of credit, between productive capability and consumption possibility. This is a period of instability, economic tensions, and slackness. During these times, business activity, after slowing down and peaking, will then decline as forced readjustments painfully take place.

Confidence is fragile, and the business confidence that characterized the preceding period of expanding activity has changed for the worse. When a boom breaks, confidence can collapse. Caution becomes the rule of the day as the excesses of the boom go into reverse. Psychology plays an important role. The seeds of the down-swing were sown in the time since the last business cycle trough. That is, during the period of the upswing of recovery and expansion, when imbalances first appeared and gathered strength. This downswing period marks the period of readjustment from those imbalances.

This stage in the business cycle features a widespread contraction in business activity across many industries and economic sectors. The tendency on the part of any industry or sector to curtail activity has a similar impact upon other fields, with the result that as the period (or duration) of decline lengthens, the situation cascades, becoming more pronounced. After over-production in some industries becomes apparent in light of perceived decreased demand or opportunity at prices that are profitable, producers in that line of business cut-back, setting in motion a vicious cycle of curbed production and purchases, reductions in payrolls, falling incomes, and a duller pace of spending. This is the sequence and order of causation. It is a vicious cycle. The reaction does not immediately occur in all industries, but eventually spreads to others.

Industrial production is substantially restricted and falls off during this stage. Buyers are either unwilling or unable to purchase and, as a result, demand declines as well. Unfilled orders shrink, and inventories rise to new levels relative to output. Apprehension of future prices has the natural effect in causing producers to lessen the risk of loss from further weakness in prices. At this point, inventories are more than adequate to meet existing demand, which is increasingly a faction of its former volume. Construction volumes, reflecting prior commitments and plans, however, may increase during the early period of decline. Transportation weakens and falls off. Supply chain congestion eases, and deliveries quicken. If the downturn is worldwide, both exports and imports will be dull. That said, should the downswing be confined to the United States, the tendency would be for American exports to increase and imports to decrease. With industrial and other business activity slumping, purchasing power will be reduced, which results in falling retail sales. Many service industries may suffer as well. Present agricultural production is usually not affected by worsening of business, but in the 18th and 19th centuries, crop failures often played a very large role, affecting a variety of industries.

Reflecting upon the interaction of supply and demand, and the imbalance between the two, commodity prices decline, rapidly at first and then more gradually, only to reach their ebb when the downswing is at its deepest stage. Other prices and wages also may be soft, but because of current rigidities or stickiness, they were more likely to weaken in the periods prior to World War II.

In the downswing, labor conditions become unfavorable for workers as unemployment rises and pressure mounts to reduce labor costs. The trend in wages is moderated, and in earlier times (prior to the 1940s) was downward. Labor strikes and other industrial controversies continue at a strong pace at first, but then lessen as reality sinks in. Amid increasing unemployment, low consumer confidence, and contracting production, consumers cut back on purchases.

Corporate earnings are affected during this stage of the cycle as profits decline and credit is scarce for virtually all firms and across all sectors. Credit becomes quite scarce, and lending standards tighten appreciably. Losses occur in the fall of the value of inventories held over from the expansion period. Liquidation becomes the norm. Debt defaults increase. Business failures increase with the decline in corporate earnings, as debt levels tend to be fixed to some extent. New security issues decline abruptly with the beginning of contraction, due to lessened demand for new capital. Offerings during this period are limited to refunding operations that extend maturities. As improvement in business conditions fosters a boom in equity markets and valuation, retrogression of conditions fosters a bust, or a slump. With equities, the movement from a bull market to a bear market often occurs before the business cycle peak.

During the downswing, excess capacity is apparent and prior demand forecasts are seen to have been too optimistic. As profits decline, business leaders and management teams often change, capital expenditures are reduced, and industry consolidation begins. Capital discipline becomes the norm. The reduction in capital investment and contraction in industry supply will eventually pave the way for a recovery of profits. This stage of the cycle is marked by price declines, private equity losses, marked reductions of valuations, collapsing IPO (initial public offering) activity, and reduced M&A (merger and acquisition) activity.

Equity transactions decline during a downswing. That said, a recovery in equity valuations usually precedes the cycle trough and a recovery in business conditions.

As prices soften, bank clearings, bank and non-bank loans, non-bank securities, and other conditions of finance weaken during the downswing. Often, lower interest rates encourage firms to restructure debt obligations by issuing (if they can) long-term bonds. Interest rates closely follow the trend of business conditions. Interest rates do not decline at first but usually follow. In this stage, monetary policy becomes more accommodative, and inventories are gradually reduced, despite low sales levels, setting up for the next recovery. For over 100 years, a primary focus of monetary policy has been to increase economic activity by lowering interest rates and increasing the money supply.

The transition from cyclical contraction to one of expansion is usually of gradual change. Unlike the peak, the transition at the trough may be uneven and difficult to ascertain with month-to-month declines mixing with month-to-month gains among various lines of business. Just as productive activity is overdone prior to the peak, it is underdone during the later timing of the downswing. Low costs of production through greater efficiency and lower unit labor costs, low interest rates, and abnormally low costs of commodities encourage an opposition to inaction among business leaders, leading to a revival of activity.

Excess inventories of goods get worked off and shortages begin to develop. Idled workers seek employment. Business leaders initiate undertakings, the essence of entrepreneurship. Decreased costs of construction and capital goods stimulate investment. These forces ferment silently and invisibly, hence the readjustments needed for recovery work for themselves through relatively gradual periods of time. That said, the transition sometimes is distinct and pronounced.

Characteristics of the Upswing – History shows us that every downswing is followed by an upswing. This is a period of recovering and eventually expanding activity. Business cycle theorists and practitioners sometimes divide this upswing stage into two sub-periods: 1) recovery and 2) expansion. The recovery is usually marked from the trough to where recovering activity results in measures of business output and other metrics regaining the most recent peak. The expansion extends these gains and sees additional improvements to new highs in activity, eventually culminating at a new business cycle peak.

I first discuss **recovery**, the period of persistent rising activity following a trough in business. Firms stop cutting back on business activities. After under-production in some industries becomes apparent in light of perceived increased demand or opportunity, firms in that line of business expand, setting in motion a virtuous cycle of rising production and purchases, increased hiring, rising incomes, and a quicker pace of spending. This is the sequence and order of causation. The reaction does not occur immediately in all industries, but an improvement in one or more of the important industries has a stimulating effect on others, and it gathers momentum. Sometimes a sharp recovery occurs, marked by a distinct inflection point from declining to gains in activity, and the latter is often at an accelerating pace.

A rebound and increase of productive activity is the chief feature of the cyclical upswing, and sentiments reflect expectations of permanency in improving business conditions. Agriculture is less affected, but industrial production and construction activity (especially housing) lead the way. Business inventories are drawn down as sales growth improves. Transportation volumes improve, and retail sales increase, slowly at first, but gathering momentum as time passes and purchasing power, arising from greater productive activity, advances.

Prices generally advance during the upswing; dull at first, then slowly rising and then gathering momentum. That said, prices do not change uniformly. Commodities are most sensitive to supply and demand conditions and are thus more volatile, followed by prices for intermediate and semi-finished products, then by finished products and finally, services. Consumers become more positive about their prospects and start taking advantage of the low interest rates by increasing their discretionary spending.

Labor conditions generally improve during the upswing; slow at first but gradually gathering momentum. Payrolls increase, while the number of unemployed workers decreases. Discouraged workers return to the labor market. Wages slowly increase, gradually adding to the virtuous cycle.

With improved efficiency gained during the downturn and lower cost structures, corporate earnings can improve rapidly during this stage of expansion. As output rises, capacity utilization improves and total costs often moderate. Prices advance more rapidly than costs and, as a result, profit margins become larger. The rise in profits stimulates further activity.

Amid still easy monetary policy, credit conditions stop tightening, and eventually lending standards begin to loosen. Business leaders of courage and initiative take advantage of low interest rates to float bond issues. New security issues gain in volume as firms desire to expand their capabilities, and although interest rates may begin rising, it is not enough to discourage borrowing. Business failures show a sharp decline as rising selling prices may bring profit to even less efficient producers. Bankruptcies and insolvencies become rarer as time proceeds.

The recovery in business conditions fosters a boom in equity valuations. These tend to lead the recovery rather than follow. Prospective profits are a driver, and investor optimism gains.

Eventually, business activity reaches its most recent peak. Thus, recovery transitions into expansion when activity returns to normal (prior peak) and ends with the month preceding the next peak.

Turning to **expansion**, the upward swing in measures of business activity, just as a pendulum swings, rises from the trough, and carries improvement above the prior peak. Some mark this as the end of the recession, but that is false. The recession (or downswing) ended at the trough of activity, which is often gradual and not sudden as at peaks. Although slow at first, the gains in activity intensify. Psychology continues to play an important role, and as activity gains, a spirit of optimism rises and eventually becomes pervasive. This further stimulates productive activity, and increasing selling prices can result in higher profits as business continues to grow. That said, higher prices can serve to moderate the quantity demanded. With rosier prospects and increasing corporate profits, companies begin to allocate capital to expand business and improve productivity to meet increasing demand. Business has now grown from its slump and regained what was lost. Optimism often transforms into enthusiasm, which at times, can be unfounded and unhinged from reality, as the sign of abnormally high profits sets the stage for the eventual transition to the peak. Both production and sales grow, and business activity gathers momentum. Firms become over-enthusiastic regarding future requirements, and with capacity utilization high, they embark on ambitious plans to further expand capabilities further. This is often aided and facilitated by central banks continuing to maintain low interest rate policies as firms borrow money. Firms begin to order beyond current requirements, and speculation affects business. Unequal expansion or imbalances begin to arise. These potential problems, or imbalances, if left unattended, have a habit of becoming crises.

Industrial production reaches new highs as the apparent demand for goods seems limitless. Selling prices seem to be of secondary importance to the emerging problem of securing deliveries. Deliveries of goods slow, and supply chains become extended and less elastic. Firms (and consumers) are often willing to pay a premium for prompt delivery. Transportation follows suit and rises to new highs, with congestion along the supply chain rising. Shortages of labor begin to emerge, and in many cases, hinder production. Wages rise, along with purchasing power and retail sales. Overheating is now occurring as capacity is now constrained.

Construction is mixed at this point. An increase in interest rates is usually at play, and labor and raw material shortages present challenges and rising costs. Projects in the non-residential sector are now underway and even if interest rates rise, firms may be reluctant to cancel projects or abandon work. Housing, however, tends to be more sensitive.

Overall prices continue to advance as long as demand for goods and services continues to outpace the ability to supply. At some point, however, wages and other costs begin to rise faster than selling prices, and profit margins are crimped. A decline in sensitive commodity prices usually indicates the end of expansion and peak, with the transition to a downswing. Prices in general do not stop suddenly, but increasing resistance mounts, and towards the end of expansion, they appear to be stabilizing at a high level. Higher prices will work to reduce demand in some market segments (i.e., price conscious consumers) and often spread to other segments. This is often referred to as demand destruction, but sometimes price gains do stop suddenly. Moreover, a decline in price impinges upon profit margins, and in some cases because of high fixed costs, firms may speed up production, exacerbating the imbalance.

Labor begins to demand an increasing share of income as unemployment ceases to be problem and shortages emerge. Bargaining power shifts in their favor. The difficulty is now that of recruiting and retaining talent and of finding workers for jobs rather than jobs for workers. Wages rise and increase most rapidly during expansion, especially before the transition (i.e., cycle peak), as the cost-of-living increases. Workers seek higher wages, and wages begin to trend upward. If the power of labor unions is sufficient, this later period may be marked by industrial controversies. In early phases of the recovery, pay raises are typically granted, as rising profits and increased efficiency offset the effects but later in the upswing, as costs rise more quickly than prices, leading to lower profit margins, employers are less inclined to further increases. Industrial controversies are more likely to lead to strikes and longer strikes.

Keep in mind that rising prices (and then wages) are a symptom of inflation, not the cause. A primary cause is the expansion of credit. Credit conditions and lending standards loosen further, and towards the end of the upswing, lending standards are often non-existent, as exuberance becomes the norm. Business profits at this point of the cycle have increased significantly. In addition to margin expansion, the continual advance in pricing magnifies earnings. Business failures continue to decline in numbers as expansion lengthens. New security issues reach their highest point, but rising prices often result in higher interest rates and lenders need to be compensated for the loss of purchasing power. Higher demand for credit also tends to push up interest rates. Higher interest rates then begin to confine corporate borrowing to the short-term. Credit growth becomes strong. Monetary policy is still accommodative but is becoming increasingly neutral. Although the pace of inflation may not always be high, it is higher than at the start of the upswing and eventually leads to tighter monetary policy. That is, interest rates start rising from their relatively low level. Monetary policy eventually becomes more restrictive to steer the economy away from overheating.

Higher prices boost profitability, and bubbles begin to froth. Improving profitability soon loosens the capital discipline that characterized the downswing well into the recovery. Business leaders are inclined to boost capital expenditures. Competitors are likely to follow, and new entrants may arrive, encouraged by optimistic demand forecasts. Investment bankers aid the process, fostering the expansion of capacity and consolidation, as capital is attracted into industries with high profits. Exuberance prevails as private equity, IPOs, and M&A activity rise to new levels. There is a lag between a rise in capital investment and new production. This varies from industry to industry, and for some capital-intensive industries, this can be five years. New supply can be slow in coming on-stream which with rising demand reinforces profitability, adding to capital expenditures. All of this implies that supply changes are lumpy and due to the lag, lean towards overshooting. This eventually leads to market instability. The lags have long been known as the "cobweb effect" in economics. Eventually, supply will increase, and demand will disappoint, setting up the eventual cyclical turning and a reduction in industry profitability and shareholder returns.

The world gets caught up with chasing its own version of a future "golden age" and ends up repeating the same mistakes of the past. Equity market exchanges are large, and sentiments such as fear of missing out (FOMO) and there is no alternative (TINA) to stocks lead investors and then individuals to enter speculative markets. Over-optimism results in the pursuit of securities of higher yield, but greater risk and poorer quality. Bank clearings, bank- and non-bank loan activities, non-bank securities and other conditions of finance continue to improve and reach their maximum towards the end of the period. At this time, prices are highest and the volume of transactions greatest. There is a marked decrease in the ratio of cash reserves to obligations as the gains in business activity are increasingly facilitated by bank credits. Credit facilitates the expansion of business far beyond where it would go otherwise. Eventually, credit availability reaches a point of exhaustion, and the end is near.

The period of expansion tends to work out its own undoing. Trees don't grow to the sky, as the law of gravity asserts itself sooner or later. A prime factor is a decrease in earnings as rising costs, decreasing efficiency, and higher interest rates eat into selling prices which increasingly cannot be raised further. In addition, investment decisions made during the upswing can result in production of goods and services that cannot be sold at prices that cover their cost of production, or when credit availability is exhausted.

There is a clear link between rising prices and "demand destruction" among many industries. The chemical industry provides a good example. Purchasing agents and buyers down the value chain know that chemical prices are correlated with the price of oil. If oil prices rise, and buyers anticipate further gains, these companies in downstream customer industries will build inventory ahead of expected higher prices. Buyers may double or even triple order in times of scarcity. At some point, the chemical companies discover that consumers cannot afford the higher prices. Demand then suffers a double blow. Chemical companies have to work off their excess inventory at a time when end-user demand is falling. This was the case in the 1973-75 downturn. Multiply this behavior across a wide number of industries (steel, other metals, oil products, etc.), and it can lead to recession.

At the end of the expansion, production rises faster than unfilled orders, and the latter are likely to decline at the peak. Reports of cancellations emerge. Inventories begin to climb faster than production. Commodity prices cease to rise and may begin to decline.

A financial crisis often marks the end of the period of expansion and the beginning of the next contraction. Often a "crisis" will emerge, set in motion by some inevitable development. These could include failure of some important bank or business or some political development (e.g., looming passage of a major tariff in 1929). In the 18th and 19th centuries, major crop failures could bring about a crisis. Again, the seeds of business crises are found in the period of recovery and expansion.

The business cycle has now swung back to the peak, the period at the start of recession (or downswing) which was the point of origin in this present discussion. Examining over two centuries of history, each business cycle is unique in its own way, but some patterns tend to repeat themselves over time.

The Role of the Entrepreneur

The entrepreneur is central to economic growth and the business cycle. Entrepreneurs regulate the activity of the resources under their control using their judgment. They do so at the risk of their firms, and even their own personal risk. Thus, it is in the mind of the entrepreneur and in the influences arising from his/her circumstances that we may find the key to cyclical change in business activity. Economic growth begins with the entrepreneur, and an increase in productivity, new products, and new markets. Some economists refer to entrepreneurship as the fourth factor of production, in addition to land (or natural resources), capital, and labor.

We currently think of the term entrepreneur to mean an innovator, laboring in a garage or dorm room to develop a new product, new app, or new business venture. However, the original meaning of the term "entrepreneur" was more inclusive.

Entrepreneur is a French word said to be coined by the Classical economist Jean-Baptiste Say, from the word *entreprendre*, which is usually translated as "undertaker" or "adventurer." That is, one who undertakes, or manages. It can include the innovator, or founder of new business venture, but also a business leader. In modern terms, this would be a CEO, managing director, managing partner, or some similar leadership position. I use this term to mean all business leaders, not only of start-ups, but also of Fortune 500 companies and enterprises in all forms of commerce. It also applies to the owner of a small business. The entrepreneur is the strategic decision-maker.

Production is carried on in anticipation of demand. That is, ahead of demand based on an estimate (or forecast) of demand and/or price by the entrepreneur. Working from an estimate involves the risk of loss when a wrong estimate has been made. The entrepreneur organizes this production, which implies production for the market with its accompanying risk.

Among the circumstances facing the entrepreneur is the condition of mutual interdependence among individual producing firms. The output of each firm, creating the earnings of that firm, establishes the purchasing power of the firm for the output of all others. As result, the total output of all the producing firms constitutes the total power to purchase. Any rise (or fall) in the business activity overall is reason for a rise (or fall), in varying degree, in the activity of the individual producing firms of which it is composed. Investment in new capital takes time (design, ordering of equipment, construction, etc.), and resources must always be set in motion in anticipation of future demand. The entrepreneur must base his/her current activity and investment plans not on known facts, but on estimates of the future condition of markets, pricing, costs, consumer tastes, etc. The entrepreneur operates and regulates activity and makes decisions on the relationship between two sets of prices: selling prices and the prices of inputs (e.g., costs), the difference being profits. As a result, arbitrary and irregular non-market changes in prices due to the result of monetary policy, misleads in decision-making, etc., fosters instabilities (or maladjustments) of output relative to demand, in many markets. These instabilities come about through the sinking of capital in unprofitable investments. Disturbances originating in the monetary system or in changes in profits of specific industries lead to variations (i.e., cyclical fluctuations) in business activity and can propagate throughout the economic system. Cycles are reinforced by business confidence. Changes in business confidence can lead to the cumulative growth of an error of optimism or pessimism in business judgment, which in times of rising activity, unduly stimulates activity, while in times of falling activity unduly depresses it. The error can grow cumulatively because of our tendency to exaggerate success or failure. It acts directly on the judgments of the future conditions of markets, and indirectly on those judgments by its influence of the supply of money and prices. An active principle stimulating business cycles is found in changes in the general level of business confidence, which is essentially fragile. Near business cycle peaks (and troughs), there is an infection of confidence (or utter lack thereof), and a psychology of the crowd, which dominates current opinion and often carries it to extremes. These feed into entrepreneurial judgment and decision-making.

Modern production takes time and usually involves a lengthy period to design and construct capital goods. Resources must be set in motion in anticipation of demand. The entrepreneur must base his/her current activities not on known facts, but on judgments of future conditions. As the middleman of operating between two sets of prices (selling and factor inputs), the entrepreneur adjusts the level, timing, composition, and direction of the resources he/she controls. Absolute and relative prices provide signals for these adjustments. Arbitrary and abnormal changes in price due to the imperfect operation of the monetary system mislead the entrepreneur in his/her function as society's agent for the adjustment of resources to needs. This can cause or reinforce maladjustment of output to demand. Thus, in many ways, the influence of the monetary system is to be regarded not as the primary, but as the reinforcing cause of business cycles.

Law of Markets

First proposed by Jean-Baptiste Say, the "law of markets" correctly argues that when a good or service is provided, from that instance, it affords a market for other goods and services to the full extent of its value. When a provider of a good or service produces that good or service, the seller instantly becomes a buyer who has income that can be spent. To buy, one must first produce. In other words, production is the cause of consumption, and increased production leads to increased consumer spending. Purchasing power grows out of production. Say was from a Huguenot family, and the law of markets may have been derived from Ecclesiastes 5:11:

> "When goods increase, they are increased that eat them: and what good is there to the owners thereof, saving the beholding of them with their eyes?" (KJV).

The total volume of consumption thus depends upon the total volume of production, not the other way around. Every kind of good or service brought to market adds to the supply of its own kind but also confers upon its owners (both capital and labor) the purchasing power necessary for taking off the market every other kind of good or service. Buyer power exists in the products produced. Thus, the general demand for goods and services is in direct proportion to the amount of production. As Classical economist John Stuart Mill writes:

> "Could we suddenly double the productive powers of the country, we should double the supply of commodities in every market; but we should by the same stroke double the purchasing power. Everybody would bring a double demand as well as a double supply, everybody would be able to buy twice as much, because everyone would have twice as much to offer in exchange."

Every increase in the volume (and value) of production constitutes an increase in the power to consume, or an increase in purchasing power. It is production that generates the necessary purchasing power. The buying power of the farmer comes from his/her crops. The buying power of industrial firms comes from their manufactured products. The supply of goods of one type necessarily constitutes demand for goods of other types. The same proposition holds true of all areas (or sectors) of economic exchange. If they produce, they have something with which to buy, and if production is in the right proportions all around, markets will be cleared. Producers need to produce goods and services that consumers want (thus proving salable) at cost-covering prices.

Production is the wellspring of prosperity. What really drives a nation (and an individual) is not demand; it is production. Mankind was created to produce. We are wired that way. One must produce to consume. One works to buy, not what one makes, but what one needs. Consumption comes out of production. Production comes before consumption and leads to it. It is the presence of supply that creates a demand. Prosperity can only be secured out of production. We can only consume after we or others have first produced. We live by rendering services to others. As independent investment strategist Russell Napier puts it, "investors spend 90 percent of their time thinking about demand and 10 percent thinking about supply. It should be the other way around." To put this on an individual level: to demand things we must first produce. The buyer must have produced something first to be a buyer, or the buyer must have accessed the production of someone else (through credit) in order to be a buyer.

Overproduction in the sense of the overproduction of all goods and services in the aggregate is inconceivable. The supply of everything constitutes the demand for everything, and the two are essentially equivalent. In the aggregate, the actual power of production can never outrun the potential power of consumption. Thus, there is but one way by which the volume of consumption can be increased, and that is by increasing the volume of production. The impossibility of general overproduction, however, does not imply the impossibility of imbalances in production in certain business lines. The chief industries in which imbalances are likely to arise are those which provide production goods (e.g., capital goods) as distinguished from those providing goods and services for direct consumption. Economic growth occurs through the organic, natural, productive activity in which firms produce goods and services that consumers are demanding. This is the essence of human economic exchange. This is fundamental to my understanding of the business cycle and provides a framework for monitoring and assessing business conditions. Thus, production is primary, and consumption is secondary. This was economic orthodoxy (i.e., Classical economic theory) for over 160 years until the 1930s when this was reversed, to where production serves consumption. That is, consumption as primary, and production secondary. Economics was turned on its head. An outstanding, modern formulation of this Classical theory of the business cycle can be found in Kates (2020).[4]

It's been my experience as a business economist of five decades, that it is the indicators of production (or business activity) that first decline before and during downswings, well ahead of the indicators of consumption. When the economy begins to recover, and an upswing begins, indicators of production turn first. It's because production starts first, followed by consumption. Production spending is always ahead of consumption spending. Indeed, most of the indicators used to construct the Conference Board's index of leading economic indicators are production or supply-side oriented. This is the same for other similar leading indicators developed by other groups.

---

[4]   Steven Kates currently teaches economics at the RMIT University in Melbourne but spent most of his working career as the chief economist for the Australian Chamber of Commerce.

The strength of the economy does not come from the ability to spend money or consume. This has been a major fallacy in economic thinking since the 1930s. It consists of the belief that government can fix economic problems by spending more money. On the household side, it consists of the belief that economic strength arises from the ability to buy things. Economic strength, however, always emanates from production. This has been the case since the Garden of Eden, to the present. This old philosophical principle of production, not consumption, as primary, has long-standing economic and even religious underpinnings. There is no question that consumers are very pleased to spend money as long as they can. When consumption does drop during the business cycle, it is always the result of falling productive activity, and because of credit. The demand is always present. It is that the ability to spend more goes away when banks tighten, debt becomes too large, and credit becomes scarce. In every case, this line of reasoning (start with production and then consumption) can be used to assess all 47 complete historical business cycles. A focus on the production (or supply) side of the economy should be first and foremost in assessing business conditions.

Internal Forces: The Cause of the Business Cycle

Long-term economic progress depends upon allowing entrepreneurs to make decisions without the burden of onerous regulation, high taxation, or high levels of public spending that do not provide added value but rather consume resources and are unproductive. In addition, an environment where increased competition is the norm facilitates production, employment, and investment. That is, free markets.

A wide variance of opinion exists as to the cause of the business cycle. Historical cycles are irregular with no two cycles alike, but they do share many similarities.

Forces internal to the economic system are economic in origin and are created by imbalances of production, trade, consumption, wages, interest rates, security issues, and the prices of goods, services, and securities. These forces are inherent within the economic system and are manifested in the increasing imbalance in the production of primary goods (e.g., raw materials), intermediate goods, and final goods and services for consumers and business, as well as in the demand for these goods (and services), and in prices.

Economic phenomenon center on exchange values and prices, and on the centrality of profits. Business cycles relate to supply, demand, prices, and profits at a very distinct industry and market level. Cycles arise out of imbalances in these. These imbalances may differ in degree, in the industries and markets affected, and in duration, but some imbalance is always present during the cycle.

Fluctuations in demand occur because what consumers want, how much they want, and how much they are willing to pay is always changing. Production is carried on ahead of demand, based on the entrepreneur's estimate of that demand, and on the notion that the entrepreneur can make bad estimates. This can result in products and services that cannot be sold at a profit, resulting in excess inventories, and ill-advised ventures.

Downswings are caused not by failure of demand (as per Keynes), but by failure in the structure of supply and demand. That is, the relationship between the two. Downswings are fostered by entrepreneurs miscalculating what consumers wish to buy, thus causing unsold goods to pile up (i.e., inventories), production to be cut, incomes to fall, and finally, consumer spending to drop. That is the vicious cycle. It is errors in production and planning during upswings which cause some goods to remain unsold at prices at which costs (including the cost of capital) are covered.

Sometimes the miscalculations are modest in scope. For example, during and after the COVID pandemic, consumers bought bicycles and other exercise equipment. Retailers of such goods mistook the increased demand as permanent and boosted orders in 2021 and into 2022. When the lockdowns ended, consumers demand for such goods declined, and by mid-2022, retailers of bicycles and other exercise equipment were left with high, unwanted inventories. This was in a narrow segment of the economy. At other times, the miscalculations affect industries that have economy-wide negative implications. For example, the years leading up the Great Financial Crisis saw the unhealthy expansion of housing and related real estate, mortgage banking, etc. that affected wide swaths of the economy.

The imbalances may originate, for example, through mistakes of producers in assessing the wants of consumers, through mistakes of optimism and pessimism, through competition, through incomplete knowledge of markets and plans of other producers, through control of markets, through disruptions in supply chain logistics, changes in consumer tastes, misuse of credit, and myriad other factors. The textbook characterization of competitive markets as large number of buyers and sellers, homogeneous products, perfect knowledge of the market, freedom of entry and exit, and a single price simply does not exist (or at best rarely exists) in the real world. There are exceptions to the assumptions of rationality, as well as biases that creep into decision-making among entrepreneurs. One of the best applied books on these biases for the business forecaster is John Silvia's *Dynamic Economic Decision Making*.[5]

What causes these imbalances that generate business cycles? There is only one way Ito seek the seeds of these imbalances. We must look for them early in the recovering phase of the cycle. Once a recovery has started, a peak is inevitable. Nothing goes on forever. There is no economic perpetual motion machine. At the peak of the cycle, the downswing (i.e., recession) is the outcome of the imbalances that arose during the upswing, or the recovery and expansion.

---

[5] John Silvia is the former chief economist at Wells Fargo, a prominent business economist, and currently CEO of Dynamic Economic Strategy.

And once the cycle is clearly at "boom" levels, business activity will certainly fall before necessary readjustments are complete.

Imbalances generated within the economic system largely arise from one of two types of disturbances: 1) business as it involves production, inventories, profits, etc. and 2) financial as it involves credit, capitalization, and securities markets. Both are closely interlinked. Business imbalances include those between cost of production and price; those among commodity prices; between wages, interest, and profits; and money wages and prices. Financial imbalances include those between credit and volume of business and between short-term interest rates and the cost of capital. In a nutshell, it concerns values and profits.

All business activity is based on the decisions made by individual suppliers of goods and services. That is, entrepreneur's estimates of the future. In the effort to maximize profits and minimize losses, firms will decide how much to produce, using their best estimate of the demand for their product. Production and other decisions are usually made prior to when one can tell with certainty whether they will lead to profit or to loss, and as a result, business leaders inevitably make mistakes in production decisions. As producers move to maximize profits, the dependence of profits upon costs, and of costs on volume of output, establish a sequence of relations that reveals the motives which induce producers to over-produce. These are manifested in numerous small mistakes (often building upon each other), in decision-making, and some large mistakes. These mistakes in decision-making affect supplies of raw materials, change production methods, or alter demand. The mistakes may arise from changes in taste, technology, the weather, and a myriad of other factors.

In market economies where businesses produce for profit, supply errors can occur across sectors but are often concentrated in certain sectors. All commerce, trade, finance, and industry are based on businesses being able to anticipate demand with supply, generally before the goods are purchased. Profits are an incentive to produce more and a reward for the risks undertaken by entrepreneurs (or business leaders). When the outlook for profits is good, business expands. When profits are cut, business activity (or production) will contract. It's that simple.

Mistakes in supply decisions (often collective in nature) will inevitably occur. Downswings in business activity (e.g., recessions) are the result of widespread errors in supply (or production) decisions. These are engendered by factors that led many businesses into activities that proved unprofitable and for which there may be no demand. Changes in industry dynamics and business models also play a role. These supply (or business) errors result in misguided investment projects (and acquisitions), bad debts, and impaired balance sheets, all based on unreasonable expectations. It is in the downswing when these errors are redressed.

Price collapses often accompany these downswings, as the mistakes in supply decisions lead to over-expansion of supply vis-à-vis limitations in demand. Falling (or low) prices often exacerbate these downswings, leading to the demise of smaller, less well-capitalized firms, either through bankruptcy or consolidation.

Every broad slowdown in commerce and industry (i.e., recession) has both impulse and propagation mechanisms. The impulse causes the recession (or slowdown), while the propagation mechanism perpetuates the crisis. Causes of the impulse most likely originate internally from collective mistakes by business leaders or originate externally (unanticipated large changes in energy prices and interest rates, technology shocks, credit curtailment, policy mistakes, etc.). There are over 600 distinct industries within the U.S. economy, many of which are dominated by a handful of firms, although many are very competitive with hundreds if not thousands of producers. These industries (and firms) are highly integrated, and changes in one industry can affect others.

Globalization has extended the division of labor, specialization, and economies of scale. Integration among industries is now global in nature, and impulses from one industry to another may cross borders. Periods of globalization include the early 20th century and the first decades of the 21st century. With rising geopolitical tensions, COVID, and a variety of other factors, it appears that globalization may be reversing.

These effects are illustrated by the collapse of oil prices, from a peak of roughly $115 per barrel in June 2014 to under $35 at the end of February 2016. During the years after 2010, American oil (and natural gas) production grew rapidly, the result of the combination of several technological developments (horizontal drilling, fracking, on-site computational modeling, etc.) that combined with property rights, price signals, and learning curve effects to eventually foster a doubling of American oil and gas production. In 2014, an oil glut appeared to be emerging, and prices began to weaken, aided by a high U.S. dollar. At the time, Saudi Arabia was faced with a decision between letting prices continue to drop or giving up market share by cutting production to support prices. Saudi Arabia kept its production stable, deciding that low oil prices offered more of a long-term benefit than giving up market share. Lower oil prices caused production in the United States to ease, as producers pulled back on exploration. The rig count plummeted. This adversely affected diverse industries such as oil services, steel and oilfield machinery, as orders for tubular products, equipment and servicing declined. Chemical companies producing oilfield chemicals saw business decline sharply. Miners producing sand for fracking were affected, as were trucking companies and the railroads. Prices declined, affecting other industries as well. For example, weaker pricing affected oil refining, petroleum wholesalers, and gasoline stations. Revenues declined. In addition, industries such as chemicals (whose selling prices are correlated with oil prices) suffered as well. As these industries' revenues declined, the purchasing power associated with those revenues declined as well. Companies that had taken on large debt now faced liquidity (and in some cases solvency) issues, and debt defaults increased. Further cut backs occurred. As the ripple effects spread, the U.S. economy slowed to what I have referred to as a "near recession." This is how a contagion spreads, and the same logic and string of interlinkages can be used to explain many recessions. Substitute housing and all the linked industries (real estate, mortgage brokers, staging consultants, banks, homebuilders, lumber mills, cement producers, building materials suppliers, tool manufacturers, etc.) and the purchasing power wrapped in each one of these producing industries cause one to appreciate the inter-linkages of a modern economy, and how downswings intensify and spread throughout industry, commerce, trade, and finance. The 2007-09 recession was a typical business-cycle downturn, but it was preceded by an economic boom led by speculative excesses, particularly in the housing and related industries. When that bubble burst, a credit crunch (and panic and crisis) worsened the resulting recession.

There are other factors leading to mistakes and losses, including large and unexpected changes in interest rates, a major reduction in the availability of credit, large increases in input costs and other shocks, sudden demographic change, policy mistakes, etc. Even when losses initially affect only a small portion of the economy (e.g., oil and gas extraction value-added accounting for less than two percent of GDP), with the right set of circumstances, the effects can spread farther and wider as each industry contracts and, as a result, reduce the sector's own demand for the products of other industries. This happened during 2014-16 when oil prices collapsed and a downturn in that sector affected supplier and other industries. In a cascading manner, contraction in one part of the economy can lead to a more widespread downturn, with some industries harmed to a greater extent than others and deterioration observed not only in production but in other measures of activity (e.g., employment, income, and business sales). In this way, when the structure of demand moves out of alignment with the structure of supply (or production) in one stage of production, the economic impact can be broad, even resulting in recession. Essentially, it represents a fundamental imbalance between different industries and sectors of the economic system, and one of the results of the supply decline is the fall in consumer purchasing power.

Recessions (or downswings) are thus due to some maladjustment (or derangement) on the production (or supply) side of the economy. They are caused by a failure in the structure of supply and demand. Production has merely been misdirected into products for which there is insufficient demand at the given prices. The misdirection may be exacerbated due to monetary policy, or some other policy of government, or even external shocks. An economic downturn occurs when producers miscalculate what consumers wish to buy at a given price, thus causing unsold goods to accumulate, production to be curtailed, workers to be laid off, incomes to fall, and finally consumer spending to decline. In an economic downturn, once prices and costs readjust themselves to a new demand structure, commerce will grow again.

These occasional periods of readjustment are inevitable and useful. The period may be short and need not be severe. It is a period in which overextended industries are contracted and in which opportunities are provided for underdeveloped industries to expand. It's a period where prices and costs return towards equilibrium. It's a period in which weak areas in credit are cleaned up, and where excessive debts are liquidated, and economic distortions are repaired. Distortions are unpleasant, and cleaning up disruptions is even more unpleasant. Think of it as the inevitable hangover after a bender.

Examination of nearly 50 American business cycles has convinced this author that not one recession occurred where demand deficiency (or a general over-production) was the cause of the downturn. There is no such thing as a general overproduction, or glut in an economic downturn. Production has merely been misdirected into products for which there is insufficient demand and at prices that do not allow recovery of all costs. After unprofitable investments have been made, capital is liquidated, and reabsorbed elsewhere in the economy.

A generalization can be made from the study of business cycles, as captured in the provision of an individual market for a good (or service): production in the end tends to outrun consumption. A shortage of goods at increasing prices tends to induce speculation, and additional increases in prices. Higher prices induce a higher volume of production, or supply. Prices then tend to fall unless increasing consumption keeps pace with the increasing amount of production. An increase of production goes too far, inventories accumulate, prices fall, and a decline is started which in turn goes too far. Prices are key signals and react upon production, consumption, financing, and prices of inputs and competing products. A change in one direction does not continue forever in that direction. It meets resistance, and the direction of price movement halts and then reverses.

Our economic system is comprised of thousands of various markets (and industries) comprised of many producers (sellers) and buyers. The aggregates do not matter, but rather, these parts do aggregate to a whole. Cyclical movements of various industries reflect the division of labor, every industry, depending upon the smooth working of other industries, and every industry, depending upon the purchasing power obtained from other industries.

The movement of business cycles can also be found in changes in the general level of business confidence. Once established, rising confidence sets in motion two streams of influence which react upon one another and upon their original cause. On the one hand, by increasing willingness to produce in anticipation of rising demand, it increases supply, and thus, the general power to buy. On the other hand, by increasing the volume of effective purchasing power, it reinforces the rising tide of demand and signals the growing profitability of business.

Inflation has Different Meanings

Inflation can manifest itself in several ways; 1) inflation of consumer prices such as food and energy, or 2) inflation of financial (and other) asset prices. These two often feed upon each other. A central bank can stoke asset inflation when it keeps money rates too low for too long, pushing asset prices higher so they are no longer supported by the value of the underlying asset. This is the classic definition of a bubble. This has occurred throughout history and has included stock, real estate, and other assets. Risk taking thrives during the upswing in prices. So does greed, arrogance, and short-term thinking. Eventually, the price of the asset will converge towards its actual value. This is when the bubble bursts, as investors or people start selling. With the bursting of the bubble, the asset price collapses, giving rise to additional selling, and additional price collapse. Misery often characterizes the downswing of prices.

Inflation in the economic sense during the 19th century generally referred to two things: 1) the growth of the money supply, particularly through printing paper currency, and 2) artificial economic expansion, a bubble, or period of unsustainable growth. Americans then often linked the increase of the money supply with an artificial expansion and eventual implosion and depression. It was less common to speak of inflation of prices, and when they did, it was nearly always spoken in connection with paper (or fiat) currency inflation.

The modern definition of inflation as "a general rise in prices" did not become dominant until the 1950s, after decades of debates that brought us a proliferation of different kinds of inflation like "cost-push" and "cost-pull" inflation. Inflation can also result from the growth of excess government spending and expansion of the money supply.

Credit Disturbances as a Cause of the Business Cycle

Forces other than the internal forces of production, trade, consumption, wages, and prices are external in origin and intrude upon these forces internal to the economic system. These external forces are largely economic in origin but may not necessarily be so, and act to throw our economic system out of balance, or sometimes to push the system back into balance. That said, in many cycles, there is little evidence that these external conditions are the primary cause. Rather, they appear to be facilitating, modifying, or augmenting factors. Causes fostering change in the business cycle can originate in unanticipated large changes in interest rates, credit curtailment, policy mistakes, and speculation, among others. Originally, business cycles could be linked with crises brought on by poor harvests, war, problems of public finance, and eventually, speculation and credit expansion.

By far, the most important external force affecting business cycles has been that of monetary and credit policy. In one regard, it is an internal force as developments within banking and other financial sectors spread to commerce, industry, and trade. The institutions of money and credit make their own contribution to the process of production and consumption. As an external force, it is often the monetary authorities or central bank that foster these unstable developments. Monetary policy as a factor influencing the path of the real economy and the business cycle is less clear.

Industry, commerce, and finance depend upon credit. Credit plays an important role in fostering booms and exacerbating busts. Credit is the promise to pay money, and inflation of credit multiplies with these credit promises. Stronger credit growth tends to boost activity and push up asset prices, thus encouraging further credit growth as banks become more confident about lending in an environment of higher asset values. It is a mispricing of risk, but it is often characterized as a virtuous cycle. It is excessive expansion of credit and then wild speculation that usually precedes the downturn. Towards the end of the upswing, investment projects are taken only because credit is available to finance them. The viability of these projects is questionable and subject to error in decision-making. After a certain point, a peak is reached, and asset values begin to fall. Banks thus become reluctant to lend. The projects become unviable, leading to financial hardship for the firms. As the credit cycle turns, the financial strength of firms, consumers and even governments take a turn for the worse. This often has effects on real economic activity, which declines, and the business cycle turns vicious.

When monetary policy is too tight, it slows real business activity, especially in industries supplying durable consumer goods and business investment. When monetary policy is too loose, however, it can damage activity. Extraordinarily aggressive monetary policies such as quantitative easing (QE) can extend the eventual damage by discouraging investments in real assets like capital equipment relative to financial assets such as stocks.

In general, plenteous supply of money or credit fosters an upward force, while tight money or credit exerts a downward force. It is apparent that tight money hurts the bond market, and that a poor bond market affects all sectors (including state and local governments) dependent upon bond issues. Tight money tends to foster scarcity of funds and makes banks tend to withhold funds from investment channels to take advantage of higher rates on loans. On the other hand, loose (or cheap) money opens up the bond market, creating conditions for banks to put more money out for loan. It also tends to encourage the carrying of larger inventories.

Credit inflation schemes have great appeal to human nature because they promise a short-cut to prosperity. Real wealth, however, can only be produced by years of industry, thrift, and capital accumulation. Credit inflation is often accomplished by central bank financial repression of interest rates, resulting in the misallocation of economic resources, capital formation, productivity, and long-run growth. It sustains "zombie" companies and fosters speculation. Credit-fueled booms are inherently unsustainable because they give rise to "fictitious capital" rather than real wealth. Most financial crises at their root feature very high leverage. Balance-sheet recessions are characterized by an overload of public and private debt. Recoveries feature repairing balance sheets.

In a fundamental sense, all crises (or boom and bust episodes) are debt crises. Regarding attempts to solve a debt crisis with monetary policy the outcome is more debt. This builds the foundation for another crisis. Thus, monetary policy exacerbates boom and bust cycles.

The seeds of each credit boom are generally sown in the preceding crisis. Liquidation of credit in the downswing results in declining asset prices that are severe, resulting in some bargains. As prices begin to rise from these depressed levels, speculation revives. Speculation is characteristic of many American business cycles as it is reflective of the speculative character of the American people from colonial times to the present. In early colonial times during the 17th century, people left Europe for many reasons, braving a dangerous Atlantic passage to settle a vast and "howling wilderness," as Pilgrim William Bradford characterized this New World. We are a nation bolstered by immigrants in the 19th and early 20th centuries who were willing to leave family and everything else behind. We see this in the more recent wave of both legal and illegal immigration. This fosters a mindset and character that is uniquely speculative. The "American dream" is an optimistic vision of an improving future.

Monetary over-expansion results in rising inflation, as measured by prices for goods and services. The resulting inflation pushes down "real" interest rates. The resulting distortion leads businesses to over-invest in capital-intensive projects (or sectors) that otherwise may not make sense in the absence of inflation. This is often referred to as asset inflation. Examples include dot-com companies in the late-1990s, canal speculation in the early 19th century, or railroads during several cycles in the 19th century. In addition, expectations of further inflation can induce individuals to speculate in real estate, essentially betting on continued price increases by borrowing funds to "invest" in these assets. An environment of easy money created by central bankers (or the banking system) channels resources into land and other real estate speculation and fuels real estate bubbles. These speculative bubbles arising from new bank credit occurred in the 1830s, 1920s, and 2000s.

To a certain extent, levels of interest rates and the lags between interest rates and other business phenomena during a business cycle vary widely from period to period and suggest little causal connection. Money and credit conditions in many ways are the result of business conditions, including speculation. They not only serve as a brake on expansion and contraction, but, likely, as a secondary factor in augmenting or restraining business cycles. The influence of monetary policy may be regarded not as the primary cause of the business cycle, but rather as a reinforcing cause.

Other External Forces and the Business Cycle

Other forces external in origin intrude upon forces internal to the economic system. Causes of the impulse changing the business cycle can originate externally from unanticipated large changes in energy prices, technology shocks, credit curtailment, policy mistakes, etc. These external factors often develop when economies enter a cyclical window of vulnerability and can be a factor triggering a crisis, panic, or downswing.

Some theorists have attempted to explain the cyclical movement of business by comparing it to the effects of the weather on agriculture. More common prior to the 20th century, agricultural cycles generated business cycles through unusual harvests. Downward forces included poor crops, while upwards forces included good crops. Droughts and other weather events (hurricanes, cold snaps, overly wet summers, etc.) play a role. The economist W.S. Jevons is often ridiculed for his "sunspot theory" of business cycles but sunspot activity (an eleven-year cycle) does correlate with agricultural activity, and in a period (18th, 19th, and even early 20th centuries) when most people were engaged in farming, this explanation had some merit. Great Britain, for example, suffered one of its worst economic slumps in history (wheat crop failed, widespread livestock deaths, etc.), in wake of the Great Frost of 1709, during an extraordinarily cold winter in Europe. The severe cold occurred during the time of low sunspot activity known as the Maunder Minimum. It affected much of Northern Europe and engendered famine (and unrest) in France. Even today, anybody who grew up on a farm or in a small rural community would understand agrarian rhythms and recognize the link between weather and crop productivity. Presently, agriculture is a minor portion of the economic system of nearly all developed nations and many emerging markets, and as a result, farm prosperity is not of major importance in business cycles.

Political developments and public policy mistakes are another external source. Changes in administration, the passage of unfavorable laws, and the creation of onerous (or prohibitive) regulations can all play a role as supply-side restraints on economic activity. Currency instability, rising (or punitive) taxes (including tariffs), and government restraints on economic exchange (trade embargoes in 1807, trust-busting in the 1900s, lockdowns in 2020, etc.) are also suspects in an economic downturn. Punitive taxes were at the heart of the American Revolution and in the economic landscape that led to the creation of the U.S. Constitution. Even expectations of passage of onerous tax and other legislation (e.g., Smoot-Hawley Tariff Act), as well as expectations of an election victory of a party favoring anti-business policies (various William Jennings Bryan scares, organization of the national Progressive Party, victory of the Democrat party in 1912, etc.), can play a role. Political uncertainty (whether Tilden or Hayes was elected president in 1876, the 2000 election, etc.) can also play a role. Tax reforms, tariff reductions, and de-regulation often serve as supply-side boosts to economic activity. Government policies thus play a large role in business cycles.

Oil price shocks have been cited as the cause of several downturns, most notably those beginning in 1973, 1979, and 1990. As an essential input across much of the economy, the price of oil influences the costs of other production and manufacturing across the United States, as well as the cost of transporting goods and people. An oil price shock, however, may reflect credit inflation and the depreciation of the dollar.

Pandemic and similar outbreaks can play a role in fostering downturns. It happened in 1918 and 2020, affecting other cycles as well. Natural disasters have also played a role in fostering downturns. New mineral deposits, or technologies to extract them, can set in motion changes in economic structure. Rising prices foster an upward force, while falling prices exert a downward force. Freedom from labor troubles fosters an upward force, while strikes exert a downward force. Major labor strikes have played a role in downswings. As seen in our nation's history, wars and other international events affect the American business cycle. With globalization, international events have become more important. Other technological innovations have an effect as well. The advent of the internet, for example, likely had an effect on extending the upswing in the 1990s.

Lengths and Types of Business Cycles

The economic factors just discussed are always in interaction. A business cycle can be characterized as a series of changes in the conditions of commerce, industry, trade, and finance (i.e., business) which are characterized by an upward movement in activity to a peak, followed by a downward movement in activity to a trough. In one sense, business cycles are periodic expansions and contractions of business which involved characteristic stages of instability and rearrangement, or maladjustment and readjustment. The idea of rhythm in these flows of business is involved. In assuming rhythm, one must be careful not to assume absolute regularity in the rhythm. These periods of expansion and contraction do not recur with any precise mechanical regularity. The cycles are of varying length and periodicity, as well as magnitude. As there is no regularity, there is no simple rule or formula for determining when change may be expected. Rather, the only safe procedure is to study the causes at work and assess probable outcomes.

A good way to consider business cycles is to think of them as logical sequences of development in business activity, consisting of recovery, expansion, and contraction. They are periodic and can be expected every four or so years unless some significant event or fundamental change imposes upon cyclical trends. Business cycles vary widely in the degree of expansion and contraction and do not affect all industries (and markets) equally and at the same time. There are minor and major cycles. Table 1.1 provides a summary of peaks and troughs for American business cycles from the 1780s until now. I used the NBER dates from Cycle 14 to present. The dates used for prior cycles are based on the peaks and toughs suggested by the index of business activity developed for this book. This index measures the real gross output of all economic sectors in the U.S. economy. It measures output (or production) on a volume basis. The index is discussed in more detail in the next chapter.

In the book of Genesis, Joseph's "seven years of plenty followed by seven years of want" may or may not be the story of the American business cycle. Depending on which periods one examines, a seven or so year cycle may or may not fit the pattern. The annals of American business cycles and crises, as well as the data on real gross output, find that major crises occur on average every 10 years or so, but the intervening intervals have not been sufficiently regular to substantiate a theory of true periodicity. John Calverley — formerly of Standard Chartered Bank and American Express Bank and now CEO of Tricio Investment Advisors Ltd. — found that a typical U.S. economic cycle lasts seven to 11 years. His study confirms cycles of nine to 10 years that were first observed by Clement Juglar as far back as 1860 and later confirmed by Joseph Schumpeter, as part of his three-cycle scheme in his comprehensive two-volume *Business Cycles* back in 1939. Since Schumpeter wrote, Calverley found that we have had cycles of roughly that length in the 1960s, 1980s, 1990s, 2000s and 2010s. Only in the 1950s and 1970s did cycles not conform. John's reasoning was that the former likely reflected the stop-go fiscal policy, while in the 1970s the massive oil shock of 1974 upset the pattern. Therefore, the Biblical paraphrase above approximates a norm for American business cycle history.

Table 1.1
U.S. Business Cycle Peaks and Troughs, 1782-2020

Cycle #	Trough	Peak	Trough
0	March 1782?	March 1785	June 1789
1	June 1789	February 1796	October 1798
2	October 1798	July 1801	April 1803
3	April 1803	November 1807	April 1809
4	April 1809	January 1811	December 1812
5	December 1812	November 1815	February 1821
6	February 1821	June 1822	June 1823

Cycle #	Trough	Peak	Trough
7	June 1823	August 1825	July 1828
8	July 1828	August 1833	August 1834
9	August 1834	January 1837	June 1838
10	June 1838	March 1839	February 1843
11	February 1843	March 1846	August 1846
12	August 1846	August 1847	November 1848
13	November 1848	March 1854	December 1854
14	December 1854	June 1857	December 1858
15	December 1858	October 1860	June 1861
16	June 1861	April 1865	December 1867
17	December 1867	June 1869	December 1870
18	December 1870	October 1873	March 1879
19	March 1879	March 1882	May 1885
20	May 1885	March 1887	April 1888
21	April 1888	July 1890	May 1891
22	May 1891	January 1893	June 1894
23	June 1894	December 1895	June 1897
24	June 1897	June 1899	December 1900
25	December 1900	September 1902	August 1904
26	August 1904	May 1907	June 1908
27	June 1908	January 1910	January 1912
28	January 1912	January 1913	December 1914
29	December 1914	August 1918	March 1919
30	March 1919	January 1920	July 1921
31	July 1921	May 1923	July 1924
32	July 1924	October 1926	November 1927
33	November 1927	August 1929	March 1933
34	March 1933	May 1937	June 1938
35	June 1938	February 1945	October 1945
36	October 1945	November 1948	October 1949
37	October 1949	July 1953	May 1954
38	May 1954	August 1957	April 1958

Cycle #	Trough	Peak	Trough
39	April 1958	April 1960	February 1961
40	February 1961	December 1969	November 1970
41	November 1970	November 1973	March 1975
42	March 1975	January 1980	July 1980
43	July 1980	July 1981	November 1982
44	November 1982	July 1990	March 1991
45	March 1991	March 2001	November 2001
46	November 2001	December 2007	June 2009
47	June 2009	February 2020	April 2020
48	April 2020		

Students of the business cycle have identified different types of business cycles of varying lengths. French economist Clement Juglar (1819-1905) is one of the founders of business cycle theory, basing his work on extensive observation of prices, interest rates, and other financial variables. Austrian economist Joseph Schumpeter (1883-1950) linked Juglar to the cycle when he devised the term **Juglar cycle** to refer to cycles lasting between seven and 11 years. Juglar's explanation was monetary, emphasizing the role of the expansion and contraction of bank credit. Juglar cycles are also linked to fluctuations in business fixed investment, especially for machinery and equipment. These are major cycles.

In his three-cycle schema, Schumpeter also identified the **Kitchin cycles** of about 40 months (or 3.5 years) in length. These are named after British statistician Joseph Kitchin (1861-1932) who identified both minor cycles of 40 months and major cycles of seven to 10 years. Price levels and interest rates movements were linked to these 40-month cycles. They are linked to inventory accumulation and de-stocking. These are minor cycles.

Schumpeter attributed this three-cycle schema to innovation and identified the **Kondratieff cycles** of 45 to 60 years in length. These are also referred to as the long cycle or long waves. Russian economist Nikolai Kondratieff (1892-1938) examined long-term trends in prices in England, France, and the United States. The price phenomena is apparent, but there is some controversy whether it is manifested in real economic growth. These cycles are linked to major innovations and the flow of investment. Some economists consider these cycles to be deeply hidden.

Although not part of Schumpeter's cycle schema, a fourth type of cycle is said to exist. Named after economist Simon Kuznets (1901-1985) who first identified long-term movements in secondary movements, the so-called **Kuznets cycles** last 18-25 years. These may reflect longer-term movements in population and housing, and population-sensitive infrastructure investment. It has been referred to as a building cycle.

What is clear is that there is no agreed manner of defining major and minor cycles. Some major cycles may consist of two or more minor cycles. The National Bureau of Economic Research (NBER), the official arbiter of business cycle dates in the United States, features chronologies that cannot be differentiated into major (Juglar) and minor (Kitchin) cycles.

Examination of the nearly 50 American business cycles (the focus of this book) found that since the 1780s they have averaged 59 months, of which 40 months of upswing occurred on average, and 19 months of downswing occurred. We segment these over 230 years into three periods: 1785-1865; 1865-1945; and 1945 to the present. Longevity of cycles in American business cycle history is provided in Table 1.2. Examination of the depth of these downswings is left to the discussion of each cycle in later chapters.

In the first period (1785-1865), business cycles averaged 58 months and in the second period (1865-1945) 50 months. The shorter cycle time of the second period may reflect the greater importance of the goods (agriculture, mining, manufacturing, and construction) sectors to the U.S. economy. During the third and most recent period (1945-2020), the average cycle lasted 74 months. This may reflect the greater importance of the less cyclical services sectors, the waning of the importance of goods (and inventory imbalances), and better decision-making tools and information available to firms.

Major cycles are those usually attended by crises and in much of our nation's history, occur about every 10 years, thus confirming Calverley, Schumpeter, and Juglar. Minor cycles occur about every four or so years and are often associated with inventory imbalances. In general, our examination of cycles indicates that upswings last longer than downswings. The average since the 1780s is 40 months. In contrast, downswings averaged 19 months in length. That is, for every month of contracting, there were 2.2 months of expanding activity, or 2.2:1. If upswings weren't longer than downswings (or the period of expanding activity shorter than the period of contracting activity) there would be no economic progress. A dynamic economy has an underlying bias towards expansion.

Table 1.2
U.S. Business Cycle Upswings and Downswings

# of Cycles	Period	Upswing	Downswing	Ratio Upswing/ Downswing
15	1785-1865	36	22	1.7:1
20	1865-1945	29	21	1.4:1
22	1945-2020	64	10	6.2:1
47	1785-2020	40	19	2.2:1

In the first period, upswings averaged 36 months and downswings 22 months, a ratio of 1.7:1. In the second period, upswings averaged 29 months and downswings 21 months, a 1.4:1 ratio. These cycles were often associated with panics. During the third and most recent period, the average upswing lasted 64 months and the average downswing only 10 months, a ratio of 6.2:1. Again, the rise of services and relatively declining importance of the goods sectors, in combination with better policy tools, are often cited as factors behind this moderation. The prevalence of better economic statistics may be a factor as well.

In addition to these cycles affecting the broad economy, each industry has its own unique cycle. The case can be made that the broad business cycle consists of the aggregation of many industry cycles. Monitoring industry cycles provides an avenue for examining the business cycle in its particular parts. It provides a means for exploring timing relationships between industries. It provides business leaders with insight into industry turning points. A business leader who quickly recognizes a change (or turning point) in their industry cycle could foster appropriate marketing strategies for either downswing or upswing.

A clear understanding of the present situation is a condition to a clear assessment of the likely future. Good business forecasting is an accurate analysis of existing and current conditions and wise interpretation of trends that companies may be expected to follow. Business moves in cycles of expansion and retrenchment, prosperity, and recession. The data indicate that actual historical business cycles are highly irregular, with no two cycles alike in terms of <u>distance</u> (amplitude, intensity and pronounced effect), <u>ubiquity</u> (diffusion, dispersion, universality, frequency, incidence, and pervasiveness among the markets and industries), and <u>endurance</u> (duration, extent, length, and persistence over time). That is, give the upswing and downswing of each business cycle it's DUE. This is the framework I use when evaluating where we are in the business cycle.

Signs of Peaks and Troughs

One of the most important tasks for the business leaders or business economist is to see in advance or anticipate future trends, but most important for short-term performance is anticipating changes in direction of the business cycle, the transitions of peaks and troughs. It is the most difficult challenge for business forecasting and is the primary cause of errors in forecasting. Much like families in the opening sentence of Tolstoy's classic novel *Anna Karenina* (and quoted in the Preface), every business cycle is different, but may have common patterns. The following are some signs of the peaks and troughs of American business cycles. In general, turning points occur when there is a secular change in the economy's fortunes or a notable development that affects a leading industry's long-term prospects. Understanding the forces involved in upswings and downswings is important for knowing when we are entering a transition between these phases of the cycle. That is, peaks or troughs.

In the later stages of the upswing, business is good (and getting better), sales are rising, and unemployment is low. Business is booming as the cycle nears its peak, and people start believing that "things will be good forever" and "this time it's different." The longer the upswing, the more everyone is convinced that it is here to stay. Speculation runs rampant as financial markets have shrugged off past episodes (and losses). Optimism and imprudence reign, and as financial journalist Walter Bagehot (1826-1877) would note, investors become "blind" and unable to remember the past. As such, they are condemned to repeat it. Roger Babson (1926) identified extravagance, recklessness, waste, greed, and irreligion as factors. Such thinking is hard to dislodge, especially at turning points.

Indications that the peak of a business is near include: commodity prices that, after a prolonged rise begin to fluctuate near high levels and may even decline; industrial and commercial activity is well above trend and increasing; unfilled orders are high and delivery times long; new orders are falling; inventories are beginning to accumulate; employment is high, and recruiting and retaining are challenging; interest rates are high; credit is strained; consumers are spending more via credit than out of income; bank lending is significant; equity markets are at highs, but the course is erratic and little gain has been shown for months; dividends have been increased; speculation in equities and commodities is high; wages are advancing and price concessions are emerging. These may not appear in every cycle, but most do.

Signs of a trough in the cycle are the very opposite to those at the peak. Indications that the trough of a business is near include: commodity prices are stabilizing after a long decline; industrial and commercial activity is well below trend and decreasing; unfilled orders are low, and delivery times short; inventories are high relative to output but are declining; unemployment is high but rising at a slowing pace; interest rates are low; credit is difficult to obtain, and banks are unwilling to loan; equity markets have rebounded from a low point; wages are contained, and prices are stabilizing. Sometimes a specific event (war, opening of new lands, etc.) serves as the stimulus to the inevitable upswing. Sometimes, it is a change in government policy towards business (i.e., a tax cut).

During a typical cycle there is usually one dominant industry. In the 19th century, it was often the railroad industry with its boom-and bust-cycle of rail construction. In much of the 20th century, it was usually light vehicles and/or housing. In the 2001 recession, the dominant industry was that associated with the dot.com phenomena. The dominant industry in the lead-up to the Great Financial Crisis (GFC) of 2007-09 was housing and all the allied business activity associated with that sector. The GFC was preceded by an economic boom that was led by speculative excesses, particularly in the housing industry. When that bubble burst, a credit crunch worsened the resulting business-cycle downturn. By determining the chief factor in the upswing of a cycle and studying the cycle with that in mind, a better understating of circumstances is possible, as is the ability to see emerging developments more clearly. For insight into bubbles, I recommend John Calverley's *Bubbles and How to*

Survive Them.[6] His checklist (page 13) on the typical characteristics of a bubble alone is worth the cost of the book.

In all of this, the business forecaster should look at conditions of production and inventories, unfilled orders, and commodity prices, as well as corporate profits. In addition, credit is important, as is background monetary policy, political agenda, and global conditions.

---

[6] John Calverley is founding director and Chief Economist of Tricio Investment Advisors, advising professional investors on economic and market trends. He was previously Chief Economist and Strategist at American Express and Head of Economic Research at Standard Chartered.

CHAPTER 2

On Measuring Business Activity

"Can do much better macroeconomic forecasting looking at individual industries."

—Alan Greenspan

Introduction

As represented by a wide variety of data, production, commerce, trade, and finance show a persistent tendency to increase over time, decade by decade. However, disturbances and events intervene along with mistakes, resulting in interruptions to, or deviations from, the tendency of growth. More important is the definite wave-like movement (i.e., business cycles), which appears to be superimposed on the line of growth. The persistence of these business cycles can be thought of as interruptions to normal growth.

To assess business cycles in American history, this book uses a measure of economic activity — an index of the volume of (or real) gross output — developed by the author. This chapter discusses the need for measuring output, the concept of gross output, and the data and methodology used in creating the index of the volume of real gross output.

Need for a Measure of Business Activity

There are many different measures of productive activity, but, given the complexity of our economic systems and over 600 distinct industries, the data needs are overwhelming. There are many differences in the cyclical movements of various times series of data, and they may not always synchronize exactly. After all, there are over 600 distinct stories and cycles. Yet, there is enough similarity in the movement of these measures that we can speak of the business cycle. As illustrated in the last chapter, the law of markets and inter-connectedness among these industries warrants viewing the economic exchange from the production side as well as the traditional focus on demand employed by most business economists. In my career, I have presented the same forecasts as other business economists (components of GDP, real incomes, profits, etc.) but always start on the production side to guide my thinking. Most forecasters focus on the demand side. These demand-focused indicators are essential for any economic modeling and for forecasting detailed product demand.

I was often asked by reporters and members of the audience during the early stages of the last several upswings (after the business cycle trough) what type of recovery I foresee. Is it V, U (both normal and inverted), W, or L-shaped, resembles a Nike swoosh logo, resembles an inverted square root sign, or some other manner? I honestly admit that it is all the above, as each industry (and market) will experience something different. Recoveries, or upswings, come in all different shapes, sizes, and forms. They can occur for all different reasons and recover from recessions in different ways. Some of the common types of recoveries (or upswings) that have occurred in American business cycle history include:

- V-Shaped: Marked by short and sharp contractions followed by a fast and sustained recovery.
- U-Shaped: Marked by a prolonged slump in the economy, including a slower drop and a slow, long recovery.
- L-Shaped: Marked by a short, sudden downswing followed by a sustained period of contraction, often lasting years.
- W-Shaped: Occurs when business activity falls, begins to rise, and then falls into recession again before rising out again. America experienced a W-shaped recession between 1815 and 1821 and between 1980 and 1982. It is erroneously known as a double-dip recession.

This is often measured by examining the trend in real GDP. This is a very aggregated measure, but in looking at the details and production-side of the economy, various shapes are normally present. For example, at the start of the present upswing from the business cycle trough in April 2020, a V-shaped recovery is apparent in many manufacturing industries, but who would challenge that cruise lines were facing anything but a L-shaped recovery until the pandemic eased? Each industry has its own distinct dynamics and story, yet there is some co-movement together for most.

In business cycles, the variable to be measured is general business activity, a variable in a continual state of flux, although the forces that foster deviations are often self-correcting. To assess business cycles, a monthly measure is needed that captures fluctuations in a wide variety of industries into a single accurate statistical index, which will represent the general state of business of the country as a whole. Such has been the aim in this book, the construction of a monthly index of the physical volume of the productive activity of industry, commerce, trade, and finance.

Real GDP (gross domestic product) is one such measure that is widely used by business leaders, business economists, policy makers, and the media. Prior to the 1940s, policy makers had to guide the economy using limited and fragmentary information about the state of the economy. Both the Hoover and then Roosevelt administrations designed policies to combat the Great Depression of the 1930's based on sketchy data, such as stock price indices, freight car loadings, and incomplete indices of industrial production. Comprehensive measures of national income and output did not exist at the time. The Great Depression, and with it, the growing role of government in the economy, emphasized the need for such measures and led to the development of a system of national income accounts. The Department of Commerce commissioned Simon Kuznets (later a Nobel laureate) of the National Bureau of Economic Research (NBER) to develop a set of national economic accounts. Professor Kuznets coordinated the work of researchers at the National Bureau of Economic Research in New York and staff at Commerce. An original set of accounts was presented in a report to Congress in 1937. In 1942, annual estimates of gross national product (GNP) were introduced to complement the estimates of national income and to facilitate war planning. Over time, in response to policy needs and changes in the economy, the national income accounts were expanded by the Bureau of Economic Analysis (BEA) to provide quarterly estimates of GDP (gross domestic product) and monthly estimates of personal income and outlays, as well as regional accounts, wealth accounts, industry accounts, and expanded international accounts.

In the 1990s, most economists switched from using the GNP concept to the concept of gross domestic product (GDP). Both reflect the national output and income of an economy, but the main difference is that GNP considers net income receipts from abroad. GDP is a purported measure of goods and services produced in a particular country. It adds together the purchases of goods and services by consumers, business, and government during a year (or quarter). It measures and emphasizes final spending (what Keynes referred to as "effective demand"), and at its core is commonly known by the accounting identity of $Y = C + I + G$ where Y = GDP; C = consumption by consumers: I is investment by business as well as residential investment (i.e., housing and repairs) and changes in inventories and G = purchases of goods and services by government. Exports are added, and imports subtracted to complete the definition. Details on how the GDP is constructed and related accounts can be found on the BEA website at www.bea.gov.

The Y was the letter that Keynes used, and the respect for Keynes was so strong that, to this day, even monetarists, new classical economists, and supply-siders, among many schools of economic thought, use this abbreviation. The concept of GDP is essentially a Keynesian statistic. The development of these national income data (GNP and later GDP) helped advance the Keynesian revolution in economic thought and policy proscription. All three reinforced each other.

Several criticisms have been made about GDP, including not accounting for black market activities, household production, and used goods. The largest issue in my opinion is that it leaves out spending at the intermediate level before reaching the final stage of consumption.

In fact, GDP essentially represents only final spending. One of my pet peeves is when economists (who should know better), policy makers, and journalists refer to GDP as total spending in the economy. One often hears that consumer spending accounts for roughly 70 percent (or two-thirds) of the economy. These same people make the mistake of assuming that the economy is consumer driven.

Another one of my pet peeves is when I see economists discuss movements in GDP in the same sentence with non-farm payrolls. Except for the agricultural and related extractive sectors, the latter includes intermediate production. This truly is a comparison of apples and oranges.

Although the "customer is king" in marketing most economic exchange (as measured by revenues or sales) is business-to-business (B2B) spending, often defined as intermediate spending. Along with business investment, business spending represents well over half of economic exchange (and activity) in the United States and other advanced nations.

Another criticism is that it is a quarterly measure. Although several national statistical agencies (Canada, United Kingdom, etc.) have created monthly measures of GDP, there is not an official monthly measure of GDP. That said, the economists at S&P Global Market Intelligence (formerly IHS Markit) have developed an indicator of real aggregate output that is conceptually consistent with real (i.e., inflation-adjusted) GDP in the National Income and Product Accounts (NIPA). Their approach uses calculation and aggregation methods comparable to the official GDP from the BEA. The time series unfortunately only goes back as far as January 1992.

Quarterly reports such as GDP also obscure details. Employment, industrial production, and other data, available monthly, show that April 2020, for example, was the worst month in the most recent downturn, with a sharp but partial rebound in later months. GDP for the second quarter was certainly bad, but where monthly data are available, June shows generally better than April, providing more insight into the timing of the business cycle trough and transition from downswing to upswing.

Prior to the development of the national income and products accounts in the 1930s and 1940s (and consequent focus on GNP/GDP), several prominent business economists developed broad indexes of business activity. Most notable were the Axe-Houghton Index of Trade and Industrial Activity, the AT&T Index of General Business, and the Cleveland Trust Index of

American Business Activity. The index developed for this book continues this tradition.

Concept of Gross Output

When supply and demand come together, an economic exchange emerges. Networks of these exchanges are called markets. These countless interconnected markets are what constitute the economy. This bottoms-up approach is the one taken in this book.

In his 1990 book titled *The Structure of Production*, financial economist Mark Skousen first introduced the concept of gross output (GO). Since then, he has been the leading proponent. Skousen champions gross output as a more comprehensive measure of economic activity. The BEA's decision in 2014 to publish GO on a quarterly basis in its GDP by Industry data offerings is a major achievement in national income accounting. GO was the first output statistic to be published on a quarterly basis since the 1940s. Skousen finds GO and GDP to be complementary aspects of the economy, but GO does a better job of measuring total economic activity and the business cycle as it measures the production sector. GDP is appropriate as a measure of welfare. Both are needed in understanding the economy. By using GO data, consumer spending is only about one-third of economic exchange, not the two-thirds that is often reported by the media. Business spending is nearly twice the size of consumer spending in the economy.

Our economic system is one of continuous mutual exchange between those who buy and those who sell. The many decisions of firms and individuals are a network of upstream and downstream linkages across the economy, forming a complex and intricate web of economic exchange. Considering this elaborate coordination of exchange by stage of production and by examining the changes in the structure of production can shed light on what is really happening in the economy. An industry perspective can more readily illuminate the nature and causes of fluctuations in economic growth and employment. For example, the macroeconomic aggregates (Y, I, etc.) are not in themselves actual components of the economy but rather a measure of the cumulative actions taken by millions of individuals and firms. These statistics are intended to provide an overall "total," but the aggregation involved is at such a high level that they provide little insight into the economy's structure and how resources are being employed.

One can monitor these trends and the changes in the structure of production using the BEA quarterly GO by industry data. The data are released with a lag of three months and are only available back to 2005. There are also some measurement issues (e.g., wholesale and retail trade are measured as value-added and not by sales), but quarterly gross output by industry is still very useful in understanding the US economy's structure of production. The BEA Gross Output by Industry data are available on the BEA website.

Gross output is a more comprehensive (and I believe better) view of total economic activity along the entire supply chain, from primary sectors to secondary (or intermediate) sectors, to final sectors, and ultimately to the final consumer. It is more sensitive to the business cycle. The data show that about 90 percent of economic activity as measured by gross output is within private industries. That is, B2B spending. The gross output data can be used to identify the trends among individual industries across the economy and to create heat maps tracing distance, ubiquity, and endurance of propagation arising from various impulses. Heat maps illustrate the impulse inducing the slowdown and the "ripple effect" throughout the economic system. I have long looked at the inter-connectivity of these industries to better understand changes in economic exchange and business cycle dynamics. The Alan Greenspan quote at the start of this chapter, from one of the greatest business economists before his role in government and as chair of the Federal Reserve, is indicative of the need to look at the details and the production side of the economy.

Why should business economists look at the BEA's gross output data? Think of gross output as a measure of market activity or value of exchanges. It measures how much activity is taking place in the marketplace. To some extent, it is equivalent to domestic revenues, or top line growth. That is, the data measure the revenue base of the United States. Many CEOs think in headline revenue (and volume) growth terms and compare performance to the same period one year earlier rather than marginal (or incremental) change. This is particularly the case in multi-product firms. Most do not think in inflation-adjusted real terms, although CEOs in some industries do think in some specific volume terms (units or tons sold/produced, etc.), again on a year-earlier comparison basis. Furthermore, long-term growth rates used for corporate valuations are often based on the growth in the economy, as measured in nominal terms (e.g., nominal GDP). For these purposes, growth in nominal gross output may be a better measure. In addition to tracking change in the structure of production and the diffusion of change among sectors, business economists may also use this data to explain (or compare) changes in corporate revenues as well as B2B spending. In addition, an economy-wide decline in gross output may presage business cycle downturns. In a low-inflation environment, for example, a recession likely occurs if growth in nominal GDP falls below 3½ percent year-over-year. A similar rule of thumb could be developed for nominal gross output, but, with only a limited history, no conclusions can be drawn. A longer history of the BEA's gross output data is needed, as is additional research.

As a measure of economy-wide revenues, the gross output data are also more closely aligned (than GDP) with measures of profits, cash flow, fixed business investment, employment, and related data. This facilitates common-sense comparisons. Other possibilities exist for business economists. For example, gross output is a more appropriate measure of transactions (than GDP) in the economy for measuring the circulation (or velocity) of money.

Looking at the details, I continuously monitor the health of 156 industries on an ongoing basis. The major sectors are those covered in the BEA GO program, as is most of the data. I use actual wholesale and retail trade (or sales) from the Census Bureau instead of value-added. Thus, I give more weight to wholesale and retail trade. This better reflects reality. I also use data from the Census Bureau MISO (formerly M3) report to provide comparable gross output values for key manufacturing industries. Thus, my estimate of nominal GO for 2022 is $54.5 trillion, more than 18 percent higher than the comparable $46.0 billion BEA figure and more than two times the $25.5 trillion figure for nominal GDP.

I also use a systematic approach to estimating the latest quarter based on monthly and other data. I can't say that I am an expert on all 156 industries, but I can usually provide a narrative on most of these. I often publish these as a heat map.

In addition to nominal GO, the BEA also publishes quarterly indexes of real GO, or the volume of production. These form the foundation for much of the work in this present volume. Again, I provide greater weight to wholesale and retail trade.

A New Measure of Real Business Activity

In accordance with my views on the role of the business cycle causes and characteristics, underlying economic assumptions, the value on focusing on production, and the need for a composite and timely index of overall activity, I have constructed a monthly index of business activity, or rather an index of the monthly volume of output (or real gross output) of these Untied States for as long a period as possible to obtain a record of the behavior of business. I have assembled monthly figures on production, prices, interest rates, etc., as well as prepared a chronological account of economic events and developments.

It all begins with production, as measured by real GO. I use the latter term interchangeably with volume of business activity and the output of industry, commerce, trade, and finance. The work of developing a monthly index of the volume of business activity is complicated and difficult. A bottoms-up approach is taken.

The first challenge is the choice of a base for the index numbers. The main use of a base number of 100 is that it affords a relatively quick means of estimating percent change in activity. I select a base year that is a "normal" period in the economy, not too near to either period of transition in the cycle. In this case, the year 2017 is the base year, and all data are set to where 2017 = 100. The choice reflects a period four years into the upswing. In addition, some of the underlying data (e.g., industrial production) used in construction of this index of real gross output were already based on a 2017 base year. When the BEA and Federal Reserve change their base year, I will change the base year for this monthly index.

A second challenge is to construct a monthly index. The BEA real gross output indexes are quarterly, but monthly data on output (or proxies) behind the BEA indexes are largely available. For example, the Federal Reserve publishes a monthly industrial production index back to January 1919. Furthermore, there are other measures of industrial production that were compiled by business economists beginning in the 19th century. I first became aware of these sources when I authored a short history of the chemical industry from 1872 to 1997. In addition, I created a leading indicator of the U.S. business cycle that extends back to 1884, and in developing that, became aware of more historic data sources.

Several of these data sources come to mind. A good starting place is the Bureau of the Census' publication titled *Historical Statistics of the United States, Colonial Times to 1970*. This is available at www.census.gov. Since the publication of this book of historical statistics, there has been an explosion of new analyses and data by economic historians. The BEA's *Survey of Current Business* and the

Federal Reserve Board's *Federal Reserve Bulletin* were comparable sources, as were other federal government agencies.

During the first several decades of its existence, the NBER assembled an extensive set of data that covers all aspects of the pre-WWI and interwar economies, including production, construction, employment, money, prices, asset market transactions, foreign trade, and government activity. Many series are highly disaggregated, and many exist at the monthly or quarterly frequency. Details on the NBER Macrohistory Database are available at www.nber.org. The St. Louis Federal Reserve bank developed its FRED data service, an on-line source of 822,000 time series from 110 sources, including the NBER. See https://fred.stlouisfed.org/ for details. From these sources, many of the authors are cited in the Bibliography, as well as various statistical handbooks and compendiums from various trade associations. A perusal of various 1920s issues of the *Survey of Current Business* and the *Federal Reserve Bulletin* reveals the importance of many of these industry sources.

In developing a monthly index of real gross output, I utilize the available production indexes from the Federal Reserve Board as a starting point. For the non-industrial sectors, monthly indexes are calculated using much of the same underlying monthly source data that is used in the calculation of the BEA quarterly data. I start with the quarterly BEA quantity indexes of gross output and by using monthly data on production, hours worked, deflated sales, etc., have been able to develop monthly data conceptually consistent with the BEA quarterly data. As mentioned before, I give more weight to wholesale and retail trade. As a result, my headline measure of real gross output differs slightly. All of these time series are combined, with weights reflecting contributions to economic exchange, into a single series, representing an index of the total volume of business activity (or real gross output) in the United States. A consistent series (based on the 156 industries) is available back to 1997. The structure of the U.S. economy is constantly shifting, and many current important industries (i.e., Internet-based) simply do not exist in this period. I was able to "drop" some of these sectors off while re-engaging once prominent sectors. I do this working back in time. A consistent approach is available from 1947 through 1997. Again, working back through time, I was able to construct the monthly index of real business activity (or gross output) while adjusting for changes in economic structure and data availability. Fortunately, several indexes of business activity — Axe-Houghton Index of Trade and Industrial Activity, the AT&T Index of General Business, and the Cleveland Trust Index of American Business Activity — were available to provide guidance, as did complementary data sources on other sectors, all of which are used (along with other data sources) to extend this monthly index backward in time. Complementary annual data on economic exchange are adjusted with monthly data fitted to them using various sources on production, other economic activity, bank clearings, stock prices, bond prices, and commodity prices. These are combined, with weights reflecting economic contributions, into a single time series. This approach was used to a much greater extent in the 18th and first half of the 19th century. I am indebted to the work by Leonard Ayres in *Turning Points in Business Cycles*. A wealth of data has been developed and published since Ayres' work. The underlying data are consistent between 1919 and 1947, between 1855 and 1919, and from the start in the 1780s through 1855. As more data are uncovered or become available, I will take them into account and possibly revise this index of business activity (or real gross output). This is a work in progress, not a finished product, and in no way is it even close to being perfect.

Figure 2.1 shows annual data for this index of real gross output. The underlying monthly index of real gross output provides a means of measuring production across all industries and sectors of the economy. That is, a broad measure of industry, commerce, trade, and finance. It centers on production (or supply). This is a far bigger marker for the economy. Production must come before consumption and is key to a healthy economy. Consumption is not sustainable if it is not coming from a productive part of the economy. It is the productive capacity of an economy that affords spending. The data are presented in a linear chart, one in which values are evenly spaced. The distance between two points on the lower end of the scale is the same as if at the higher end. It shows the amount of change in a trend. A linear chart is often referred to as a "hockey stick" chart as it resembles a hockey stick lying on its shaft with the blade pointing upwards. A linear scale — also referred to as arithmetic — represents output (as measured by an index where 2017=100) on the y-axis using equidistant spacing between the designated output. A linear scale does not depict or scale movements in any relation to their percent change. Rather, a linear scale plots output level changes with each unit change according to a constant unit value.

Figure 2.1
Index of Real Gross Output: 1780-2022 (Linear)
Index where 2017 = 100

Linear charts display absolute values. This type of chart is skewed toward the higher values (i.e., recent years), and thus for long multi-century time periods this is probably not the best way to present the data. Linear charts are effective for examining distinct business cycles, and I use these in chapters three, four and five. I only present charts for the major cycles and few other selective cycles. In the period after 1945, I often combine two cycles into one chart to better capture long-term trends during a decade, or across cycles.

Figure 2.2
Index of Real Gross Output: 1780-2022 (Logarithmic)
Index where 2017 = 100

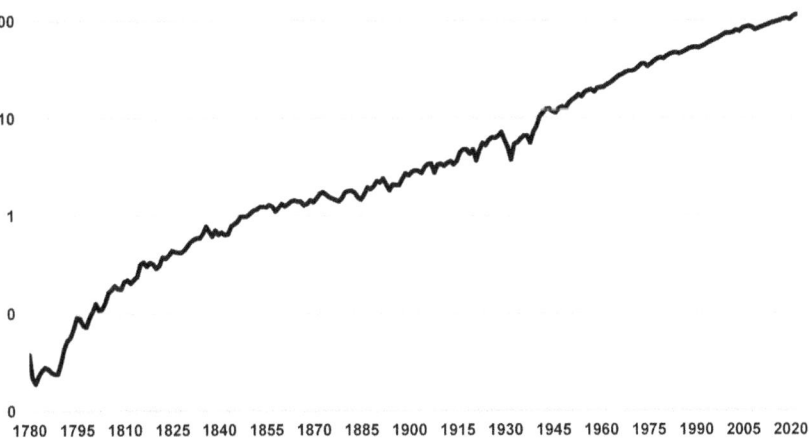

Figure 2.2 shows annual data for this index of real gross output but in logarithmic scale. A logarithmic scale — also referred to as log — represents real output (or volume) spacing on the vertical or y-axis, dependent on the percentage of change in the underlying output. A logarithmic scale is plotted so that the output in the scale is not positioned equidistantly. That is, equally from one another. Instead, the measure is plotted in such that two equal percent changes are plotted as the same vertical distance on the scale. A logarithmic scale is useful for long time periods. The data

indicate a period of very rapid growth in American real gross output in the initial decades leading to the mid-19th century. Growth then moderates and has been consistent since then over the long-term.

Another way of looking at long-term trends is per capita real gross output. In this case, the index of business activity is divided by population and re-based to where 2017 = 100. Figure 2.3 is a linear presentation of per capita real gross output for the United States. This is a better presentation of trends than Figure 2.1 and considers population change. However, it is still skewed towards the higher values of recent years.

Figure 2.3

Index of Real Gross Output per Capita: 1780-2022 (Linear)
Index where 2017 = 100

The business cycle peaks and troughs as determined by this index of real gross output generally coincide with those determined by the NBER since the 1850s. In some cases, the exact months may vary, sometimes as much as three months. Of the 69-business cycle turns (or transitions) recorded by the NBER since 1854, the index of real gross output presented in this book coincide exactly with 44 of them. Of the 25 not coinciding, 19 were off by one month, five by two months, and one by three months. The latter peak in real gross output was in November 2019, three months ahead of the NBER business cycle peak of February 2020. Revisions to data may cause both to be more closely aligned.

Hopefully, this monthly index of real gross output provides another means for measuring the economy and the business cycle. Again, this is a work in progress.

The monthly record for this index of real gross output (or business activity) is available from January 1785 to the present. A spreadsheet containing the index is available from the author upon request.[7] High-frequency data can also be employed to determine near real-time trends in real gross output. For example, by the third week of the month, one can make a reasonable assessment of the broad (or aggregate) changes that month, and I do provide this during the third week of the month for the current month.

Real gross output has increased at a 4.1 percent annual pace from 1785 to 2019. This compares with a 3.7 percent annual gain in GDP and an estimated 4.4 percent annual gain in industrial production for this 130-year period. Population has grown at a 2.0 percent annual pace during this period.

---

[7]   The author can be reached at tks@swiftecon.com.

Figure 2.4

Annual (Year-over-Year) Change in the Index of Real Gross Output: 1780-2022

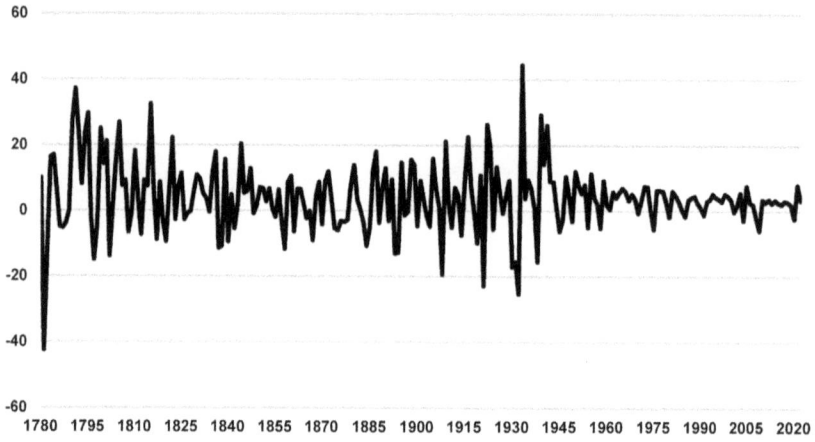

Figure 2.4 shows the year-over-year change in this index of real gross output. The data show that general business activity — as measured by this index of real gross output — is variable in nature. Periods of high activity are followed by subpar performance, and even decline, which in turn gives way to new upswing. Such has been the case in the United States since the 1780s. From the 1780s through 2020, there have been 47 complete business cycles as measured from trough to trough, and in mid-2020 a 48th cycle began. The length of the swings is most pronounced early in the American experience as well as in the first half of the twentieth century. The swings moderate after that. The subsequent three chapters graphically present the measure of real gross output, along with a short discussion of each one of these cycles. In the course of these cycle discussions, I will bring in supplementary data on inflation, unemployment, interest rates, trade, production of leading industries, and other economic measures.

CHAPTER 3

Revolutionary War to Civil War

"The farther back you can look, the farther forward you are likely to see."

—Winston Churchill

Introduction

America is one of the most blessed of nations in terms of geography and natural resources, which in time led to the rise of what Peter Zeihan (2014) referred to as "Accidental Superpower." The nation is endowed with a temperate climate, abundant forests, and fertile agricultural land as well as vast oil, natural gas, iron ore, copper, coal lead, silver, gold, and other mineral deposits.

By some estimates, the lower 48 states have more miles of navigable inland waterway than the rest of the world combined. The Mississippi, Missouri, and Ohio rivers (along with major tributaries) flow diagonally uniting the entire temperate, agricultural area of the nation, an area of rich, arable soil. This river network facilitates the movement of people and farm produce to domestic and foreign markets. The lower 48 states are protected by two vast oceans and significant, protected, and natural deep-water ports on both coasts. The ports on the East Coast allowed for strong economic development. This sets the background for the remarkable growth of American industry, commerce, trade, and finance.

The annals of American commerce and industry (and the data on real gross output) from the Constitutional Convention until the Civil War include eight major downswings, which developed in the following years, namely 1785, 1796, 1807, 1815, 1825, 1837, 1839, and 1857. The elapsed time between the major downswings averaged 10 years. Minor downswings occurred in 1801, 1811, 1822, 1833, 1846, 1847, 1854, and 1860.

Economic conditions were vastly different in the closing years of the 18th century and the first half of the 19th century. Agriculture was the chief occupation and engaged more than 75 percent of the population, and early in this period was essentially subsistence in nature. There were a few cash crops for export. Tobacco and later cotton and grains were most notable. The population was relatively small; just 3.5 million in 1785, and only 34.8 million in 1865. This period witnessed the invention of the steam engine and its application to transportation and to industry; the first industrial revolution; and the rise of the factory system. It is during the early years of this period, with the advent of the market economy and entrepreneurial decision-making, that the economy was able to improve living standards on an almost annual basis.

Grain production soared during the 1800s, thanks to new technologies, more acreage, and rising yields. Still predominantly an agricultural economy throughout this period, major crop failures occurred with some regularity (every third or fourth year in the South), and business activity suffered.

With the emergence of the Industrial Revolution during this period, new perils like financial panics and the business cycle emerged. Indeed, a notable feature of downturns during this period were the various financial crises and panics. They were relatively more important than the usual business cycle dynamics with which we are now familiar.

Figure 3.1 illustrates trends in real gross output during this period of unprecedented growth. During the period from 1780 to 1865, real gross output would rise 50-fold.

Figure 3.1
Real Gross Output of the United States: 1780-1865
Index of Real Gross Output where 2017 = 100

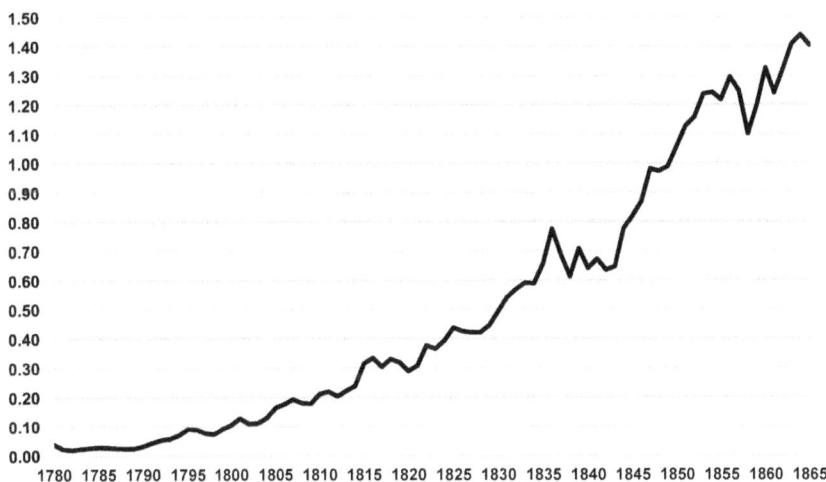

Beyond business cycles, this was an important period for the United States. The 1780s witnessed the creation of a new nation, and the 1860s witnessed a devastating civil war; that in some ways completed the American Revolution.

Prelude: The American Revolution

Great Britain's American colonies featured abundant land with plentiful timber and other raw materials. The energy of the people was paramount. After all, these were the adventurous, willing to leave what was comfortable and cross a wide ocean in search of religious liberty, fortune, and adventure. They were the risk takers.

Hard money was very scarce throughout the colonial period. Barter and the use of commodities (wampum and cod in New England, tobacco, and rice in the South, etc.) for money were common. Taxes were often payable using these commodities. Thus, the money supply was a mix of Spanish dollars and other foreign coins, tobacco warehouse receipts, beaver skins, whiskey, various commodities, and later, paper monies printed by the colonial governments. Some forms of money were perishable, not very portable, and of varying quality. Credit was in part provided by British merchants. Bills of exchange from these merchants circulated as money, as did promissory notes from well-known persons.

The use of paper (or fiat) money first emerged in 1690 (Massachusetts issued bills of credit as payment to soldiers of an unsuccessful expedition against the French) and would plague some colonies. Land bank notes (or loan office notes) appeared after 1710 and were reprinted as a second type of paper money. In the late colonial period American merchants would begin to take a role in providing credit. Financial "innovation" was not limited to the 20th and 21st centuries. The issuance of paper bills and notes caused prices to rise in terms of paper money.

Although population and economic activity expanded, led by exports of commodities (timber, tobacco, naval stores, etc.), the colonies had an adverse balance of trade as most manufactured goods were imported. Beyond these export-oriented commodities, the nation was agrarian and largely subsistence farming.

The Seven Years War (called the French and Indian War on this side of the pond) was a drain on the British economy. The period from 1765 to the breakout of the American Revolution (or Revolutionary War) in 1775 were years of depressed industry, commerce, trade, and finance in nearly every colony, as a series of navigation, trade, and other acts were imposed by Parliament. These acts and this period of economic disruptions stiffened the colonials' resolve and fed into the push for independence. The seafaring colonies, in particular Massachusetts, were especially hampered by taxes and oppressive regulation that stymied trade and commerce, and thus employment and incomes. Prior to the war, the various colonies were separated, each having its own political life and commerce. Trade was largely with Great Britain, the mother country, rather than with each other. The American Revolution would bring them together.

During the protracted war, economic exchange in the country was seriously disrupted. Resources were lean and decimated by the war and destruction of property. The South experienced the most systematic destruction.

The War for Independence needed to be financed. Monies were borrowed from France, Spain, and the Netherlands, all of whom were mercantile nations opposed to Great Britain, and some borrowed domestically, with the rest obtained by printing money. Having limited means to borrow or tax, the war obligated Congress and the various colonies/states to issue paper money, and a rampant inflation of prices ensued. By the end of 1770, the Continental Congress had authorized 42 issues of paper money, a large debt for a group of 13 states with a population of only three million. So much so was the depreciation of the various issues, notwithstanding patriotism, by 1780, the paper money — so-called "Continentals" — was no longer taken for custom fees. Prices doubled each year from 1776 through 1778. In some regards, it was hyper-inflation. By 1781, at the time of Washington's defeat of Cornwallis at Yorktown, it had virtually no rating and was not even taken at one percent of face value. In some respects, inflation lightened the burden of debts, but, as always, inflation was corrosive and destructive. Many were ruined. In 1781, financier Robert Morris persuaded Congress to form a bank — the Bank of North America — to, among other goals, help the national finances. Similarly, in Great Britain, the period from 1777-81 was also one of depressed economic activity.

Although the Treaty of Paris, signed in Paris by representatives of Great Britain and representatives of the United States of America in September 1783, ended the war for practical purposes, the major hostilities had already ceased. The treaty set the boundaries and other details concerning fishing rights, restoration of property, and prisoners of war. British occupation of New York continued until 1783, and occupation of the Northwest Territories lingered as well. Immediately after the war, an upswing of activity occurred. Some would even characterize it as a business boom. Trade revived, but all was not to last.

Cycle 0: Depressed Conditions and Emergence of a New Republic

I name this cycle as Cycle 0, as the nation was not yet complete, and it was during this period that depressed economic conditions led to the Constitutional Convention and the creation of the United States. The cycle began after the short post-war downswing ended in March 1782. Real gross output grew until March 1785, a 36-month upswing and a 57.1 percent gain in activity. A variety of factors (discussed below) led to a lengthy downswing that lasted 51 months until June 1789. Real gross output declined 19.7 percent over this period. Figure 3.1 illustrates this cycle.

The 1780s were a critical time in U.S. history. The Revolutionary War had ended. The Articles of Confederation, a loose compact between the former colonies (now states), had created a central government that was weak. It had no power to tax, no legal currency, no standing army or navy, no ability to regulate commerce, nor any real authority. During this Confederation Period, the United States was essentially a federation of independent republics, with the Articles guaranteeing state sovereignty and independence. Attempts were made starting in 1783 to secure a five percent tariff on imports, but not all states approved. This was a disappointment for many in Congress.

For three years following Yorktown, economic conditions improved. A feeling of victory and getting on with life prevailed. Americans were relieved to have the strain of war behind them. In addition, the British and French armies left comparatively abundant specie before removing from the 13 former colonies, now 13 states. It was a time of rebuilding. For some time, Great Britain would remain the principal supplier of manufactured goods to the American market and the leading buyer of American commodities.

This did not last long, and a depression of economic activity occurred from 1785 to 1789. Causes cited were over-expansion in some industries (e.g., shipbuilding), a buildup of public and other debt amid credit inflation, intense competition in manufactured goods from Great Britain, and lack of a sound currency. In addition, American export trade now had to compete in world markets without the advantages of the British mercantile system. Prices collapsed. The government of the Confederation could not meet its own small expenses, and interest on domestic and foreign debt went largely unpaid.

The downswing lasted much longer than expected and was exacerbated by the loss of export markets. In addition, intra-state trade, as in the colonial period was minimal. Similarly, in Great Britain, the period from 1783-87 was also largely one of depression.

The end of the war inflation also led to the downswing by eroding incomes. The nation was burdened by debt and was particularly onerous for farmers, as the various states raised taxes to pay for the war. This was an early example of a money-induced boom-bust cycle. The Bank of Pennsylvania was founded by Robert Morris in 1781 with the purpose of helping to finance the war. The bank was granted a national charter as the Bank of North America in 1784 by the Continental Congress and was founded on specie. Two other specie-based commercials banks (in New York and in Boston) were founded in 1784 as well.

Credit expansion by the Bank of North America combined with trade disruptions to upset an economy that was already weak and still recovering from the war. People refused the notes. Credit became impossible to obtain, and bankruptcies followed. Despite previous disastrous experiences during the war, many states started issuing paper money (bills of credit) to ease a shortage of money. Various state governments attempted to pay war debt without onerous taxation. Prices of commodities soared at first, but the money depreciated in value to virtually nothing. This further eroded confidence. A general scarcity of real (or metallic) currency existed. Other states imposed burdensome taxation.

At one time, economic historians credited the post-war economic hardships to a surge of inexpensive British goods once the hostilities ceased. More current thinking is more nuanced, having the hardships partly reflecting that, after the war, the United States faced all the mercantilist restrictions that the United Kingdom applied to other nations. Prior to the war, when the 13 colonies were still within the British Empire, many of the navigation laws and other restrictions did not apply although some policies were onerous and a factor behind the push for independence. The mother country had been the colonies' major trading partner, and independence presented challenges to renewed American trade. Now the nation could no longer enjoy an open market within the British Empire. The closing of the British West Indies to American shipping was a major factor in the economic disruption. A variety of British trade and navigation laws largely destroyed American exports for years after independence. Great Britain refused to conclude a commercial treaty, and other nations were laggard as well. Exports fell in half in the wake of heavy duties on tobacco, rice, and other commodities. The fishing industry depended on foreign markets and was particularly reduced, along with whaling. Although American tobacco found new markets (e.g., France) by 1785, a postwar boom in tobacco was over, and prices dropped sharply. Naval stores (pitch and tar), rice, and indigo (used as a dye) all declined, although the latter was partially offset by gains in cotton. Trade in crude iron did not revive. After surviving during the war, shipbuilding dwindled by mid-decade. New England and the South suffered the most during the 1780s.

As economic conditions deteriorated, prices became severely depressed. Falling prices and the loss of export markets hurt producers and traders. Both the people and the government were bankrupt. The funds to pay ministers (i.e., ambassadors) to foreign countries was lacking, and many had to beg foreign governments for support. After slipping on payments on its debt interest, and an inability to make all payments on principal, attempts to borrow from France were futile. Foreign debt accumulated, and private indebtedness was heavy.

A major economic problem during this critical period was the debt from the war. Although several states aimed to ease the burden by new issues of paper money (i.e., inflating their way out of it), the various state governments increased efforts to collect taxes both on individuals and their trades. These rose to new heights to service the interest and principal on these debts. Taxes in some states were two to three times higher than prior to the Revolution, with many taxes falling on property in addition to poll taxes. Farmers and debtors urged greater reliance on tariffs and issuance of paper money, while merchants and creditors advocated for higher taxes on land instead of tariffs, as well as less paper money. Massachusetts, in particular, was aggressive with taxes, which were as high as one-third of incomes and insisted on payment in specie. There was a rise in actual and pending defaults among many groups. The property of many who defaulted on their taxes was seized, and courts threw those who could not pay into jail. These depressed economic conditions led to Shays' Rebellion in the western part of Massachusetts during 1786-87. This was essentially a tax revolt, much like the Revolutionary War a decade before. Discontent, uneasiness, and radical ideas became widespread. The rebellion was put down, but conditions were ripe for further unrest. Although the tax burden was most severe in Massachusetts, all of the states were hindered by the tax burden, which aggravated the downturn.

The promise of a new life beyond the Allegheny Mountains was thwarted by a continued British military presence in the Northwest Territory, in violation of the peace treaty. Native American resistance was encouraged by the British. Although emigration from the seaboard occurred, development of the area was hindered. Shipping down the Mississippi was closed.

Unemployment rose; houses and land depreciated in value. Economic activity languished. Manufacturers and other business interests clamored for protective tariffs, citing the "infant industry" argument. During this period, interstate tariffs and barriers to trade were minimal, but Hamilton's Federalist Paper #12 raised the potential of future trade restrictions between the states. The frequent changes in tariffs and lack of permanency in laws and regulation fostered uncertainty. The political and economic situation was grave. Merchants, as well as artisans and mechanics (primarily in the North), desired a more powerful government that could enact laws protecting American shipping, as well as protective tariffs for fledgling American manufacturers. Some individual states did impose import duties or raised tariffs, but the situation was uneven.

By 1786, with a sense of panic and crisis growing among merchants, Congress and much of the nation began to demand a stronger federal government. Concerns over public finance and trade policy were central and echoed in the newspapers and public discourse. The depressed economic conditions were a large element in development and ratification of the Constitution and subsequent new form of government. Under these conditions, business of every type was awaiting adoption of the Constitution.

The Constitutional Convention took place from May to September 1787, and the agreed-upon Constitution was then submitted to the states for ratification, pursuant to its own Article VII. Ratification occurred in June 1788, and the Constitution was officially established. The first presidential election under the new Constitution was held, and in early 1789, the Electoral College was convened. George Washington was unanimously elected to be the nation's first president, and John Adams was elected its first vice president. In March, the federal government began operations under the new form of government, as members of the 1st United States Congress convened. Upon the adoption of the Constitution, the state issuing of paper money ceased, and gold and silver became the only means of circulation. Treasury Secretary Alexander Hamilton established a sound financial system. With uncertainty removed, confidence returned, and gradually improvement in industry, commerce, trade, and finance appeared, and an upswing was underway. The Constitution might never have occurred without these depressed conditions and the realization that a greater industrial, commercial, trade, and financial future was possible.

Signs of recovery appeared in 1788, but in 1789 weak copper prices led to a loss of confidence in copper coins, largely due counterfeiting (and to a lesser extent debasement), with disruption in New York as well as Pennsylvania. The bordering states of New Jersey and Connecticut were also affected. In mid-1789, the Bank of North America printed small change notes (using special paper) to help alleviate the small change problem. This solution was greeted with enthusiasm, and confidence returned. The downswing — often referred to as The Copper Panic of 1789 — was not severe enough to hinder recovery across all of the nation, and I view this episode as another (and last) leg down in the long depressed economic conditions of the 1780s that eventually gave way, allowing the nation to grow and prosper. With stability returning, the value of copper also rose again.

Cycle 1: Seaborne Commerce and the Panic of 1796-97

With a stronger central government, sound public finances, the lessening of uncertainty, and other favorable developments, confidence returned, and the long 1785-89 downswing ended within the context of a new republic. The upswing (Cycle 1) started in June 1789, as economic disruption gave way to improvement. Steady gains were apparent by mid-1790, and real gross output grew until February 1796, a long 79-month upswing and a 312 percent gain in business activity. This has been associated with a long Kondratieff upswing that centered on canal construction and factory organization of the production of manufactured goods. This cyclical upswing would be the longest in American business cycle history, a record that would last until the 1940s. Across the pond, after nearly a decade of depression, a boom emerged in Great Britain in the late-1780s and extended into the early-1790s. It was led by the "canal mania" of the period.

Several factors came together during the opening years of the upswing. These include stronger central government, sound public finances, the growth of overseas trade, and domestic development of manufacturing, agriculture, and other commerce. In 1792, President Washington was reelected without opposition, and in 1796 John Adams, a Federalist, was elected president. A wave of "republican" sentiments would mark his administration of one term.

The difficulties associated with the Bank of North America and the 1780s led Treasury Secretary Hamilton to propose to Congress in 1790 the founding of a national bank. It began operations in 1794, as the Bank of the United States, and had a 20-year charter (1791-1811). It was capitalized by the federal government and private individuals based on specie and promised to redeem notes it issued in gold and silver coins. One purpose was to serve as a financial agent for the federal government. By 1805, it would have branches in Boston, New York, Baltimore, Savannah, New Orleans, and Washington, DC. It was a large institution, and because of its size and favored position with the federal government, it would generate both fear and hostility among privately-owned banks and the public. One point was that the First Bank retained the ability of state banks to issue bank notes and would therefore over-issue paper money and inflate the money supply, so Hamilton focused on paying off the national debt and assuming all of the war debts of the states starting in 1790. This demonstrated to Europe the new nation's creditworthiness and attracted investment.

Figure 3.2

Cycle 1: Seaborne Commerce and the Panic of 1796-97
Index of Real Gross Output where 2017 = 100

The Constitution gave the federal government the exclusive right to coin money. The Coinage Act of 1792 adopted the dollar as the primary unit of money and specified sliver (371.25 grains) and gold (24.7 grains) content. Thus, the nation was established on a bimetallic standard at a rate of about 15 units of silver to one unit of gold. If the market price of silver or gold fluctuated above or below this 15:1 ratio, one or the other metals would be "chased" out of circulation, reflecting Gresham's Law. The problem was eventually solved by going on a de facto gold standard. The U.S. Mint offered free and unlimited coinage of silver and gold.

The creation of the Bank of North America and a uniform currency provided for a stable currency. It also relieved the need of the states to tax as they did in the 1780s, and state taxes were lowered. By mid-decade, the tax burden returned to its pre-Revolution levels. Business prospects improved.

Still largely an agricultural economy, the country's economic cycles would continue to be influenced by crop success or failure. An abundant wheat crop in 1790 aided the upswing at its crucial early stage. The South was more rural and agricultural and was depressed in 1791 and 1792. This period witnessed a diversification in the Tidewater away from tobacco to wheat, corn, and other crops, as well as livestock. With the development of the cotton gin, the perennial problem of removing seed was solved, and production of raw cotton would rise to over 3,000 bales in 1790 and exceed 167,000 bales in 1796. It would lead to Southern economic revival, and as a growth industry, cotton production would continue to rise every year through 1807, despite the 1796-98 downswing and disruptions to trade during the Anglo-French wars. Unfortunately, this fostered the expansion of the evils of slavery in the Carolinas and Georgia and further across the South.

During 1792, a minor panic took place. Its causes included the extension of credit and excessive speculation. The panic was largely solved by providing banks with the necessary funds to make open-market purchases. The Treasury allowed importers to pay their import duties using promissory notes instead of cash. Lenders were asked not to call in their loans. Calm was restored, helping to promote recovery. Overseas, the 1793 outbreak of the war between Great Britain and France caused a run on the banks in England.

Tariffs provided revenue for the new government but also protected the development of American industry. This cycle would witness the beginnings of manufacturing, particularly in the North. Many new projects were launched. In 1793, for example, the Slater Mill, the nation's first cotton mill, was established in Pawtucket, Rhode Island. This would be the first in America's industrial revolution and the beginnings of a large industry. Other developments included improved transportation and communication, as well as newspapers and magazines. The former expanded from around 90 to 235 during the decade. Development of the postal system occurred with the number of post offices growing more than ten-fold during the 1790s.

Infrastructure investment in canals, roads and ports also played a role in this upswing as internal trade became more active and land speculation emerged. Western development expanded in Ohio, Kentucky, and Tennessee. An unsuccessful Native American War in 1791 hindered development in Ohio and westward. This would continue until 1794, with the Battle of Fallen Timbers, the final battle of the Northwest Indian War. The Treaty of Greenville in 1795 concluded hostilities between the United States and a Native American confederation. The end of hostilities made British evacuation of forts and posts in the Northwest inevitable. A subsequent Treaty of Amity, Commerce, and Navigation (aka Jay Treaty) settled outstanding issues between the two countries, and Britain finally agreed to remove themself from American territory. This opened settlement of the Northwest Territory above the Ohio River. Spain reached an agreement with the United States in the Treaty of San Lorenzo which recognized borders and free navigation of the Mississippi.

In 1791, a "whiskey tax" was enacted to generate revenue for the war debt incurred during the Revolutionary War. The excise tax applied to all distilled spirits, but because whiskey was a predominant product, it was known as the whiskey tax. Due to transportation costs, farmers on the western frontier fermented and distilled surplus rye, barley, corn, or grain mixtures to make (or monetize as) whiskey, which was easier to transport to market. On the frontier, whiskey often served as a medium of exchange. Farmers resisted the tax, and resistance was most pronounced in western Pennsylvania, where armed rebellion emerged. President Washington responded by mobilizing the militia to suppress the rebellion. In 1792, higher tariffs were enacted, and in 1794, new excise taxes on snuff and sugar were enacted.

With the exception of some brief armistices, from 1792 until 1815, Europe was torn apart by a struggle between "republican" and revolutionary France, and later Napoleonic France, with many European opponents, including Austria, Prussia Russia, and especially (and most consistently) Great Britain. Neither Great Britain nor France thought anything of seizing the merchant marine of a largely unarmed America. This would be an issue for two decades. It would, however, provide a boom for American agriculture, and farm prices generally rose for two decades.

Trade began to recover in 1790 and would expand from $20 million in 1790 to $67 million by 1796. It was a golden age for American shipping. In addition to Western Europe and the West Indies, American traders operated in the Baltic and Mediterranean seas. In the latter, Barbary pirates preyed upon American shipping and increased their attacks after 1793. At the same time, British attacks hampered American commerce. Trade in 1794 was temporarily checked by embargo. The wars in Europe would enable American merchants to push trade into Central and South American. At this time, Americans expanded their markets in Africa, South Asia, Java, Hawaii, and even China. Total U.S. exports faltered in 1797, reflecting a set-back to the Atlantic trade, the result of financial disruption emanating from England. Despite the broadening of markets, Great Britain remained the leading trading partner, accounting for three-quarters of American exports. After 1791, American merchants increasingly re-exported goods they imported. After 1793, wartime demand and the progress of the Industrial Revolution led to Great Britain expanding its purchases of American grain and flour. Britain would remain a large source for American imports, largely manufactured goods. In 1794, British policy changed to widespread seizure of American ships trading in the French West Indies. This ceased with the Jay Treaty negotiations. Rising seaborne commerce resulted in a large increase in shipbuilding, which in turn fostered greater demand for lumber, canvas, rope, tar, and other marine supplies. French hostilities emerged in 1797, and French privateers seized more than 300 American merchantmen. This eventually resulted in an embargo during 1798, further exacerbating the downturn.

Although liquidity constraints existed in the early-1790s, the Bank of the United States soon engaged in credit over-expansion, resulting in rising general prices, abnormally low real interest rates, speculation, and the financial distortions that led to over-investment. The Bank was not a central bank in the technical sense. It had no regulatory powers over commercial banking, nor a monopoly on note issues. However, it was the only bank free from nationwide restrictions on branch banking, and the only bank whose notes were accepted by the government for payment of customs duties. "Boom" conditions emerged as early as 1792, and price inflation ensued over investment in manufacturing, banking and infrastructure projects and endeavors. The number of commercial banks would expand more than seven-fold from 1790 to 1796. A series of canal projects were organized, many of which would fail once the bubble burst. Finally, financial distortions led to over-investment in factories, most notably in cotton and woolen mills, as well as glass and other sectors. These boom conditions did not last, and in 1795, credit soon began contracting, falling every year until 1798. Eventually a correction occurred in early 1796 and led to a contraction of commercial activity, falling selling prices, and rising real interest rates. With fear of insolvency, banks began contracting credit, making many projects unprofitable and resulting in business and personal bankruptcies. The latter were sometimes referred to as "embarrassments" by chroniclers of the time. Most notable of personal bankruptcies was that of Robert Morris, the financier of the Revolution, and at one time, the wealthiest man in America.

In February 1796, business activity (or real gross output) peaked, and a downswing emerged. This was a classic bursting of a credit bubble, which was termed by Senator Theodore Sedgwick as a "bubble of speculation." The downswing lasted 32 months until October 1798. This was a long downturn, and real gross output declined 25.2 percent over this period. It was a major downswing.

A yellow fever epidemic in 1797 killed 10 percent of the population of Philadelphia, then America's largest city. It would be the first of many such epidemics. This disrupted business, but like many epidemics of this and the next century, the disruption would be local or regional. Panic, tight money, and many failures marked 1797 and into 1798. Land speculation collapsed. In 1797, Napoleon's attempt to invade England also fostered a "run" on English banks. The Panic of 1796-97 was exacerbated by the suspension of specie payments in early-1797 and widespread deflation in the Bank of England, which crossed the Atlantic and furthered financial panic in America. The disruption of credit particularly affected merchants involved in the Atlantic trade. Interestingly, the South largely escaped this panic, but business activity in the North was stagnant for nearly three years.

Cycle 2: Carrying Trade Prosperity, Peace of Amiens, and the Recession of 1801-03

With the revival of activity in the North and of seaborne trade, plus other favorable developments, the downswing associated with the Panic of 1796-97 ended. A new upswing (Cycle 2) started in October 1798, and depressed business activity gave way to improvement.

Real gross output grew until July 1801, a 33-month upswing and an 84 percent gain in business activity. Cycle 2 was a minor cycle.

In the decade of the 1790s, the population of the United States grew from 4.17 million in 1790 to 5.31 million in 1800. About one-fifth of the latter were slaves. About 95 percent of the population was rural, and about 90 percent of the workforce was still engaged in farming, many of whom moved from subsistence farming into the market economy. The upswing continued to see French seizures of American merchant ships, leading to the creation of an effective American army and navy. This led to a surge in government spending. To finance this, the government levied new taxes and raised new loans.

In July 1801, business activity peaked, and a downswing emerged. The downswing lasted 23 months until April 1803. This was a typical duration, and real gross output declined 21.3 percent over this period. In 1800, Thomas Jefferson, a Republican[8], was elected president after a tie vote with Aaron Burr. This was the first popular election in history that resulted in transfer of power from one party to another. The Federal government moved from Philadelphia to the new Federal District on the Potomac, now referred to as the District of Columbia.

Industrial activity in the North showed marked improvement early in this cycle, with further improvement in subsequent years. With large gains in productivity, this period marked the evolution from small shops to increasingly larger cotton, woolen, iron, lumber, paper, and other mills. There was continued prosperity in the South, as production of raw cotton rose from nearly 42,000 bales in 1799 and tripled to over 125,000 bales in 1803, the end of this

---

[8] Not to be confused with the modern Republican Party. The modern Democratic Party can trace its heritage back to Thomas Jefferson and James Madison's Democratic-Republican Party, often referred to in those times as the Republican Party. The modern-day Democratic Party was founded in the late-1820s by supporters of Andrew Jackson, making it the world's oldest active political party. The modern Republican Party was founded in 1854 by opponents of the Kansas–Nebraska Act, which allowed potential expansion of slavery into the western territories.

cycle. This period witnessed the development of cotton as a major crop in the Southwest and the accompanying flourishing of slavery. Ohio and elsewhere in the Northwest saw rapid development as well. The year 1800 saw an excellent wheat crop, along with high wheat prices, which aided farmers into 1802.

Infrastructure development included turnpikes, which lowered the cost of transporting produce. Turnpike companies continued to be formed, with development centered in the North. In 1802, Congress authorized the building of the National Road to extend from the East Coast to the Ohio River.

Despite continued diplomatic conflict with France, trade continued an upward trajectory. With Great Britain and France engaged in struggle and most of Europe pulled into conflict, America captured market share in trade throughout most of the Western Hemisphere, and American shipping tonnage was second only to Britain. However, America was caught between the two belligerents. Shipping was complicated, and re-exports (also called the carrying trade) figured prominently as a means of getting around the British (Rule of 1756 and the "broken voyage") trade restrictions. Re-exports thrived, and in some years, re-exports exceeded the value of exports from domestic production. Trade boomed and brought prosperity as America supplied the belligerents. Exports of wheat and flour expanded from 2.347 million bushels in 1799 to 6.59 million in 1803. Similar gains occurred in other farm products as well. Overall exports would rise from $71 million in 1799 to a peak of $94 million in 1801, before falling to $56 million in 1803 after the boom of war-time activity. This brought prosperity to America, especially in New England. After the Peace of Amiens ended the war between Great Britain and France and led to a brief period of peace, the subsequent slump in demand for wartime materials and supplies led to a significant decline in commodity prices. Trade was further disrupted by the Tripoli pirates who began seizing American merchant ships, leading to the First Barbary War. War between France and Great Britain continued in 1803, with the latter forming the Third Coalition with Austria and Russia.

Commodity prices rose into early 1802 but then collapsed. Banking would continue to evolve. When the Bank of the United States was chartered in 1794, there were only four state-chartered banks. By 1800, there were 28, and by the end of the decade, over 85 banks. Most of these were in the North. The South lagged in banking as well as emergence of institutions and infrastructure (turnpikes, canals, etc.) supporting commerce. The year 1800 saw rapid gains in security prices, which continued until the collapse in 1803. Prices would begin to recover later in the year. A yellow fever epidemic disrupted business in New York during the fall of 1803. The effects were generally local.

France regained possession of Louisiana as a bid to reestablish a French colonial empire. However, large war debts along with France's inability to reverse a revolt in Saint-Domingue (modern Haiti), coupled with the prospect of renewed warfare with the Great Britain, prompted France to consider selling Louisiana to the United States. This would lead to the Louisiana Purchase in 1803, essentially doubling the size of the United States, and would be a factor in American development well into the 1890s. The recession of 1801-03 provided a short set-back, but as recovery emerged, it provided the framework for a large expansion of trade during the first decade of the 1800s.

Cycle 3: European War, Maritime Commerce, and the Embargo Depression of 1807-09

With Peace of Amiens, trade revived as did development and expansion of industry, and the downswing associated with the Recession of 1801-03 ended. A new upswing (Cycle 3) started in April 1803, and reduced business activity gave way to improvement. Real gross output grew until November 1807, a long 55-month upswing with a 93 percent gain in business activity. This was a major cycle.

Iron smelters and forges were developed, as were related metal-working industries, along with flour, lumber, glassmaking, sugar refining, meatpacking, printing, furniture, and machinery. There was rapid improvement, development, and expansion of industry. Commodities and other prices began to improve during the initial phase of the upswing. New companies were formed.

Figure 3.3

Cycle 3: European War, Maritime Commerce, and the Embargo Depression of 1807-09

Index of Real Gross Output where 2017 = 100

Banking underwent further development, and the number of banks began to multiply and was associated with rapid expansion of paper money circulation. Indeed, a sort of banking mania began in New England. Security prices were weak in 1803-05, but with improving trade and industry, active speculation emerged and pushed security prices higher. Foreign gold and silver were still used in circulation.

In 1804, President Jefferson was re-elected. Political stability would continue until 1807, when Aaron Burr's attempt to establish an "empire" in the Southwest failed.

Additional infrastructure development in the form of turn-pikes continued. In 1806, Congress authorized the building of the Cumberland Road to extend from Maryland to Cincinnati and eventually to the Mississippi. Canal development and improvement of rivers and ports also led to construction. In 1807, Robert Fulton would construct the *Clermont,* which inaugurated steamboat trans-portation and a new industry. It was a success. New Orleans would emerge as the second largest port (after New York), as it was the gateway to the world for the entire area drained by the Mississippi, Missouri, and Ohio rivers. It would retain this position into the 20th century.

Settlement of the Northwest and Southwest continued apace. The first years of recovery saw good wheat crops with generally high prices. Cotton development continued as well, with produc-tion of raw cotton rising from slightly 125,000 bales in 1803 to 167,000 bales in 1807, the peak year before trade disruption. It was a period of prosperity. That said, the year saw lower wheat prices and security prices, along with slackening activity in many corners of commerce. Security prices would weaken further in wake of the economic downturn starting in 1807.

Trade relations would be the defining characteristic of this cycle, and the upswing was marked by reviving trade. First, America needed to deal with long-standing problems with the Barbary pirate states who seized American merchant ships and imprisoned sailors. A peace and commercial treaty with Tripoli ended an undeclared war, but there were other Barbary States. By 1805, the Barbary pirates were largely subdued, but events in Europe would play a role in threatening foreign trade.

Demand from the European belligerents would push American wheat exports from 3.77 million bushels in 1804 in to 6.80 million in 1807. In 1805 the Royal Navy began searching and seizing American merchant ships and impressing sailors. With Nelson's victory at Trafalgar, the year marked the end of France's hopes of invading

England, but soon launched economic sanctions in what came to be called the Continental System, which forbade all trade with the British Isles and ordered the confiscation of ships that had landed in England or its colonies. This was directed at neutral trade, largely American. In 1805, there was a de facto British blockade of New York for inspection of ships. Soon, both France and Great Britain, by blockade and retaliatory measures, were seizing American ships. Britain's larger navy allowed it to plunder about one of every eight American ships that were put to sea between 1803 and 1812. Nearly 1,600 American ships and property were seized by the two belligerents. British agents also instigated the Native Americans in the Northwest, and the Royal Navy stepped up seizures, even going so far to seize the Danish fleet in neutral Copenhagen.

America's response was perhaps the dumbest move by a nation. There was great resentment against the British even though France originated the blockade policy. The Non-Importation Act, passed in April 1806, forbade the importation of certain British goods to coerce Great Britain to suspend its impressment of American sailors and to respect American sovereignty and neutrality. It came into effect in 1807, a year in which the president announced a new policy which expanded economic retaliation. Incredibly, President Jefferson launched a trade embargo with the Embargo Act of 1807, which forbade Americans from sending their ships and goods abroad. It was a general but rigid trade embargo on all foreign nations as it halted all American ships from trading in foreign ports. The thinking was that withholding might bring pressure on Great Britain to cease capturing American ships and cargoes and impressment of sailors. That is, to respect American sovereignty and neutrality, while also pressuring France and other nations in pursuit of general diplomatic and economic leverage. The announcement of the embargo came with little notice, causing a violent supply shock. It led to a significant decline in product prices and trade, fostering significant hardship for shipping industries.

The embargo led to falling trade volumes, a sharp drop in commodity prices and securities prices. Overall exports had risen from $56 million in 1803 to a peak of $108 million in 1807, and with this self-inflicted wound, exports fell to $22 million in 1808 after the embargo was enacted. Imports fell from $139 million in 1807 to $57 million in 1808. Wheat exports collapsed from 6.80 million bushels in 1807 to just 1.27 million bushels a year later. Although there was leakage (i.e., smuggling) in Maine and the Lake Champlain borders, the embargo was a shock that tipped the American economy into recession. Trade was nearly completely checked. In February 1807, business activity peaked, and a downswing emerged. The downswing lasted 17 months until April 1809. This was a slightly shorter duration than pre-Civil War downturns, and real gross output declined 17.8 percent over this period. Leakage from the embargo and outright smuggling lessened some of the depressive forces. Macon's Bill ended the embargoes in May 1810, at which time a firm recovery was underway.

Along with trade restrictions imposed by the British, shipping-related industries were hard hit by the Embargo Act. The economic devastation emanated from shipping to the various supportive industries. The embargo caused paralysis on the East Coast, gradually spreading inland. Custom receipts fell from $16 million to $7 million in 1808, resulting in a federal deficit. Prices of foreign goods rose, while prices of many domestic goods fell below the cost of production. Commodity prices would fall to a very low level, and security markets were dull. Bankruptcies increased and affected not only merchants and manufacturers, but also farmers. Farmers, who had been buying land on credit during the upswing to meet expectations of rising demand for American crops, suddenly were placed in difficulty, and many were forced into failure along with their merchants. New York and New England particularly suffered, and the South and West felt the adverse effects of the embargo as well. Banking became unsound.

So widespread were "republican" sympathies that even with economic distress and what must be seen as a failure of American foreign policy, Secretary of States James Madison, a Republican, was elected as fourth president of the United States. He would serve two terms.

The Depression of 1807-09 was thus brought on by this government-induced stoppage of trade. It caused British merchants to capture much of the trade in the West Indies and South America. Economic distress continued into 1809, with near complete stagnation in New England where a banking crisis emerged. Many failures ensued. Some revival of activity emerged in other regions as larger crops and prices rose.

The downturn led to calls by New England to suspend the embargo and also fostered sentiment to succeed from the Union. Congress went further and granted the administration powers to capture and punish violators. Pressure to repeal these measures mounted, and the recession ended when President Jefferson and Congress yielded to pressure and removed the embargo with the Non-Intercourse Act of 1809 in March. By May, a more targeted foreign policy replaced the general embargo, and trade began to improve, and business activity stabilized and was soon again on an upward trajectory.

In a related matter, Jefferson's embargo along with Napoleon's blockade in Europe, prevented exports of British manufactured goods. A panic ensued in Great Britain, as English banks had loaned credit to British merchants who had lost their traditional markets. Loans had increased significantly in 1809, and goods soon glutted domestic markets, prices slumped, and British industry and commerce became stagnant in 1810-11.

The downturn marked the beginning of an earnest development of domestic manufacturing and commerce, as capital turned from shipping to manufacturing, in particular cotton mills. Despite tight money, in 1809 alone, more than 60 new cotton mills were erected in New England, as a turn towards developing domestic resources and meeting American markets emerged. The American Industrial Revolution had arrived.

Cycle 4: European War, Restricted Carrying Trade, and the Brief Recession of 1812

The Depression of 1807-09 ended with the Non-Intercourse Act of 1809, and the Macon Bill of 1810 further reopened trade, as development of American industry led to a gradual improvement and the start of Cycle 4, while depressed business activity gave way to improvement in April 1809. Real gross output grew until May 1811, a 28-month upswing with a 38 percent gain in business activity.

A strong revival of activity in the North began in 1810, and prosperity continued in the South, despite cotton production lingering during the upswing, easing from 171,000 bales in 1809 to 157,000 in 1812. Prices were high.

Cycle 4 marked a period of domestic development. Companies were formed to build harbors and canals. Development of the postal system occurred, with the number of post offices growing four-fold during the first decade of the 1800s, which expanded the number of newspapers to over 375. Other infrastructure included postal roads and turnpikes. By 1810, a postal road ran continuously from Maine to Georgia. Development of the Northwest would normally have been aided by victory at the Battle of Tippecanoe, but war with Great Britain was on the horizon.

In the early stages of the upswing, money remained tight, and a bank crisis occurred in New England. The legality of using foreign coins was terminated, and money markets remained tight into 1810. Security prices were steady at first. Money would become tight again in 1811.

Opposition to the Bank of the United States emerged from Southern agrarians and from the state-chartered banks, who resented restraints on their issuing paper money. Presidents Jefferson and Madison both opposed re-chartering the Bank of the United States. In 1811, the bank's charter expired, another factor said to contribute to the next downswing. Money became tight, and security prices declined.

With the release from the financial constraints of the Bank of the United States, the number of state banks nearly tripled in five years, from 88 in 1811 to 246 in 1816. Along with the war, this period of rapid expansion of banks caused rapid inflation of paper currency to emerge. The over-issue soon became widespread, and depreciation followed. It would foster a boom-bust cycle that would end in a downswing later in the decade.

With the partial lifting of the Embargo in 1809 and its complete ending in 1810, foreign trade was among the first sectors to improve. Overall exports would rise from $52 million in 1809 to $67 million in 1810, and $61 million in 1811 as the next downturn gained traction, before collapsing to $39 million in 1812, as hostilities ensued. American wheat exports rose from 4.20 million bushels in 1809 in to 6.72 million in 1811 and were accompanied by rising wheat prices, which supported prosperity. These exports would ease slightly in 1812 as war began. Imports rose from $39 million in 1809 to a near-term peak of $69 million in 1812.

Still at war, Great Britain (and to a lesser extent France) continued seizures of American shipping. Macon's Bill of 1810 provided provisions to re-impose trade embargoes, should both nations do not change policy by rescinding orders against neutral shipping. France complied, but Great Britain refused. Congress had approved the Non-Intercourse Act in March 1811, which prevented trade with Britain. Thus, the economic downturn was likely brought on by international trade restrictions. It would also heighten hostilities between the United States and Britain, ultimately leading to war.

The recession was brief, likely starting in May 1811 and ending in June 1812, a 13-month downswing and an 11.8 percent decline in activity. In 1812, a more stringent embargo was enacted in April. Commodity prices declined, and the downturn was more pronounced in the South, although activity in New England was soft as well. Foreign trade was depressed, as the British blockaded the East Coast. Money was tight, and financial distress emerged in New England. The financial distress was short-lived, as war production infused the American economy with cash. The trough largely occurred with the declaration of war in June, and by year-end security prices improved amid rapid expansion of paper currency. The recession ended quickly, as the United States ramped up production for the War of 1812.

In the initial phases of the war along the border in 1812, the United States suffered a series of reverses. Fort Mackinac fell, Fort Dearborn was evacuated, and Fort Detroit surrendered without a fight. American attempts to invade Canada across the Niagara Peninsula and toward Montreal failed completely. Despite these reversals, President Madison was re-elected.

As "Republicans," both President Jefferson and Madison favored limited government and called for further reductions in government debt. By 1813, even with the monies spent on the Louisiana Purchase, both administrations had reduced the federal debt to $45 million, nearly half of its peak ($86 million) in 1805. With the declaration of war, expenditures would more than double, from $8 million in 1811 to $20 million in 1812. If would expand further as the war progressed.

Cycle 5: War of 1812, Post-War Depression, Expansion, and the Panic of 1819

With 30 years of progress, the nation was on a better economic footing in 1812 than in 1775. With the declaration of war, Cycle 5 started as a short downturn, but gave way to improvement in June

1812, as the nation went on a war footing. Real gross output grew until November 1815, a 41-month upswing with a 74 percent gain in business activity. As would occur in many subsequent wars, a post-war downturn would occur. It would be a long downturn, as this was a major cycle.

Figure 3.4

Cycle 5: War of 1812, Post-War Depression, Expansion, and the Panic of 1819

Index of Real Gross Output where 2017 = 100

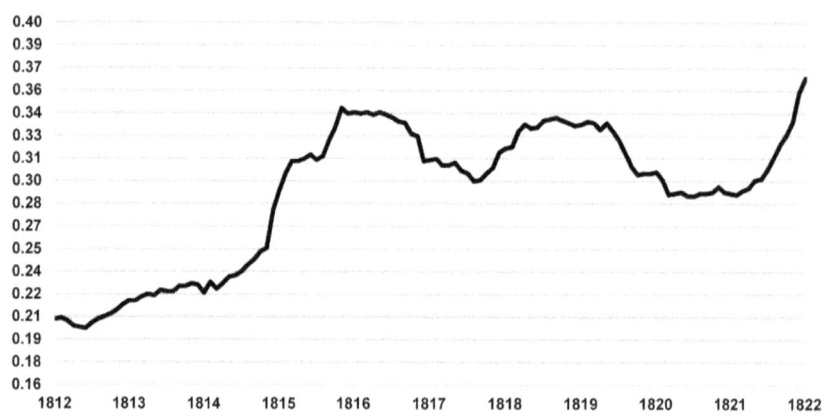

The War of 1812 would dominate this cycle and was referred to by historian Gordon Wood as the strangest war in American history. With British disruption of shipping and impressments of American sailors as the cited cause for declaring war, the United States was woefully unprepared. Just as America was declaring war, Great Britain repealed its policy of seizing American ships and impressing American sailors. Poor transatlantic communications played a role, as did national pride and sectarian philosophy. In many ways, the United States had been in commercial conflict with both Great Britain and France since 1806, and the actual war was the consequence of failure in finding a peaceful solution. Congress soon added authorization for additional troops.

The war did create some financial distress, but also opportunities. New England was the section of the nation most hurt and least in favor of war. It was the South and West that were most in favor. The latter had regional motives of removing the last British influence over Native Americans in the Northwest. The year 1812 was marked by plans to invade Canada, which largely resulted in disaster, culminating in the surrender of an American army in early-1813 at the River Raisin in Michigan. The American navy fared better and was enhanced by additional construction of frigates and ships of the line and by the nation's privateers who, during the war, captured some 1,300 British merchant vessels. Naval successes may have helped President Madison win a second term. In 1813, the tide would briefly turn in the Northwest, with victories on Lake Erie and at the Battle of the Thames in Ontario. The situation along the Niagara and St. Lawrence fronts remained deadlocked. The year 1814 was mixed, with British plundering of towns on the Chesapeake and burning of Washington, DC. In the Southwest, General Jackson's successful campaign occurred, culminating in victory at New Orleans, which occurred after a peace treaty — Treaty of Ghent — was signed. Again, the inadequacies of oceanic communications delayed peace.

British naval superiority was manifested by 1813, resulting in an effective blockade from New York down into the Gulf of Mexico. New England suffered the most, but regions producing staples and other crops for export were affected as well. American exports would fall from $61 million in 1811 to $39 million in 1812, $28 million in 1813, and only $7 million in 1814. Imports would shrink from $69 million in 1812 to a low of $13 million in 1814. American wheat exports, for example, fell from 6.55 million bushels in 1812 to 5.96 million in 1813, to only 870,000 bushels in 1814. With the reduction of foreign trade, American shipping entering the United States would fall from 667,000 tons in 1812 to only 59,000 tons two years later. A general stagnation ensued. Smuggling along the northern border undermined embargo and efforts to restrict trade and provided some support for New England. Privateering did this as well. The British blockade cut off coastal traffic, forcing Americans to rely on overland routes. This restricted communications and commerce.

With the secession of hostilities, wheat exports rose to 3.90 million bushels in 1815 and overall exports to $53 million. The shipping business experienced a revival, and exports would rise to $82 million in 1816, $88 million in 1817, and $93 million in 1818, as markets expanded in the years after the war. Imports grew strongly in 1815, rising nearly ten-fold to $113 million. Imports would expand further, reaching $147 million in 1816. The Tariff of 1816 was the first tariff passed by Congress explicitly protecting American manufacturing from overseas competition. Prior to the War of 1812, tariffs served primarily to raise revenues to fund and operate the national government. As new tariffs were enacted in 1816, imports then fell back to $99 million in 1817, but revived to $122 million in 1818.

Until 1815, Americans looked across the Atlantic to Europe. It was a large export market with the focus of American shipping. One result of the war (and the Battle of New Orleans in particular) was a gradual change to a domestic focus and to the West. This would last throughout the 19th century. Innovations in transportation and communications made this possible. Northern manufacturers took advantage to replace foreign manufactures.

Despite surpluses on the prior decades and debt retirement, the Treasury and financial markets were not prepared for war. Presidents Jefferson and Madison both favored limited government and called for further reductions in government debt. By 1813, even with the monies spent on the Louisiana Purchase, both administrations had reduced the federal debt to $45 million in 1813, about half of what it was in 1801. Excise taxes were raised during the war, but taxes would cover only a portion of the war, and with borrowing the logical means of funding, the federal debt would mushroom from $45 million in 1813 to a then record $120 million in 1815.

War finance was divided between short-term notes and long-term Treasury bonds. Following the war, financing of the debt was aided by the sale of public lands.

During the war, the Barbary States took advantage of the situation and once again captured American merchant ships and imprisoned their crews. With the War of 1812 over, Congress declared war on Algiers, who capitulated and signed a treaty with the United States. Tunis and Tripoli soon followed.

The war fostered demand for iron, firearms, cloth, and other goods. Domestic manufacturing picked up some of the slack from exporting. The War of 1812 marked a change in the American economy, with New England merchants shifting capital from shipping to manufacturing. The reduction of foreign trade induced capital to be invested in domestic industries, and a turn towards developing domestic markets emerged and was centered largely in the North. Explosive growth would occur in textiles and supplier and related industries. Domestic manufacturing and internal trade were seen as important to the wealth of the nation. Prior to the 1806 beginnings of trade difficulties related to tensions with France and Great Britain and the war, there were perhaps a dozen cotton mills in the United States. By 1815, there would be some 250. In 1813, there was widespread activity and expansion of manufacturing accompanied by rising commodity prices. This continued into 1815, when progress was checked by a flood of imports, as hostilities ceased. New England was particularly affected. Manufacturing would continue to be distressed into 1821 despite brief improvement during 1817 as a result of tariffs. The iron industry especially suffered. This resulted in many failures and rising unemployment.

The close of the war did bring a modest recovery of trade, commerce, and other real activity but was marked by speculation, reckless banking, and inflation. With the war's end, the United States consisted of 18 states and five territories. The rapid development of domestic trade fostered the need for additional infrastructure development in the form of canals, roads, ferries, and bridges. Many of the canals were financed in the same way as toll roads. Development of this infrastructure would increase the speed and lower the cost of moving goods within the nation. Increasingly, the focus of commerce would be internal to the nation.

Banking would further develop, and with the end of the war, finance rebounded appreciably, and securities gained. In 1811, there were 88 state-chartered banks. By 1815, there were 208 banks, and in 1816, the number rose to 246 banks. In 1820, there were 307 banks. With the multiplication of banks came excessive paper issuance and loose credit. Many of the banks commenced business without adequate capital and issued paper currency without sufficient security. This, combined with the failure of Congress to raise sufficient taxes, resulted in excessive borrowing and the expansion of notes and deposits, which resulted in a depreciating currency.

The capture and burning of Washington in August 1814 was a shock. A crisis soon emerged as banks, primarily in Philadelphia (but also in New York and Baltimore), issued an unprecedented amount of bank notes. The expansion of money and credit led to the depreciation of paper currency, which led to higher prices for most everything. Overall prices rose well above a level compatible with a gold standard. Looked upon as a real increase in prices, it was an illusion and resulted in further extension of credit and speculation, and inflation. Security prices fell in both 1814 and 1815 and resulted in some financial chaos. The shipping trade had largely been brought to a standstill. The British blockade of eastern ports added to the effects of the over-extension of credit and led to the suspension of specie by Philadelphia and then New York banks. Money was tight and banknotes depreciated. This situation lasted into 1815, and although the New England banks were largely spared, it led to the consideration of a national bank. These economic disturbances would linger, and it wasn't until mid-1817 that many banks resumed specie payment. The United States had entered a period with bank notes rapidly depreciating because of inflation following the war. Continued depreciation of currency occurred in 1816, although some security prices would be revived. Speculation in bank stock fostered volatility, rise and collapse. President Madison became convinced that a national bank should be reconstituted.

The Second Bank of the United States was organized and opened for business in early-1817, with nominal resumption of specie payment. It had a capital of $35 million, a large concentration of money in its day. Twenty percent of the capital was provided by the federal government. This bank also served as the fiscal agent for the federal government. It too had a 20-year charter.

To a certain extent, the 1815 eruption of Mount Tambora (in current Indonesia), the most powerful volcanic eruption in human history, may have played a role in this cycle. The ash from the eruption column dispersed around the world and lowered global temperatures in an event known as the "year without a summer" in 1816. In New England, it was a disastrously cold summer (with hard frosts), and it even snowed in June. This period of significant climate change triggered extreme weather and harvest failures in North America and Europe. Agriculture followed the weather. Wheat was depressed, with higher prices during 1815-1818. Wheat crops remained below average into 1821. After small cotton crops in 1813 and 1814, a revival occurred, and the latter half of the decade would witness rapid expansion of cotton acreage and larger crops. Production of raw cotton rose from 157,000 bales in 1812 to 377,000 bales in 1821. High cotton prices fostered this increased supply, although 1818 witnessed a small cotton crop and in 1820 lower prices. America would soon surpass India, the long-leading producer of cotton. By 1820, cotton replaced tobacco as the nation's leading export.

This expansion of cotton acreage led to rapid western migration. Between 1810 and 1820 the population of Louisiana and Mississippi doubled, and that of Alabama increased 12-fold. Speculation in western lands occurred and was said to be wild. Confidence led manufacturers, merchants, farmers, etc. to take on too much risk and leverage. A generation had passed since the last period, and lessons were forgotten. These years saw over-rapid expansion of commerce and manufacturing, as well as increased competition from British manufacturers. Several years of mildly depressed activity followed, and then a major financial crisis emerged.

In Europe, most nations were impoverished after more than two decades of war. A collapse of credit occurred, and on the Continent, paper currencies were largely worthless. A decline in prices and the failure of many banks transpired. A crop shortage in England during 1818 was a harbinger of a banking crisis and depression in 1819. This would be manifested in the United States and result in a commercial and industrial crisis.

Land speculation in the South and West, along with continued excessive issue of paper bank notes and extended leverage, led to a new crisis emerging in late-1818, which derailed recovery efforts, leading to widespread economic pain across the nation. Largely stagnant activity since 1815 was prolonged by this panic. The value of bank notes rapidly depreciated, and credit contraction caused widespread difficulties. The so-called Panic of 1819 was the first great financial crisis in American history. The resulting economic disturbances (and hard times) were characterized by falling security prices, liquidation, and forced sales of goods (often below their purchase price), credit contraction, scarcity of money, restriction of commerce, bank failures, illiquidity and insolvency, widespread foreclosures, closed and idled factories and mills, and increased unemployment among laborers and artisans. A slump occurred in agriculture and manufacturing. Money was very tight, and security values declined, reaching a bottom in 1820.

General bankruptcy spread across the land, affecting all industries, regions, and classes. Land prices collapsed. There were many failures and severe unemployment. The West felt distress due to land speculation. Within one year after opening in 1817, the Bank of the United States was foreclosing on properties in Ohio and Kentucky.

A variety of factors thus led to a lengthy downswing that lasted 63 months until February 1821. Real gross output declined 16.7 percent over this period. It can be seen as a classic primary post-war recession. The economic disturbances during this cycle (in 1814 and 1819) were largely due to unsatisfactory banking practices, as the old evils — over-issue and depreciation of value — of the Continental period appeared. Due to strengthening economic interrelationships, the downturn was widespread across the nation and could be said to mark the first modern business cycle. A recovery emerged, and with the absence of war, a new commercial and industrial era commenced.

Europe suffered commercial losses as well. Exports fell to $70 million, and imports fell to $87 million in 1819. This period of depressed economic activity was lengthy, with business conditions in 1819 particularly poor. Foreign trade would fall even further during 1820 and into 1821. So severe was this leg of the downturn, that even the chartering of a Second Bank of the United States in 1816 failed to provide adequate assistance until after 1820. The depression in activity resulted in widespread calls for government action. Various state legislatures passed laws to strengthen the banking system.

The end of the war resulted in what historians refer to as the Era of Good Feelings, a period (1817-1825) in the political history of the United States that reflected a sense of national purpose and a desire for unity among Americans. The term had nothing to do with the economy and reflected an end to bitter partisan disputes. American political sentiments had turned decidedly "republican" in nature such that amidst all this depressed activity, Secretary of State James Monroe was elected in 1816 and was re-elected in 1820. In his two terms he strove to minimize partisan affiliation in his nominations for postings, with a goal of national unity. The Era is largely associated with his presidency and lasted until 1825. Among policy developments, Florida was purchased from Spain in 1819, and the first immigration law passed. In 1820, Congress passed relief acts for holders of public land, and a political crisis concerning slavery ended with the Missouri Compromise. Congress also appropriated funds for building a section of the National Road through Wheeling, Virginia (now West Virginia). It would later be extended across Ohio, Indiana, and Illinois. It is currently U.S. Highway 40, although portions have been incorporated into Interstate 70.

In 1819, a voluntary association of banks in Boston called the Suffolk Banking System was created in wake of concern for the inflationary danger posed by country banks in the Berkshires. The latter banks kept a reserve of specie at the Suffolk Bank of Boston, which took the lead in arranging this cooperative system, which lasted until 1858. Cooperative and voluntary stems of decentralized monetary control are possible.

New industries continued to emerge. The forty-year period after 1815, for example, would mark the golden age of American whaling, as whale oil was used for lighting. By the mid-1830s, four-fifths of the world's whaling fleet would be American and centered in New Bedford, Massachusetts. Eventually, petroleum would replace whale oil, a classic example of Schumpeter's creative destruction. More recently, Yardeni has characterized this creative destruction as creative construction.

This cycle also witnessed the formal founding of New York Stock Exchange in 1817. Between 1792 and 1817, the stockbrokers of New York operated under the Buttonwood Agreement, but in 1817, they instituted new reforms and reorganized. This made it easier for entrepreneurs to raise capital from investors and was essential in the economic progress of the United States. Capital would flow more easily to where it was needed.

Cycle 6: Era of Good Feeling (I) and the 1822-23 Recession

Confidence returned, and the long 1815-21 downswing ended. After all, it was the now the Era of Good Feelings. The ensuing upswing (Cycle 6) started in February 1821, and economic disruption gave way to progress. By October, a marked improvement was in place. Commodity prices reached bottom in mid-1821 and then advanced. Credit became easy, and security speculation revived. Demand generated by farming fostered new industries, especially in New England. With steady improvement apparent by late-1821, real gross output grew until June 1822, a short, 16-month upswing and a 36 percent gain in business activity.

Although foreign trade remained depressed in 1821, it was largely in balance, with both exports and imports at $55 million. With the recovery of activity in 1822, imports would rise to $80 million and exports to $61 million. Exports would expand further into 1823, but with the onset of a downturn, imports would fall back. Exports were dominated by wheat, tobacco, rice, lumber, naval stores, hides and pelts, and increasingly cotton. Across the pond, the first modern boom in British economic history occurred in the period leading up to 1825.

Production of raw cotton rose from 377,000 bales in 1821 to 439,000 bales in 1822 before falling back to 387,000 in 1823, largely due to crop failure. Cotton prices were good at first but declined as recession set in. The crop failure in 1823 would result in higher prices and eventually greater supply. A depression in other agricultural areas occurred and resulted in record low wheat prices during 1821, but prices would recover in 1822 and into 1823.

Commodity prices continued to rise, but just when America began to see some light after six years of depressed activity, commodity prices turned in March 1822. Money tightened, and security prices declined. The revival of activity continued until May and then faltered, with a mild recession beginning in June. This resulted in failures and higher unemployment. The recession was short-lived and considered a minor disturbance, ending in June 1823 after 12 months in duration. Output would fall 9.8 percent peak to trough. By the second half of 1823, a marked improvement in business activity was apparent.

Attempts by the Second Bank of the United States to prevent the overissue of state bank notes (by buying them and presenting them for redemption in specie) under the leadership of Nicholas Biddle would lead to widespread resentment. This resentment would be centered in the western states beyond the Appalachian Mountain range, where bankers were looser in issuing banknotes. In addition, the democratic spirit accompanied by the Jacksonian revolution led by President Andrew Jackson, fostered fear that the Second Bank was an institution of eastern bankers and monopoly.

With technological innovations in printing and paper making, the 1820s would mark the expansion of newspaper publishing. The drop in prices would produce a significant rise in circulation. Newspapers would constitute a significant portion of the mail carried by the U.S. Post Office, which expanded from three thousand post office branches at the end of the War of 1812 to eight thousand by 1830. The Post Office would give contracts for carrying mail, which aided the stagecoach and steamboat industries. It was the lifeblood of our communication system. This revolution in communication and transportation would make goods and information broadly available.

The explosion of the cotton industry extended the evil of slavery. Debate over slavery extending to the West led to the Missouri Compromise. Increasingly, the North would come to resent the constitutional clause in which three-fifths of the slave population counted for representation in Congress and the Electoral College. The 1820s saw the rise of the abolitionist movement. The South would further dig its heels in on the issue, and this would characterize national politics for four decades, leading to the Civil War.

Cycle 7: Era of Good Feeling (II) and the Panic of 1825

The Era of Good Feelings continued, and the upswing (Cycle 7) started in June 1823. With steady improvement apparent by late-1821, real gross output grew until August 1825, a 26-month upswing and a 30 percent gain in business activity. Thus, the nation got only a slight reprieve before the Panic of 1825, a stock market crash that would prove devastating to the economy. It was during this cycle that Edward Chancellor (2000) noted the beginning of a close connection between speculation and the business cycle.

A marked improvement took place in the second half of 1823 and would continue into 1825. The upswing resulted in the formation of new manufacturing enterprises and a renewal of banking. This cycle marked the completion (after eight years of construction) of the Erie Canal in November 1825, a revolution in transportation and a great step in the opening of the West. The canal contributed to the prosperity and rise of New York, making it the Empire State. The cost of production would be paid off using tolls collected within nine years. It served as a stimulus to similar projects throughout the North, as other states rushed to imitate New York's success. Canals further extended the advantages of low-cost water transportation and would support the emerging Industrial Revolution. It would also lead to state promotion in canal construction and speculation in this infrastructure.

Still a growth industry, production of raw cotton recovered from 387,000 bales in 1823 (a year of crop failure) to 732,000 bales during 1826, before falling back to 565,000 in 1827. With excellent crops, production rebounded to 680,000 bales in 1828. Cotton prices were high from 1823-1824 but fell over 50 percent in 1825 and would remain soft through the rest of this cycle.

Figure 3.5

Cycle 7: Era of Good Feeling (II) and the Panic of 1825

Index of Real Gross Output where 2017 = 100

After excessive speculation (a boom) in cotton, iron, other manufacturing and mining, a financial panic in Great Britain began in late-1824 and was complicated by a crop failure in England that fostered the exporting of gold to buy grain. At the same time, the Bank of England raised interest rates. It was a classic example of a speculation-fueled boom and bust. Speculative investments in Latin America, and alongside other investments, led to a bubble that inevitably burst and spread. At the same time, mining stocks fell, causing even more financial upheaval. Credit was exhausted and caused a reaction in other European nations, as obligations were recalled. English cotton mills curtailed production, adversely affecting cotton prices, and leading to distress among New Orleans banks. This spread to other areas, but the Bank of the United States mitigated some of the damage. By 1826, liquidation had largely run its course, but recovery was slow among sectors.

Commodity prices were generally weak in 1823 and into 1824 and would then start rising amid speculation. Security prices started off slow, and with the expansion of financing and speculation, would also begin to rise. Many new banks were chartered, and money soon became easy. Prosperity was reached in 1825 with further gains in activity, rising commodity prices, and heated speculation. The collapse then occurred with tightening money and panic. Falling equity prices were fueled by excessive speculation and reaction in London, which soon spread to America. British and American financial markets were severely disrupted. Security prices fell sharply in the second half of the year, and business activity then slackened and declined. Unemployment rose sharply, and there were many bank failures. In 1826, trade and industry remained dull but stabilized and improved slightly in the closing months of the year. Money remained tight, and bank failures continued with depressed securities.

Commodity prices remained low but improved in 1827, as did some aspects of industry and commerce. Money eased and speculation revived. From 1822 into 1828, the Bank of the United States more than doubled its circulation of bank notes, largely supplanting notes from other banks. Early in 1828, money was plentiful, but this turned quickly, and credit markets were again tight near the end of the cycle in 1828, as difficulties in specie circulation cropped up. Activity continued into 1828 and then slumped, another leg down. This was particularly the case in New England. Commodity prices, trade, and other activity were depressed. The recession was longer (35 months) than the previous downturn, ending in July 1828. Output would fall 9.7 percent peak to trough. It can be seen as a classic secondary post-war recession.

Secretary of State John Quincy Adams was elected in 1824 after a tight election. Initially a Federalist like his father, he won election as a member of the Democratic-Republican Party, and in the mid-1830s became affiliated with the Whig Party. Like his father, he served only one term. Senator Andrew Jackson was elected in

1828 and would usher in a new period in American political life. His presidency coincided with a period of relative prosperity.

The Tariff of 1824 was a protective tariff designed to protect American industry from cheaper British commodities, especially iron products, finished wool and cotton textiles, and agricultural goods. In 1826, Great Britain forbade American trade with her colonies, and the United States soon issued counter-trade measures. The Tariff of 1828 was another protective tariff designed to protect industry in the North. Created during the Adams presidency and implemented during the Jackson presidency, it was labeled the "Tariff of Abominations" by opponents. It set a 45 percent tax on certain imported raw materials and a 38 percent tax on certain imported goods. By the end of the decade, the average tariff on dutiable imports would reach its highest level in American history, over 60 percent for some products. Trade subsequently suffered at a time when credit became tight for manufacturers in New England. As a result, the decline in trade was a factor behind this recession. The development of the textile industry in New England would foster protectionist sentiment in a region where maritime interests had long favored free trade.

Exports rose from $68 million in 1823 to $91 million in 1825, before easing to $73 million in 1826 and $64 million in 1828. Imports rose from $72 million in 1823 to $90 million in 1825, before easing to $71 million in 1827 and then rebounding to $81 million in 1828.

Cycle 8: Jacksonian Era and the 1833-34 Recession

With an easing of money, depressed commerce and industry gave way to increased activity by late-1828. Wheat prices were high and there was a large cotton crop. This continued largely unabated for 61 months until August 1833, with a 45 percent gain in real gross output.

In 1829, purchases of public land began to revive. There was a constant movement westward into the Northwest (and old Southwest) causing a large increase in agricultural production. The availability of cheap land and rapid settlement, along with easy money, would expand agricultural production faster than markets could absorb, leading to boom-bust cycles for decades. Another development was the beginning of sizable immigration.

Growth in transportation was a mark of this cycle and the next one. During this cycle, the success of the Erie Canal fostered the start of construction of numerous canals in Ohio, Pennsylvania, New Jersey, Illinois, and other states. However, with the development of railways in Great Britain, it was during this cycle (in 1828) that steam railroads proved practical in America, beginning operations in 1830. Extensive construction ensued within a few years and would eventually supplant canal construction. Miles constructed were 72 in 1831 and would rise to 253 miles in 1834. Thus, miles operated would rise from only 23 in 1830 to 633 miles by 1834. Eventually, rail would overtake canals.

Production of raw cotton eased from 764,000 bales in 1829 to 732,000 bales in 1830, before rising to 805,000 bales in 1831, 816,000 bales in 1832, and 931,000 in 1833. Even with recession, production would rise to 962,000 bales in 1834 and would continue to expand in the years following. Cotton prices remained low into 1831 but would begin rising in the following years. Wheat crops were mixed in this cycle as well.

Exports rose from $64 million in 1828 to $72 million in 1830 and 1831, and as difficulties limiting trade with British colonies were removed, would rise further to $102 million in 1834. Imports eased in 1829 and 1830 from $81 million in 1828, before rising to $96 million in 1831, and with lower tariffs even further to $109 million in 1834. Trade was fostered by internal improvements such as dredging harbors and building lighthouses. In addition, trade relations with Great Britain improved. The most important American export was cotton, with Great Britain as the largest customer. The Tariff of 1832 was billed as a compromise tariff that reduced existing tariffs to remedy regional contention arising from the Tariff of 1828; however, it was deemed unsatisfactory by many in the South.

In 1830, there were 329 state-chartered banks, up from 307 a decade before. Money soon became easier, but in 1830, President Jackson started a policy of increasing hostility to the Bank of the United States. The year marked progress in real activity amidst soft commodity prices. The latter began to rebound in 1831, and money began to tighten in late 1831. Security prices rose for much of the year. It was during this cycle that New York supplanted Philadelphia as the nation's financial center. The Second Bank would become an election issue in the 1832 election.

The 1830s would witness an expansion of industrial activity. The rise of the textile industry was central to industrialization in the United States, and by the early-1830s, most of the largest corporations in the nation were textile companies. Gains in industry and other lines of business improved further in 1831, although the pace of expansion slowed amidst ongoing financial strain. This is likely the first instance of a growth recession. In 1832, President Jackson vetoed the Bank of the United States charter renewal and was reelected, despite money becoming tighter. This election marked the gradual transition from presidential campaigns centered on individuals to political party oriented presidential campaigns. Other events of the year include flooding of the Ohio River, a cholera epidemic in New York, and the Black Hawk War in the old Northwest.

In 1832-33, the nullification crisis emerged. This involved a confrontation between the state of South Carolina and the federal government. It arose after South Carolina, in its Ordinance of Nullification, declared the federal Tariffs of 1828 and 1832 as unconstitutional and therefore null and void within the boundaries of the state. Courts at the state and federal level, and ultimately the U.S. Supreme Court, rejected the theory of nullification. Congress in March 1833 passed both the Force Bill — allowing use of the military if necessary to collect tariff duties — and a compromise tariff that reduced those duties. South Carolina responded by rescinding its Ordinance. This sectional political crisis created considerable uncertainty, one factor leading to the next panic.

Activity continued into mid-1833, but prosperity gave way to uncertainty, panic, tightening credit, decreased business activity, commercial distress, and many failures. President Jackson in 1832 demanded the Bank of the United States give up $10 million in federal funds and disperse them among state banks, resulting in a contraction of credit by the Bank of the United States. Money became even tighter, and security prices declined. Business activity as measured by real gross output, slackened with rising unemployment. Commercial dullness continued into 1834. The recession was shorter (only 12 months) than the previous downturn, ending in August 1834. The modest decline was more of a slowdown of activity, as real gross output fell only 2.1 percent from peak to trough. It was a brief and mild recession. Increased cotton and other exports softened the distress, as money remained tight. The amount of gold backing the dollar was reduced. A marked improvement in the cotton market, along with other good crops, fostered improving activity by late-1834, as the next cycle emerged. The upswing would be driven by land speculation, a great boom led by a decline in interest rates and a rise in security prices.

With the demise of the Second Bank, another period of money inflation emerged, as the number of state banks increased from 329 in 1830 to 506 in 1834. These banks would over-issue notes, leading to another boom-bust monetary episode and would end in another financial panic and downswing.

In 1829, the state of New York created the New York Safety Fund System, a deposit insurance system. Each private bank would be required to set aside a three percent reserve that would be held by the state. This system was a forerunner of the current Federal

Deposit Insurance Corporation (FDIC). It seemed to be sound but collapsed during the Panic of 1837.

Cycle 9: The Panic of 1837

A marked improvement in cotton markets emerged, and with rising land speculation, strong exports, a relaxation of interest rates, and the upswing of security prices, steady improvement was apparent by late 1834, and real gross output would grow until January 1837, a 29-month upswing and a 39 percent gain in business activity. Ayres (1939) referred to this upswing as a "bank credit land boom" and to the whole decade as "the turbulent thirties." Cycle 9 was a period of marked expansion of industry and commerce, as well as that of land speculation.

President Jackson's refusal to extend the charter of the Second Bank of the United States and its consequent withdrawal from business was a key factor aggravating the difficulties that come after a season of unbridled growth in speculation. With the end of the Second Bank of the United States in January 1836, the nation entered what is known as the "Free Banking Era" where banks are free to issue their own paper currency (banknotes) but were subject to few regulations beyond those applicable to most enterprises. So-called "wild cat" banks that would issue irredeemable paper currency proliferated. The period prior to 1837 featured cheap and easy money, which never ends well. A principal cause of the panic was the excessive issue of paper money. The years 1835 and 1836 were a period of astonishing speculation in farmlands and real estate, as European capital flooded the United States. Ayres felt the speculation of the 1830s was comparable to the stock speculation of the 1920s in its intensity and widespread participation by people throughout the nation and in all walks of life.

Figure 3.6
Cycle 9: The Panic of 1837
Index of Real Gross Output where 2017 = 100

Canal and railroad construction continued in this cycle as did development in the West. All this was led by steady increases in population and foreign trade. Canal construction in particular, played a role and was speculative in nature. Over-trading and speculation spread to most parts of the nation, particularly centered in the West. Money was easy and led to speculation. New banks were formed. British lending to America surged during these years. A flood of British capital poured into the United States, inflaming land and other speculation.

The years 1834 and 1835 were a period of low prices and characterized by an improving abundance of money, credit, and a rapid increase in construction and activity in other business sectors. The increase in railroad construction is illustrative of this upswing. Miles built were 253 in 1834 and would nearly double the next year to 465 miles. Demand for materials for this effort exceeded supply, resulting in advancing prices. With tighter money, this would fall back to 175 miles in 1836 and 224 miles in 1837. As rail construction eased, inventories accumulated, resulting in a reversal of prices, nearly a year before the panic.

In 1836, industry, agriculture and commerce were largely prosperous, leading to an abundance of incomes. Commodity prices rose, and foreign trade was active. Speculation in land, railroads, canals, mines, and other enterprises reached new heights. This was especially the case in the West and the South. In some cases, land prices increased ten-fold. State-chartered banks continued to lend actively against land and building. Credit was available from overseas, most notably from Great Britain and The Netherlands. In order to stem the flow of capital to America, the Bank of England raised interest rates so perhaps one-third of the speculative schemes were no longer viable. Panic and bank failures in Great Britain during 1836 would spread to the United States. Cotton prices fell, and panic ensued. New York and other banks suspended payment, and bank notes depreciated.

Widespread land sales temporarily doubled Federal revenues in 1834-36. The financial position of the Federal government had so improved that the entire national debt was redeemed by 1835, the only time in American history. Still, the revenues kept rising, as land sales and tariff revenues continued at a strong pace. At the start of 1836, a surplus of $27 million was on hand. In 1836-37, the Federal government distributed excess revenue to the states. At over $28 million, it was equivalent to over 15 percent of typical spending. It was distributed to each state according to its electoral votes, including three-fifths for slaves. This furthered the speculative boom.

The Coinage (or Gold Coin) Act of 1834 changed the ratio of the relative value of gold and silver. This had the effect of devaluing the gold dollar by 7 percent without altering the silver dollar. This was another factor leading up to the downswing.

In 1836, a wave of public projects (canals, railroads, banks, etc.) were undertaken, many of which in the enthusiasm of the times, were made without regard to added value versus the resources consumed for their completion. Speculation, especially in land, became rampant and was aided by an expansion of credit and banks.

Following the Coinage Act, President Jackson instituted the Specie Circular, an executive order that stipulated that federal land must be bought with silver or gold. This resulted in severe credit restrictions for smaller financial institutions, precipitating the recession. Starting in 1836, the Treasury Department refused to accept anything but specie for public lands, thus placing a check on land speculation. It would be the pin that would puncture the bubble. Commodity prices were high in early 1837, indicating that the period of prosperity was coming to an end. Indeed, real gross output peaked in January and was already weak. The panic came in April 1837 and spread. Within 10 days, 128 commercial failures were reported in New York. The drain on reserves was severe, and money became scarce. Specie payments were suspended by banks in May and were not resumed until the following year. The panic spread from New York to Philadelphia. New England banks were affected to a lesser extent. Suspension was an admission of illiquidity, and this resulted in an extreme loss of public confidence in currency, which led to many bank runs by consumers and a general (and spreading) suspension of specie payments. Altogether, over 600 banks would fail during 1837 and 1838. It was a paralysis of credit. Jacksonian policy was thus a major factor behind the panic and downswing in business activity. It was widespread. The failure of a New Orleans cotton broker would spread to New York creditors. The mercantile house of Arthur Tappan and Company, founder of the *Journal of Commerce,* failed.

Innovations affected not only manufacturing, but agriculture as well. John Deere's forged steel plows, along with the reaper developed by Cyrus McCormick, initiated large gains in agricultural productivity. Agriculture still represented the largest sector of the U.S. economy. The failure of wheat crops in 1835 was an unfavorable factor. Crop failures again in 1837 left farmers without the ability to meet their obligation in Western states, where the troubles began. Cotton production rose from 962,000 bales in 1834 to 1.06

million in 1835, 1.13 million in 1836, and would soon peak at 1.43 million in 1837. The South was the engine of the national economy during this period. Cotton prices were high in 1835 but collapsed in February and March of 1937. The failure of cotton crops falling back to 1.093 million bales in 1838 was a factor reinforcing the unfavorable situation.

The start of 1837 was marked by strong activity and speculation. It would not last. The panic in 1837 marked the close of land, bank, railroad, and commodity speculation. A reduction in British commercial loans to American merchants was another factor. The cotton market largely collapsed. Commodity prices declined, and foreign trade was restricted. Money was tight, and the panic began. A period of depression followed. The downswing was sharp, with real gross output falling 29 percent until June 1838, a 17-month recession. A period of liquidation ensued and resulted in many failures. Factories closed, and unemployment rose. The downturn had both foreign and domestic causes. Some economic historians place the trough in activity as late as 1840. It was one of the nation's great economic catastrophes.

Widespread deflation was avoided by suspending payment. Paper was widely issued, especially in the South. Just as the decline was sharp, a rebound was sharp as well. An attempt at revival was made. The recovery of railroad construction marked the year 1838. Stagnation gave way to improvement and increased activity. Still, it would not last, and a case could be made that the next cycle, along with the Panic of 1839 and its aftermath, could be included within this cycle, as the peak of business activity reached in January 1837 was not reached again until mid-1845. Most scholars differentiate between this cycle and the next, and I concur. Failures continued, and foreign trade declined.

In 1836, Vice President Martin Van Buren was elected president. A Jacksonian Democrat (and one of the founders of the party), he largely continued the policies of his predecessor and, as a result, his term represents an extension of the Jacksonian Era. Outgoing President Jackson, however, left the U.S. economy in poor condition, with high interest rates, little bank lending, and collapsing land speculation.

Other domestic events during this cycle include the Seminole War and the War of Texas Independence, a war fought from October 1835 to April 1836 between Mexico and Texas colonists. Texas was increasingly populated by American settlers who migrated into the area from the United States. The war resulted in Texan independence from Mexico and the founding of the Republic of Texas (1836–45).

Finally, the political scene was such that what was essentially a one-party rule disintegrated into two distinct political parties that viewed the economy quite differently. This would foster uncertainty. Democrats blamed the banks (they still do), and the Whigs blamed Jackson and his Specie Circular.

During downturns, new industries can arise. In 1837, William Procter and James Gamble (brothers-in-law) formed a partnership to use excess lard (as Cincinnati was a center for meatpacking) in making soap a mass consumer product, replacing what had previously been produced by households. The 1830s were a period of rapid gains in other industries.

Cycle 10: Brief Boom, the Panic of 1839, America's First Great Depression, and Debt Repudiation

Money eased in 1838 and was accompanied by a gradual resumption of specie payment in 1839. There was soon an inflation of currency. The decision of New York and Michigan in 1838, and then other states as well, to adopt "free banking" and granted bank charters to any comers, amplifying sources of credit. It would lead to an explosion of state banks and money inflation.

With a gradual resumption of specie payments, an upswing emerged in the second half of 1838. The American economy appeared to be undergoing a recovery. There was a fair wheat crop but lower prices while cotton yield was low (1.093 million bales), resulting in high cotton prices. Ayers referred to this as the Cotton Boom. Improvement continued, and there was a revival of land speculation. Speculative activity briefly resumed and was extraordinarily violent in the cotton market. It was all an illusion and created the real estate bubble that would burst, sometimes referred to as the "second revulsion." The upswing would be short-lived (only nine months), which pushed real gross output up an incredible 31 percent in this short period from June 1838 to March 1839. Thus, a case could be made that this cycle, along with the prior cycle, should be included as one. As most scholars differentiate between this and the previous cycle, I do so as well. Cycle 10 was a major cycle.

Figure 3.7
Cotton Production in the United States
(Thousand Bales)

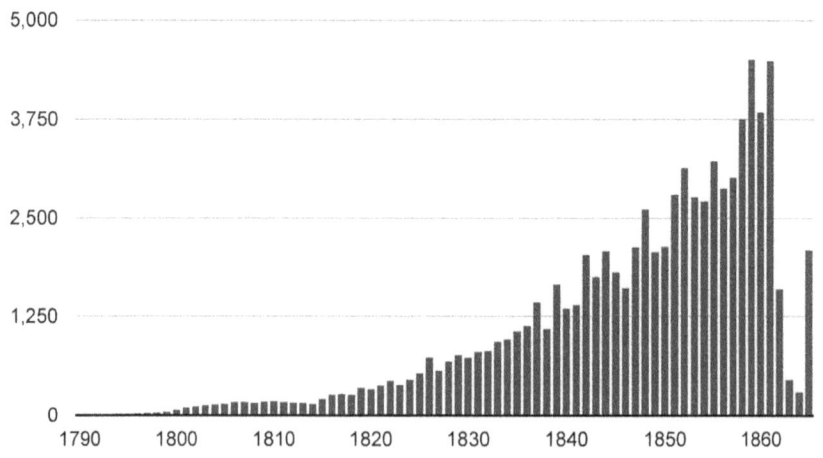

Source: Statistical Abstract of the United States

In 1839, a reaction occurred and would burst forth with renewed fury. Some scholars felt that it was precipitated by the withdrawal of credit from America by British banks, most notably the Bank of England. A crop failure in England resulted in large overseas purchases of wheat from continental Europe. The Bank of England was weakened by the outflow of gold, and credit restriction resulted. Credit collapsed in America, starting first with Philadelphia banks and spreading to banks in New York. The panic was so severe that confidence was nearly destroyed. Money markets tightened, resulting in rapidly declining activity, panic, and many failures. Liquidation followed the panic. By the fourth quarter, specie payment was suspended again, with the exception of New England and New York. In the background were tensions with Great Britain over the border with Canada. This fostered some uncertainty. There was a large wheat harvest and record cotton crop (1.654 million bales), resulting in lower prices. The downturn in Great Britain affected American exports (especially cotton) and restricted credit availability. In 1839, cotton prices would fall to half of 1836 levels.

Figure 3.8

Cycle 10: Brief Boom, the Panic of 1839, America's First Great Depression and Debt Repudiation

Index of Real Gross Output where 2017 = 100

Although specie payments resumed in 1839, economic stagnation and depression lasted for years. By some accounts, it was not until 1845 that a sustained business recovery emerged. In some regards, the 1839 downturn could be characterized as the second leg of a W-shaped recession piggybacking on the Panic of 1837. Peak activity reached in March 1839 fell short of the previous peak in January 1837, and it would not reach that volume until mid-1845. At 47 months, the downturn was long, with real gross output falling 21 percent. It has been referred to as America's First Great Depression. Indeed, Ayres (1939) referred to the whole decade as "the depressed forties." A multitude of failures occurred. The situation was aggravated by the suspension of the United States Bank and other banks. Indeed, bank failures (959) were even more numerous than in 1837 (618). This long depression of business activity resulted in extreme debt repudiation. The nation was burdened by a large volume of indebtedness that had been incurred by all sorts of land speculation, private ventures, and public ventures. Many states had floated bond issues for construction of highways, canals, and railroads, as well as for the founding of state banks. Borrowing abroad was politically easier than raising taxes to finance projects. As the downswing in activity got underway, there was a decline in commodity prices that greatly increased the weight of indebtedness. This long, grinding downturn fostered more hardship on the nation than any other period. Wholesale prices declined 39 percent, on par with the decline during the 1930s. Manufacturing slumped, and many new cotton mills halted production. The slump would extend to woolen goods, shoes, metalworking, and other industries. As businesses cutback production or failed altogether, unemployment rose. Finance suffered as well.

The year 1840 was an important year for the nation. At 17.1 million, the population of the United States was on par with that of Great Britain. In 1840, commodity prices further declined, exacerbating financial strains, especially in the West. Security prices decreased, and activity was depressed. During 1840, business activity descended month after month. The downturn was so severe (with high unemployment, falling prices, debased currencies, and bank failures) that President Van Buren was not reelected, ending a long stretch of Democrat administrations. It was a contested election, and many feared violence. Public opinion turned against Jacksonian policy. Former Senator and General, William Henry Harrison was elected. He was a Whig and had unsuccessfully run against Van Buren (in a spilt Whig ticket) in 1836. The Whigs nicknamed Van Buren "Van Ruin" because of the economic problems. Harrison would not serve long, dying of pneumonia only 31 days into his term, becoming the first president to die in office, and the shortest-serving U.S. president in history. He was succeeded by Vice President John Tyler in April 1841.

The 1841 wheat crop was large, while cotton production fell to 1.348 million bales, a poor level compared to prior years. The Land Act of 1841 was designed to "appropriate the proceeds of the sales of public lands... and to grant ' pre-emption rights ' to individuals" who were living on federal lands. This landmark legislation was important in encouraging settlement of the West. Commodity prices continued to decline in 1841, adding to financial strains, further affecting the West. Activity was dull, and there were many failures. State finances collapsed. Attempts to open the Bank of the United States failed, and security prices declined, most notably in the closing months of the year. Congress passed the Bankruptcy Act, a depression-relief measure which established a uniform system of bankruptcy throughout the nation, but it was found to ruin debtor's credit, and was repealed two years later. During this depression (in 1841), the Tappan brothers started The Mercantile Agency in New York. The Mercantile Agency was the precursor to Dun & Bradstreet (D&B) and modern credit-reporting services.

By 1842, there were widespread demands that the Federal government assume all state debts, but legislation, to that effect, did not go far. Congress passed the Tariff of 1842, a protectionist tariff that reversed the Compromise Tariff of 1833. Social unrest mounted. It was also referred to as the Whig Tariff or the Black Tariff. It raised tariff rates to 20 percent on most goods.

Commodity prices continued to decline in 1842, resulting in many bank and other failures. Activity remained dull. This marked the nadir of security prices and gradually, tight money eased with specie payments resuming in many eastern cities. Security prices soon began to rise. Crops were largely abundant, especially cotton, the production of which reached a new record of 2.035 million bales. However, crop prices were generally low. The Seminole War was brought to conclusion. The Webster-Ashburton Treaty of 1842 established the boundaries between the United States and Canada, alleviating some uncertainty surrounding differences and tensions. Exports reached a cyclical low of $83 million in 1843, off from the recent peak of $124 million in 1840. Imports slumped to a low of $42 million in 1843, off from the peak of $156 million in 1839. Recovery would then take place.

The depression was severe. There was a dramatic and grinding decline in business activity over nearly four years. Rail construction fell from 453 miles in 1838 to 386 miles in 1939. It would rebound to 491 miles in 1840 and 606 miles in 1841, before falling to 505 miles in 1842, 288 miles in 1843, and then bottoming out at only 140 miles in 1844. Nonetheless, the emergence of this industry was staggering. The 1830s encouraged construction, and by 1840, rail mileage totaled as much as canal mileage and was more than twice that in all of Europe. The extensive distances in America fostered a need, and availability of cheap land and low-cost wood as a fuel were factors.

The depression was followed by defaults (i.e., debt repudiation) by eight of the 26 state governments at that time, resulting in a general mistrust (and avoidance) among foreign creditors of American banks, state governments, and other institutions. States had chartered too many state-supported and state-owned banks (many of which proved to be unstable) and undertook too many transportation infrastructure projects. State infrastructure investment collapsed.

By 1843, America was essentially frozen out of international financial markets as non-defaulting states were affected as well. There are consequences of debt repudiation. The mood in London turned grim, and although the Federal government had an impeccable record and was largely debt-free for a decade, it too would have issues selling bonds to European investors. There were reports of Americans being verbally accosted on the streets in London. A key feature of the downturn was the collapse of trust within the financial and business communities. With this collapse, economic exchange ground to a halt.

The Federal government also faced a budget crisis, in that many of its revenues were deposited in state banks, some of which suspended payment, and some of which failed. Gridlock would emerge in Washington as to remedies for the nation.

The economic turmoil resulted in social and political disorder; the Dorr Rebellion in 1842 is an illustrative of this unraveling order. The rebellion was an attempt by the working- and middle-class to force broader democracy in Rhode Island, where the voting was largely limited to landholders. Falling agricultural prices affected farming and attempts to extract rents in New York were met with resistance. Strikes and riots would plague Philadelphia, then the largest manufacturing center. There was violence between groups of workers. Riots spread to other cities.

It was in the summer of 1843 that the downturn would reach its end, marking the conclusion of one of the longest and deepest depressions of the 19th century. It was a period of pronounced deflation and large-scale debt default/repudiation. A recovery of security prices first emerged in 1842 and continued, eventually selling over to the productive side of the economy. Dullness gradually yielded to improvement, and by the summer, money had eased, and speculation again appeared.

This long downturn was not limited to the United States. After 1837, Great Britain entered a period of recession and stagnation in which recovery would not begin to emerge until 1843. The recovery there was marked by gains in nearly all manufacturing industries. It would, moreover, revive interest in railway construction, and soon a speculative railway boom would occur there, proving fodder for the next British downturn.

Even with protracted downturns, new innovations, and industries arise. Most notable was the concept of mass production and interchangeable parts in manufacturing, the "American System" as it was called. It would upturn industries as diverse as manufacturing clocks, guns, hardware, and machinery, leading to integrated industrial sites.

Liquidation was thorough in Cycle 10. The next three cycles (11-13) would feature milder downswings. Many scholars characterized the downturns associated with these as mild recessions. I follow this assessment.

Cycle 11: The Mexican American War and the Mild Recession of 1846

From the long recession of 1839-1843, business activity stabilized at a low level in February 1843 and began to recover in early 1843. Gradual improvement ensued, and by the summer revival, was clearly in place and would lead to a 37- month upswing (to March 1846) and a 46 percent gain in real gross output.

In 1843, commodity prices reached a low in the summer and improved, as did prices of manufactured goods. Exports improved, and harvest brought a good corn and other cereal crops. Cotton yields were poor, and production fell to 1.75 million bales. Money was easy, and a recovery of security prices and speculation occurred. The years 1843 and 1844 were a period of generally low commodity prices. In 1844, industries started to revive, but full headway was checked in part by a sudden, large advance of prices in the spring of 1845. A carry-over of construction contracts moderately helped business for a while.

Rail construction would resume, leading the upswing with miles built, rising from 180 miles in 1844 to 277 in 1845 and 333 in 1846. This would stimulate mining, iron production, and the machinery industries. The year 1845 saw further revival of manufacturing and other business activity, and aspects of prosperity emerged. Prices of manufactured goods improved. Cotton production improved to 2.079 million bales, and speculation appeared. There was an excellent oat crop but poor wheat and corn. A failure of European crops in 1845 contributed to the expansion of activity, but in general, agriculture remained depressed.

Across the pond, a speculative boom in railway investment was underway, which also provided support for a variety of industries. British and American business cycles tended to follow each other.

The lingering effects of the long depression furthered the gridlock in Washington, and the year featured another contested election. But with the "hard times" having largely passed, economic issues seemed less important. President Tyler was not reelected, and James Polk, a Democrat, was elected in 1844. Polk was an advocate of Texas annexation. He won by a small margin in popular votes but with a clear majority in the Electoral College. Not until 1845, with Democrats controlling both houses of Congress and a Democrat administration, would change be possible. Texas agreed to annexation in mid-1845, and this was concluded by year-end.

Easy money tightened in 1844. Both bond and stock prices turned downward in 1844 and 1845, and interest rates rose. A stock market correction occurred after the election. There followed a modest easing of business activity but no real recession. In 1844, the Treaty of Wanghai was negotiated with China and gave the United States most-favored-nation status in trade. This opened additional markets for American goods, but from 1842-1846 exports were largely stagnant. Later in 1845 there was an improvement in the South and prosperous activity in other regions. The wheat crop was good, while cotton (at 1.806 million bales) and oats were fair. The corn crop was poor, and prices rose. Speculation in wheat emerged in the closing months. In mid-year, money tightened, and the stock market was depressed but revived afterwards, along with railroad speculation. Commodity and other prices rose and would carry over into the next year.

The year 1845 witnessed the demonstration of the telegraph by Samuel Morse, which would revolutionize and integrate finance, commerce, and other sectors of the economy. Competing networks would emerge, but the Western Union would dominate. Unlike the telephone, developed three decades later, the telegraph was used more frequently for commerce rather than social purposes. The telegraph would dominate communications until supplanted by other technologies, remaining a prominent feature of American life well into the 20th century. It would foster American nationalism and territorial ambition. Texas was accepted into U.S. statehood, which would provoke the Mexican War. Also, there were tensions with Great Britain over the boundaries for the Oregon territory.

In 1846, President Polk would sign into law establishment of the Independent Treasury System, which would remain in place until the introduction of the Federal Reserve System in 1913. States adopted stricter banking laws, banks adopted conservative practices in lending, and many insolvent banks were removed. With the recovery, manufacturing would lead the way.

A surplus of seven million dollars remained in the U.S. Treasury, a product of tariff increases in 1842. One suggestion for paying for the war was tapping this surplus, but this would not come close to funding such a protracted war. Between 1846 and 1849, the Federal government issued $49 million in debt to finance the war.

Enacted by the Democrats, the Walker Tariff of 1846 repealed many of the high duties of the Tariff of 1842. It also introduced ad valorem rates for many unit duties. The tariff would prove unpopular in the Middle Atlantic and New England.

By 1846, commerce and industry rebounded, with real gross output reaching new highs. Construction contracts revived rapidly.

Cotton production would ease to 1.604 million bales in 1846, but prosperity continued in the South. A large wheat crop was harvested, and agricultural prices generally trended upwards. Early in the year, business activity began to slacken. There was pressure in the money market and a fall in security prices. The downturn would be short, only five months, with a near five percent decline in real gross output. This recession was mild enough that it may have only been a slowdown in the growth cycle.

War was declared in April, and in a limited way, the Mexican–American War provided a check on business enterprise due to the uncertainty it fostered. That said, government purchases would certainly provide a supportive effect for business and softened (and possibly ended) the downturn. In addition, the Oregon dispute was settled, alleviating some uncertainty.

Cycle 12: Mexican-American War and Crisis in Europe

After the mid dip in business activity in 1846, real gross output improved, and a recovery and expansion took hold. Aided by productive activity associated with the war, it would last 12 months, resulting in a 23 percent gain in business activity.

The Walker Tariff of 1846 made substantial cuts in the high rates of the Black Tariff of 1842. This proved useful for recovery. Business activity was also stimulated by government expenditures for the Mexican-American War. In addition, construction contracts revived and supported improvement, full employment, higher commodity prices, and prosperity in 1847. This prosperity was brief, and interest rates moved up sharply, and with tight money, bond and stock prices declined. This resulted in a minor recession lasting 15 months, from August 1847 to November 1848. Construction fell off and would not revive until 1850. "Embarrassments" (failures and bankruptcies) were few and brief during this downturn and concentrated among corn merchants and some commercial investment firms. Real gross output fell only 7.2 percent.

The destruction of the potato crop in Ireland had an adverse effect on that nation. It would foster starvation and mass emigration to Canada, the United States, and Australia.

English crops failed again in 1846 and were accompanied with crop failures in France. The export of gold to purchase wheat and higher interest rates, along with the bubble bursting in a speculative railway boom in 1847, resulted in panic in London. This would spread elsewhere in Europe, and the consequences would be felt in America. The year would mark significant unrest and even revolutions in Europe. Fears of another crop failure fostered speculation in grain prices, and when it was clear the harvest would be more normal, prices fell, resulting in grain merchants taking losses, liquidating positions, and failures. This spread to banks, resulting in panic. Conditions deteriorated as failures mounted, and a severe downturn ensued in Great Britain. Railway construction did remain relatively high after the Crisis and would cushion the downturn in Great Britain.

The crises overseas brought alarm to America. With the crisis in Great Britain, American activity faltered, but the failure of European crops would prove to be a boom for America. The crises occurring in Europe (which led to revolution in some nations) led to increased exports of grain from the United States, which served to cushion unfavorable effects. Great Britain and France in particular boosted their imports of grain from America.

The Mexican–American War initially provided uncertainty, but conditions remained sound, and confidence improved with favorable victories and the capture of Veracruz in March and Mexico City in September. The winding down of military production was a factor fostering "dull" activity.

Another factor in 1848 was the discovery of gold in California and the resulting Gold Rush. By the end of 1848, $10 million in gold had been mined in California, and by the end of 1851, some $220 million. Until this time, the United States largely minted copper and silver coins, but would begin to mint gold coins. U.S. gold coins in circulation would increase twenty-fold and would alleviate the shortage of currency that plagued the nation throughout its early history.

With this influx of hard money and British extension of credit, the case for creating another national bank would recede into memory. The discoveries of gold provided new resources and a new field for investment, thus preventing a severe downturn, which otherwise may have occurred. It would provide a foundation for recovery and a long upturn during the next cycle.

Revolutions in Europe would foster immigration to America, as did famine in Ireland. It would also temporarily hurt U.S. exports of cotton to Europe, but in the long-term, immigration would provide for a large expansion of the labor force and contribute to long-term economic growth.

The year 1848 started with slackened activity in trade and industry. Eventually, tight money would ease in 1848, and bond prices would advance, but equity markets were unsettled. The downturn was neither long nor widespread, and recovery would be aided by the boom in California. Record crops occurred and gradual improvement emerged. In 1848, the treaty with Mexico was concluded, and the nation made its indemnity payments.

The Mexican-American War in 1847 stimulated commerce, and with the war occurring outside the boundaries of the United States, no destruction of capital or land occurred. The war brought the telegraph to maturity. To pool telegraphed news about the war, six New York newspapers formed the first wire service, the Associated Press (AP). The war ended favorably, and with the treaty, the United States acquired a presence on the Pacific coast, as well as what would become the states of Nevada, Arizona, New Mexico, and Utah, as well as parts of Colorado and other states. It also solidified Texas annexation.

In the recovery, manufacturing would lead the way, and with commerce, would take its place in a more diversified American economy. Exports of grain and other foodstuffs supported agriculture.

In 1848, General Zachary Taylor, a hero of the Mexican-American War, was convinced by the Whigs to run and was elected as the 12th president. Whig economic policy was generally more favorable to manufacturing.

Cycle 13: Post-War, Gold Rush, and Railroad Prosperity

The difficulties of the 1840s would give way to a post-war bounce in late-1848 and a subsequent protracted period of expanding business activity. This has been associated with a long Kondratieff upswing that centered on railroads and the application of steam and metallurgy to industrial production. This upswing was aided by California gold inflation and would last 64 months, to the next peak in March 1854. Real gross output would rise 36 percent, with only a brief setback and interlude in 1851. This was likely a growth recession. In the years running up to 1857, growth and prosperity would see intermittent financial disturbances in finance and industry, none of which were major. In general, bond and stock prices rose during these years.

Revolution had swept Europe in 1848, where a severe depression in most German states fostered an uprising, and there were uprisings in France, Austria, and other nations as well. Political (e.g., various revolutions) and economic (e.g., potato famine in Ireland) difficulties in Europe fostered a tripling of immigration from 114,000 in 1845 to more than 350,000 in each of the years after 1849. Indeed, according to Dewey (1902), more immigrants arrived between 1845 and 1855 than in the prior 25 years. As labor is one factor of production, the influx of these newcomers stimulated productive activity and were a factor ending the short 1849 downturn.

The discovery of gold in California in 1849 expanded the monetary reserves of the nation. It fostered expansion of activity not only in that state, but in shipping and other industries. It would eventually lead to speculation.

Construction had fallen off in 1849 and would not revive until 1850, but the year was characterized by widening activity in industry and continued high rail construction, which would advance even further by mid-decade. As money eased, security prices advanced, and prosperity returned. In agriculture, there were excellent crops in cereals, but cotton was lackluster. A cholera epidemic had localized effects on commerce.

Significant capital was invested in canal construction prior to 1837, but this interest in canals was now supplanted by interest in railroads. Canal construction eased. Railroad expansion was rapid and a major factor in this upswing. In the years between 1848 and1854, over 12,500 miles were constructed, with annual miles constructed rising from 263 in 1847 to a peak of 3,442 in 1854. In addition, steam power began to supplant waterpower, and innovations in metallurgy led to new applications and industries.

Business activity expanded in 1850, and commodity prices advanced early in the year, although low prices would characterize the years 1850-1853. Foreign trade gained further, and railroad construction began its take-off. Money was easy, and the stock market revived with speculation in railroad securities. All of this was influenced by an influx of gold from California. The wheat crop was fair, but the cotton crop was poor, resulting in good wheat prices and very high cotton prices. The year was marked by the death of President Taylor, who was succeeded by Vice President and fellow Whig, Millard Fillmore.[9]

---

[9] Millard Fillmore (1800-1874) was the last Whig president. A former member of the US House of Representatives from Upstate New York, he founded the University of Buffalo. The author was born in Millard Fillmore Hospital in the same delivery room as his mother and grandmother. I just couldn't resist sharing this, and I share this just because I could.

Accompanied by large gains in foreign trade, business activity continued to rise throughout 1851, and prosperity marked much of the year. Rail construction averaged over 1,265 miles from 1850-51. In agriculture, there was a fair wheat crop but a large cotton crop, which rose from 2.136 million bales in 1850 to 2.799 million in 1851. Wheat prices were high, but there was a rapid decline in cotton. In financial markets, speculation in railroad stocks reached a peak and then declined into the fall. Money tightened in mid-summer, adding to a collapse of speculation in California, and various securities, and also in the real economy. The weakness was temporary.

Figure 3.9
New Railroad Construction in the United States (Annual Mileage Increase)

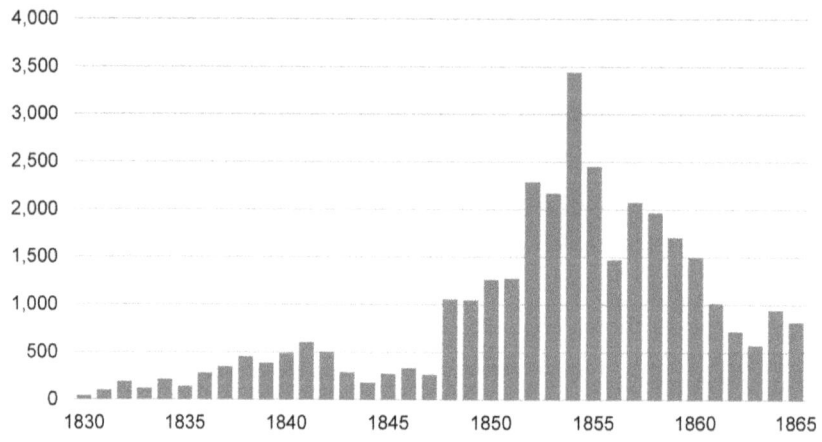

Source: *Statistical Abstract of the United States*

In 1852, the cotton crop would become even larger, reaching a new record (at 3.13 million bales) but resulting in much lower prices. Wheat prices eased. Business activity continued to rise throughout 1852, and gains were widespread among sectors. Prosperity characterized the year. Rail construction jumped to 2,288 miles, and activity so improved the demand for materials in the latter half of 1852, that prices for pig iron advanced rapidly. Security prices rose amid active speculation and railroad stocks reached another peak. A real estate boom was fostered by easy money. Also in 1852, Senator Franklin Pierce, a northern Democrat, was elected president.

Business activity continued expanding into 1853, and railroad construction added 2,172 miles. Foreign trade expanded. A record wheat crop resulted in low wheat prices, but the cotton crop (at 2.766 million bales) was good. Extensive speculation occurred, and there was a rise in commodity prices. A panic occurred in the United States after the outbreak of the Crimean War in late-1853. Credit restriction in London spread to America, where the poor wheat crop, along with an epidemic in the South delayed cotton exports, which intensified the situation. With security prices moving downward, unfavorable conditions were created for attracting new capital into business enterprises.

Prosperity reached new heights in early 1854, and money tightened, resulting in a panic in some cities and a decline in railroad stock prices. The tightening of the credit market gave warning of larger troubles ahead. The panic in London also ended a boom in railways and banks. Business activity slackened, but committed railroad projects fostered a 3,442-mile gain in rail construction. Orders fell off, and the iron industry, along with other industries, were soon depressed. Rail construction in the next year would fall nearly 30 percent and would fall even further in 1855. Unemployment appeared. With tight money, the downturn would give rise to stock market panics and many bank failures. The distress was especially severe in San Francisco. The year was marked by a small wheat crop and a lackluster cotton crop. The downturn was a short nine months (from March to December 1854) and resulted in a 13.2 percent downswing in business activity.

The 1850s would see an explosion in the number of state banks, from 913 in 1852 to 1,601 in 1861. This would lead to the expansion of the ratio of bank notes, relative to specie, as reserve. In other words, money inflation. That said, soundly operated banks existed in New England, New York, Ohio, Missouri, Louisiana, and South Carolina. Some 9,000 types of privately issued banknotes were in circulation throughout the nation. Transportation at the time, however, was limited and still local or regional. Most bank notes circulated close to the home of the issuing bank, so this note diversity did not have a great affect in any one locality.

Relations with Great Britain were tense, as American fishing interests were upset at the Royal Navy's increasing enforcement of Canadian territorial waters. This created some uncertainty but was soon resolved, and the Crimean War caused increased demand and supported prices for American products, thus offsetting pressures in the downswing. Shipping, for example, expanded on account of the Crimean War and also due to the trade with California. Also in 1854, Japan opened trade to the United States.

Cycle 14: Panic of 1857

Interest rates were declining, and bond and stock prices advanced. A business recovery got underway in 1855, and revival set in. Money eased but would tighten slightly late in the year. The Crimean War also led to increased demand and supported prices for American products, providing for recovery from the minor downturn of 1854. The recovery would last 30 months and result in a 19.5 percent expansion of real gross output. Cycle 14 was a major cycle.

In 1855, railroad securities reached a low but by year-end, recovered somewhat.

After years of expanding bank credit and speculation in the prior upturn, rail construction declined to 2,453 miles in 1855 and 1,471 miles in 1856. Leaders and investors in the industry were skittish, but railroad expansion would rebound, reaching 2,077 miles in 1857. The year was marked by excellent wheat, oats, corn, and cotton crops. Production of the latter improved from 2.708 million bales in 1854 to a new record of 3.221 million bales in 1855. Prices were actually good. The year was marked by war with Native Americans in the West.

Business further expanded in 1856 and was fairly widespread. Stocks of pig iron and other construction materials were exhausted, which provided a check on construction. Orders would begin to revive later in the year. Foreign trade recovered as well. An excellent wheat crop was harvested, but prices were weak. Cotton production fell to 2.874 million bales. Speculation in commodities was very active, and railroad stock bubble emerged. Excessive paper currency drained gold from the banks. By the summer of 1856, prosperity reached new highs. Money was easy until the fall and then tightened somewhat, resulting in a larger number of failures. In a prelude to the Civil War, a civil war erupted in Kansas over slavery. Former Secretary of State and Minister to the United Kingdom, James Buchanan, a Democrat, was elected as the 15th president of the United States

Figure 3.10
Cycle 14: Panic of 1857
Index of Real Gross Output where 2017 = 100

The years leading up to 1857 were a period of strong growth and prosperity, marred by minor intermittent turbulence. Speculation in land and railroads was supported by borrowed money and was highly leveraged. Railroad construction led this growth, as did immigration. Speculation, over-expansion, and imprudent bank credit were rife.

Led by speculation and gains in land prices and equities, prosperity would continue into early 1857, and although tariffs were reduced in March, this would soon give way to "dullness" and stagnation. A decline in the purchase of American agricultural products by Europe provided a check to foreign trade. The wheat and cotton crops were good, but prices were lower. Overall business activity would peak in June, and many industries began to decline, especially in the West. Security prices were fairly stable in the first half of the year, but signs of crisis were emerging. Prices of Western land and railroad stocks began to decline, which evolved into falling prices for stocks and other assets.

Interest rates rose, money tightened, and with many speculators highly leveraged, the inevitable crash occurred in August 1857, precipitated by the failure of Ohio Life Insurance and Trust. This failure led to panic and would burst a European speculative bubble in United States' railroads and cause a loss of confidence in American banks. A panic ensued, causing bank runs from Cincinnati to New York, and prices slumped on the New York Stock Exchange. Banks reduced lending, as reserves shrank. Interest rates rose, adding to the crisis, and specie payments were suspended by the Philadelphia and New York banks. At the height of the crisis, failures were so many that there was a general suspension of specie payment. Commercial failures were numerous, and the railroads were particularly affected. Several railroads went into receivership. The sinking of *SS Central America* contributed to the panic, as New York banks were awaiting a much-needed gold shipment. Stock and bond prices collapsed. By fall, commodity prices would decline, resulting in many failures.

Money became tight, and there were many bank failures. Every section of the nation was affected, the East as bad as the West. An exception, to a certain extent, was the Pacific states, where gold was used and was plentiful. President Buchanan urged state banks to follow federal guidelines to balance out banknotes and specie supply, specifically with the Independent Treasury, which provided federal funds to be placed in state banks. The crisis was short-lived but brought about a severe recession. Unemployment rose, and labor strikes broke out.

The crisis was not confined to the United States. Panic occurred in Germany, France, Great Britain, and elsewhere and has been called the world's first worldwide commercial crisis. In many ways, the Panic of 1857 can be said to reflect economic distress in Europe. There was a general exhaustion of credit everywhere. "Dullness" and low commodity prices continued throughout 1858. The downturn was severe, lasting for 18 months, and resulting in an 18.7 percent decline in business activity. Gorton (2012) suggests that the Panic of 1857 may have been the only panic during the Free Banking Period.

This is the earliest recession to which the NBER felt comfortable enough to assign specific months (rather than years) for the peak and trough. From now on, I use the NBER dates, even though peaks and troughs in real gross output may differ slightly from the NBER dates.

During the recession, over 5,000 businesses failed within the first year of the recession, and unemployment reached high levels and was accompanied by social unrest, especially in urban areas. The cotton crop would rise from 3.012 million bales in 1857 to 3.758 million in 1858, and other crops were good as well. By the end of the year, money began to ease, and conditions improved with a degree of stability regained. The downturn bottomed out in December 1858 after depressed security prices throughout much of the year. Some say that this recession was one of the main causes of the American Civil War. The year marked the completion of the Atlantic submarine cable.

Although the cable would fail within a month, it would eventually be the first step resulting in a "smaller" connected world.

The recession witnessed a religious revival known as the Businessmen's Revival of 1857-58 and was also known as the Revival/Awakening of 1857-1858. It cut across denominations. The most remarkable manifestations occurred in New York, but the revival also spread throughout the nation (Charleston, Cincinnati, Philadelphia, Pittsburgh, etc.) and in Canada and Great Britain.

Cycle 15: Prelude to Civil War and the Succession Recession of 1860-61

Eventually the downturn ended, and an economic revival emerged in 1859. Gradual improvement would give way to a rapid recovery and to prosperity.

Grain crops were good, and the cotton crop would rise to 4.508 million bales in 1859, a level that would not be reached again until 1875. Cotton prices were high. The wheat crop was good, although prices were low. Coal and pig iron production gained, and business in general was good. Shipping reached new records. Activity continued to advance. Commodity prices were steady, and foreign trade was active. Money was easy; however, railroad stock prices reached a low point. In October, a gold discovery in Colorado fostered excitement. The year also brought John Brown's raid on Harper's Ferry, a prelude to what was to come. The threat of war was a powerful force in shaping the course of business.

In 1859, Drake's Well was drilled by Edwin Drake along the banks of Oil Creek in Pennsylvania and was the first commercial oil well in the United States. Its success sparked the first oil boom and would usher in the Petroleum Age, first with kerosene lighting, and after 1900, with the automobile and gasoline. The latter would be synonymous with dynamic growth in the 20th century.

Prosperity continued into 1860 although the pace of advancement ebbed and would eventually decline. The election of 1860 was the most contested in history and resulted in the election of Illinois Congressman Abraham Lincoln, a Republican in the modern sense of the term and the anti-slavery party. The nation was torn apart by the slavery question, and the South threatened succession. The election fostered significant uncertainty, and there was a general fear that trade would collapse, and that the political and financial system was in danger. The succession movement paralyzed industry, and money tightened after having been easy early in the year. Bond prices had been advancing but by summer were declining, along with stock prices, as panic gripped equity markets. Real gross output peaked in October, ending a 22-month upswing that had seen a 28 percent rise in real gross output. Southern banks suspended specie payment in December. This was especially the case after South Carolina succeeded, as confusion ensued. Conditions in the North were bad, but they were worse in the South. A financial panic emerged in the summer, but a major panic was narrowly averted in 1860 by the first use of clearing house certificates between banks. Uncertainty spread, as leaders in government chose sides, leaving the Treasury, War, and other departments in poor condition. The Treasury was nearly empty.

With the bombardment of Fort Sumter in 1861, the Civil War began, and business became paralyzed. A panic arose. Business came to a standstill, stock prices collapsed, money was scarce, and distrust prevailed. Rail construction fell from 1,966 miles in 1858 to 1,707 miles in 1859, 1,500 miles in 1860, and then to 720 miles in 1861. Money conditions were marked by high rates, which dropped in the second half of the year. Prices on the stock market were low throughout the year. In March, the Morrill Tariff Act was passed, which levied higher duties and aided Northern manufacturing.

The recession was felt severely in the West, as many banks had investments in Southern securities. The South repudiated its obligations to the North, and banks in Illinois, Wisconsin, and elsewhere failed. The recession, however, was mild, lasting only eight months. Real gross output declined 14.2 percent, and with rising production for the war effort, the recession ended. Geographically, the recession was limited in scope. The great demands of the war, and the general employment associated with that demand prevented a deeper downturn.

In the North, the business of industrial firms that manufactured goods for Southern consumption were completely disrupted, as were trading concerns. Commercial failures rose. Slackened activity, unemployment, failures, and uncertainty soon gave way to rapid revival by the fall. Money eased, but the stock market remained depressed. Foreign trade was reduced. Banks quietly suspended specie payment at the end of the year. The outbreak of the Civil War threw commerce completely out of long-standing channels, resulting in changes in business methods and financing. To pay for the war, the issuance of paper money, which soon depreciated in value, made the payment of debt easier and tended to prevent bankruptcies and failures. The income tax was established. In addition, a higher tariff was enacted amid difficulties with Great Britain.

In the South, there was a different story. There was a gradual slackening of trade activity, which soon came to a halt by year-end, due to blockade of Southern ports. Cotton and other commodity prices rose amid market imbalances. The cotton crop reached 4.49 million bales, and grain and sugar crops were good as well. The Confederation was formed among the seceding states, and a constitution adopted. A tariff system was adopted as well, but trade was restricted. In an amazing and self-defeating policy move, the Confederacy embargoed its cotton crop in 1861. The move backfired, upsetting trading partners and investors, and would lead to the diversification of cotton supply to other countries such as Egypt and India. Money was tight, and paper money expanded. Many banks suspended specie payment, and gold went to a premium.

CHAPTER 4

Civil War to World War II

"The reasonable man adapts himself to the world:
the unreasonable one persists in trying to adapt the world to himself.
Therefore, all progress depends upon the unreasonable man."

—*George Bernard Shaw*

Introduction

The start of this long eight-decade period was marked by the Civil War, the conclusion of which would bring forth vast changes in commerce, industry, trade, and finance. The population would increase from 31 million in 1860 to 76 million in 1900, a period of large immigration that lasted until World War I. By 1915, the population reached 100 million. Immigration was characterized by inflows from southern, central, and eastern Europe. By 1945, it would approach 140 million.

The second half of the 19th century and the opening decades of the 20th century witnessed striking change. The further diffusion of the steam engine and its application to transportation and to industry, as well as industrial chemistry and the development of electric power, proved to be crucial factors in the rising importance of industry. This period also saw the rise of national brands. In the three decades between the end of the Civil War and end of the Spanish-American War, America would become a great industrial power, having overtaken Great Britain in the 1880s as the world's leading producer of manufactured goods. American economic growth astonished the world, and by 1914, the American economy was more than twice the size of its nearest rival.

Under a classic gold standard, prices did fall in times of peace and even during prosperity. Indeed, a flowering of technological innovation spread during the last quarter of the 19th century. It was an age of entrepreneurs (I.e., unreasonable men), marked by new products (and industries), improving productivity, and falling prices. The second phase of the Industrial Revolution brought social upheaval, along with the more pronounced financial panics and business cycles. This period witnessed large immigration and the rise of an urban society.

Vast new farmlands were opened in the United States under the Homestead Act of 1862, and agriculture's productivity rose dramatically with the proliferation of mechanical sowers, reapers, threshers, and other technologies, as well as the application of chemical fertilizers. Agricultural production soared. Migration to frontier areas ensued and fostered railroad construction, the latter often in anticipation of the former. In addition to rail, this period would be marked by the rise of the oil and steel industries, and later on, electricity, chemicals, and many other industries. Indeed, the second half of the 19th century would be one of continual scientific and technological progress.

Beyond business cycles, this was an important period for the United States. The 1860s witnessed a devastating civil war, and the 1910s and the 1940s witnessed devastating world wars. In some ways, the Civil War completed the American Revolution. The ideals boldly proclaimed in the Declaration of Independence that "all men are created equal" were now being somewhat realized. The reality was that at the end of Reconstruction, the United States was still, in fact, an "unfinished nation," and that it would be the Civil Rights era and its accomplishments that would complete the revolution.

Figure 4.1
New Railroad Construction in the United States
(Annual Mileage Increase)

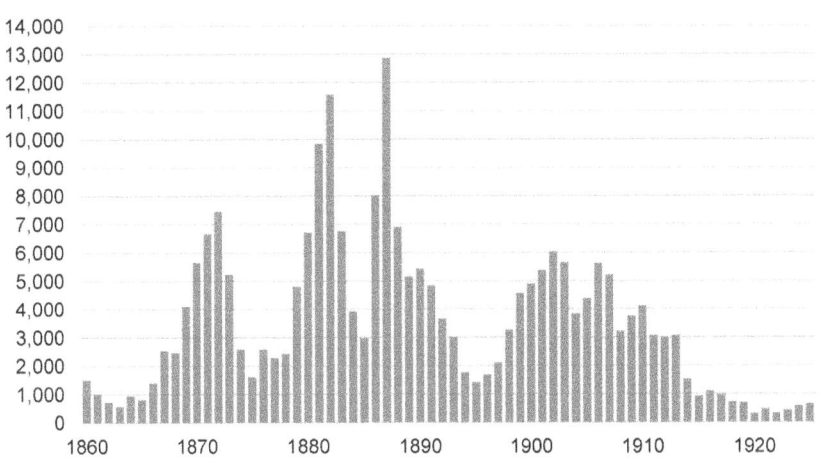

Source: Statistical Abstract of the United States

Through the 1920s, there was phenomenal growth in the ability to produce large volumes of output, as well as generate new forms of inexpensive goods and services. This was a dynamic period of wealth creation that was unprecedented in width and depth.

Financial crises and panics remained an important part of many of the downturns during this period. The annals of American commerce and industry (and the data on real gross output) from the Civil War to World War II include eight major downswings, which developed in the following years, namely 1873, 1882, 1893, 1907,

1913, 1920, 1929, and 1937. The elapsed time between the major downswings averaged nine years. Minor downswings occurred in 1865, 1869, 1887, 1890, 1895, 1899, 1902, 1910,1918, 1923, and 1926.

Figure 4.2

Real Gross Output of the United States: 1860-1945
Index of Real Gross Output where 2017 = 100

The history of American banking to this point was strewn with panics, bank runs, and failures due to real estate lending. In 1863, the National Currency Act, which allowed the creation of national banks, set out a plan for establishing a national currency backed by government securities held by other banks, and gave the federal government the ability to sell war bonds and securities. National banks were chartered by the federal government and were subject to stricter regulation and higher capital requirements. Subsequent amendments strengthened the Act, which established a uniform currency and a new national banking system that would provide a regulatory and monetary framework that would last until 1913. During this period, panics often occurred at or near business cycle peaks.

Cycle 16: Civil War Prosperity and the Primary Post-War Depression

The Civil War brought about recovery from the Succession Recession of 1860-61 as slackened activity and 'dullness' gave way to improvement in the second half of 1861. The great demands of the war effort led to a long 46-month expansion of the economy starting in June 1861. It was not a popular war, but business activity would expand 22.6 percent to the next peak in April 1865, which coincided with the end of major hostilities.

In 1862, there was marked and improving business activity in war industries, accompanied by rising commodity prices in both the North and South. While rail construction fell from 1,016 miles in 1861 to 729 miles in 1862, pig iron production expanded, as did bank clearings. Foreign trade in the North was restricted, but it came to a halt in the South, as a naval blockade took hold. In the North, wheat and corn crops were fair, but oat crops were poor. In the South, crops were poor (cotton production fell from 4.491 million bales in 1861 to 1.597 million bales in 1862), with a shift from cotton to cereal crops. In Richmond, bread riots emerged by summer.

Finance differed between the North and the South. The North had a more advanced economy, a large middle class, and an established banking system. War finance led to a large issuance of government securities. Although some greenbacks (Demand Notes) were first issued in 1861, 1862 marked the introduction of United States Notes (printed in green on the back, hence the name) that were widely issued by the U.S. Treasury during the remainder of the Civil War. These notes were legal tender by law, but were not backed by gold or silver, only the credibility of the U.S. government. Tariffs and excise taxes were raised to help finance the war effort. A stamp tax on legal documents was imposed, and the nation experimented with an income tax.

During the Civil War, the national debt would expand from $60 million to $2.7 billion. The North was able to raise two-thirds of its revenues by borrowing. Only one-eighth of the needed revenues were raised by printing money. The effects on financial markets were softened by the wealth of the North, which had more manufacturing capacity, rail mileage, and other measures of economic progress. In 1862, the stock market revived with rapid improvement of stock and bond prices.

The South was largely agrarian and had a less developed banking system. It was limited in its ability to finance a war. It could only acquire about one-third of its revenues through borrowing. One-half was raised by printing money, and inflation was terrible, with prices rising eight-fold during the first two years of the war. In the South, money was tight, and currency issued expanded rapidly. The economy was imploding, and a collapse of government bonds occurred in the summer of 1862. Inflation would spin out of control during the duration of the war.

In terms of the war, the South adopted compulsory military service. Confederate victories predominated in 1862, although the North did capture New Orleans.

Business activity in the North was widespread and improving, while that in the South was more constrained. Accompanied by speculation, commodity prices were more active in the North, less so in the South. Stock prices improved early in the year, and gold markets were very active. Money was plentiful but tightened, resulting in a slump in bond prices. The National Bank Act was passed early in the year and established a system of national banks, the United States National Banking System, which encouraged development of a national currency backed by bank holdings of U.S. Treasury securities. The Office of the Comptroller of the Currency was established as part of the U.S. Department of the Treasury, as was a system of nationally chartered banks. A uniform U.S. banking policy was supported. Only 66 state banks joined, so the Banking

Act of 1864 was passed to strengthen the system. More would join in subsequent years. Each national bank was required to purchase U.S. government bonds equal to one-third (later one-fourth) of their capital. State chartered banks increased in number in the next several decades, as checking became popular.

In the South, banking was limited. Money remained tight, and there was a rapid rise in the premium for gold. As a result of the war, development of banking in the South would remain constrained for decades.

Rail construction would fall further to 574 miles in 1863. Pig iron production continued to advance. Cotton production would fall further to 449,000 bales in 1863 but was offset by large corn and wheat crops in the South. In the North, wheat and oats crops were fair, while corn was poor, resulting in high prices. The Emancipation Proclamation was issued in 1863. The North adopted conscription, but draft riots plagued New York in the summer. The tide of war turned, with victories at Gettysburg and Vicksburg. In the South, transportation was severely restricted.

The war dragged on, but the tide turned in favor of the North, where improving industrial and other business activity in 1864 was accompanied by a remarkable rise in commodity prices and further decline in the value of the greenback. Inflation was rampant. The value of greenbacks varied according to the process of the war. At one point, greenbacks traded at 35 cents to the gold dollar. By war's end, greenbacks traded at about 80 cents to the gold dollar.

Money tightened. and early in 1864 a panic struck stock and other financial markets. Trade in gold was prohibited but soon repealed. Pig iron production reached 1.014 million tons, up from 654,000 at the start of the war. Rail construction improved to 947 miles. In the South, business was depressed with wide fluctuations in commodity prices, soft at first, and then advancing to record highs. Money was tight and currency in circulation greatly reduced.

In the North, wheat and oat crops were fair, but the corn crop was good, with high prices fostering prosperity for farmers. In the South, the wheat and corn crops were good, but currency debasement made farmers reluctant to sell. The South was impoverished. Living standard fell. By 1864, cotton production had fallen to 299,000 bales, off 93 percent from 1861. The year saw continued Northern victories, including General Sherman's march to the sea. President Lincoln was re-elected.

By early 1865, it was apparent that a victory by the North was inevitable. Industry and trade boomed and expanded rapidly early in the year, and commodity prices peaked. Still, there was a heritage of war. Speculation was active, wages and interest rates were high, the currency was inconvertible, and there was a premium for gold. Foreign trade revived. The wheat crop was weak, but corn and oats were excellent. Rail construction eased to 819 miles, and pig iron production fell back. In the North, money tightened severely, and with high taxes, stock and bond prices declined. Conditions were unstable. In the South, the currency collapsed in March, as did government finance, and as a result, economic chaos was the order of the day. Cotton production actually improved to 2.094 million bales but was accompanied by low prices.

In April, General Lee surrendered, and President Lincoln was assassinated. Vice President Andrew Johnson became president. There was a panic in financial markets. The blockade of the South was raised in June, and the war formally (and attendant bloodshed and carnage) ended. A feeling of security emerged, but the South continued in a depressed state. At the conclusion of the Civil War, the U.S. economy began to deflate. War production turned down. Real gross output peaked in April 1865 and began to decline. This was a typical post-war recession. The post-war downturn was long, some 32 months, with a 15.1 percent decline in real gross output. The recession bottomed out in December 1867.

The Civil War left many problems, not only social, but also economic. Most notable was the tremendous increase in the national debt and the monetary system of the country that was on a fiat, paper basis. The banking system of the South had suffered and with little hard cash, would lead to the sharecropping system, perpetuating slavery to a degree. The country entered a lengthy period of general deflation that would last until the mid-1890s.

The woolen goods industry was the first to feel the recession. The downturn was mild at first and continued into early-1866, but it would briefly rebound. Foreign trade improved. Domestically, a partial recovery in the South occurred. Rail construction rose to 1,404 miles and would rise to 2,541 in 1867. Manufacturing revived as well, but commercial trade was generally dull. Pig iron production rebounded to 1.2 million tons and 1.3 million tons in 1867.

Bank clearings improved slightly. Money markets were somewhat easier, but stock and bond prices remained low in 1866. Interest rates declined during much of the year, and commodity prices were generally soft. The May 1866 Overend-Gurney panic in Great Britain had a modest effect on business in the United States. Cotton production was 2.097 million bales, about the same as the year before. The wheat crop was poor (and accompanied by high prices), but corn and oats were good.

By 1867, another leg of the downturn was apparent, with dismal industrial and trade activity. Prices generally declined, and unemployment rose. Wheat, corn, and oat crops were good, as was cotton. Wheat prices reached new highs and then slumped. By summer, tight money eased, and a revival of stock prices (and prices in general for that matter) would set the stage for the end of the downturn, which occurred late in the year. The year featured the purchase of Alaska from Russia, which improved confidence.

Overseas, the 1860s and 1870s were a period in Europe of nation building, some of which was violent, much like our Civil War. The period saw the emergence of modern nation states such as Germany and Italy. This period also marked rapid industrialization in Europe.

Cycle 17: Recovery and Secondary Post-War Depression

With the easing of money, the difficulties of the post-war recession would give way to expanding business activity in December 1867. Money had eased in the summer, and there were good crops as well. This upswing would be short, only 18 months. Real gross output would rise 19 percent by June 1869. It was a period marked by rapid expansion of industry and new railroad construction.

By early-1868, business activity improved and was accompanied by steady commodity prices. This was a year of expansion. There were record corn and wheat crops, the latter characterized with low prices. Foreign trade eased, as did rail construction, but pig iron production continued to advance. Money tightened slightly, and the gold premium advanced into the summer and then declined. Stock speculation was very active due to the contest between Daniel Drew and Cornelius Vanderbilt over control of the Erie Railway, and stock and bond prices rose during the year. The year was marked by the ratification of the Fourteenth Amendment to the Constitution (also referred to as the Reconstruction Amendment) and the election of General Ulysses S. Grant, a Republican, as president.

Prosperity continued into 1869. Wheat, cotton, and oat crops were good, and cotton prices were high. The corn crop was poor. Foreign trade expanded. Pig iron production increased during the year (to 1.7 million tons), and rail construction nearly doubled to 4,103 miles. Most notable during the year was the completion of the trans-continental railroad in May. The year would mark the beginning of a lengthy period of railroad building, much of which opened the interior of the nation and would later foster a farmers' movement. Business activity continued to expand in the first half of the year, despite moderated profits. Bank clearings expanded. Bond prices trended lower. June marked the business cycle peak and also the peak of railroad stock prices. Money tightened, and the gold price rose in wake of the Black Friday panic in September. The latter was caused by railroad speculators Jay Gould and Jim Fisk. The collapse of the U.S. gold market pushed President Ulysses Grant to sell $4 million in Federal gold, which fostered a decline in the gold premium.

Fundamental conditions grew more unsatisfactory. Bankers disposed of securities, and merchants reduced their merchandise. Like the upswing, the downswing would also be short, only 18 months, with real gross output contracting only 9 percent and ending in December 1870, according to the NBER.

Pig iron production eased, and business activity declined through much of 1870, but increased foreign trade helped. A policy response to the recession was to lower tariffs. As unemployment rose, there were extensive strikes in 1870. The downturn was unusual, as it came amid a period when railroad investment was accelerating. Bank and other failures increased, and commodity prices declined. Money eased, as did the gold premium. The stock market languished, but bond prices soon began to slowly rise. The wheat crop was poor, but corn was strong, and cotton production (at 4.352 million bales) approached pre-war levels.

Cycle 18: Panic of 1873 and the Long Depression

Cycle 18 is one of the longest and most important cycles, as it includes the long and severe depression of the 1870s. With gains in railroad construction, tariff reduction, and money easing, the cycle began with recovery emerging in late-1870 and would firm in 1871. Interest rates had already turned downward, and bond prices began turning. Pig iron production improved, as did rail construction. The recovery and expansion of activity would last 34 months, rising over 31 percent to peak in October 1873. It would be accompanied by rising prosperity. This was a major cycle.

The period after the Civil War marked a wave of railroad construction, the most notable of which was the transcontinental railroad of Central Pacific and the Union Pacific, which joined at Promontory Summit in Utah in May 1869. Along with the opening of the Suez Canal in 1869, this would have an immediate and dramatic effect on world trade, as it allowed the world to be circled in record time. In 1865, 819 miles of track were constructed, and 7,439 miles were constructed in 1872, a new high. The increase in railroad construction brought a corresponding gain in pig iron production and industry in general. Pig iron shipments, for example, would triple from 832,000 tons in 1865 to 2.549 million tons in 1872. Gains were led by the perfection of methods of making Bessemer and open-hearth steel. The expansion of railroad construction progressed, resulting in a climax in 1872-73. Building construction rose as well. Construction (and associated industrial production) may have been overstimulated in viewpoint of actual requirements and financial capacity of the nation. Bank clearings improved.

Figure 4.3
Cycle 18: Panic of 1873 and the Long Depression
Index of Real Gross Output where 2017 = 100

As a new tariff became effective, foreign trade rose solidly. Money was easy during 1871, and railroad stock prices and bond prices gained. The Chicago fire occurred in October 1871, however, and fostered a financial panic in New York, Philadelphia, and Boston. Losses fell principally on insurance companies, as well as on manufacturers and wholesalers in other cities who had dealings in Chicago.

Prosperity continued into 1872, with widespread activity gains among industries and sectors. Events in 1872 included, after 10 years, the abolishing of the income tax in favor of higher excise taxes, as well as a lowering of tariffs to rejuvenate commerce. Money was not easy, and wages were high. There was a general strike in New York and a major fire in Boston. Both disturbed confidence, and the latter led to a panic. A revision of the tariff and the presidential election fostered uncertainty, but noteworthy was the reelection of President Grant.

Speculation increased and was accompanied by lax business and lending practices. It would prove to be the cause of the downturn. Borrowers went heavily into debt (at high interest rates) to foster new industrial ventures and to extend the railroads into frontier areas in anticipation of migration into those areas, the result of the Homestead Act. Railroad construction went well beyond reason and was overdone.

This was a period of extraordinary and universal inflation of prices and credit. With easy money, the value of the currency fluctuated and eroded. There was also an over-extension of credit by banks, resulting in an over-expansion of many business lines, especially construction of railroads.

Investment in railroads was financed largely from Europe, including Germany and Central Europe. This coincided with an investment boom in the latter countries. Fueled by the Franco-Prussian War of 1870, inflation and financial speculation would mark the last days of the boom. Railroad construction, however, would slacken at year-end 1872. By early 1873, business optimism began to wane, and in April, the Vienna stock market showed signs of panic amid weak business conditions. European investors sought to liquidate their positions in American equities. As a result, the international financial crisis emerging in Europe spread to the United States in September.

In the United States, many large New York banks, caught up in the boom period, made long-term loans to the railroads. Prosperity continued further as business activity continued to expand into 1873, but this would not last. With liquidation from Europe, U.S. money markets tightened in late 1872 and continued into 1873. Stock and bond prices, along with security listings, all turned downward.

A few small bank failures occurred, but it was the notable failure of Jay Cooke and Company in September 1873 that fostered a panic. The bank folded due to overextending itself in the construction of the Northern Pacific Railway. The railroad industry's misfortune and collapse were central in generating this depression. The collapse of the railroad boom led to widespread default on loans by late-1873. Railroads simply could not service their debt.

Unsound banking practices encroached on a situation that would be vulnerable to a downturn of railroad and building construction. Money tightened, land speculation collapsed, and bank runs caused the closing of many banks. Banks suspended specie payments, security prices collapsed, and the New York Stock Exchange closed for 10 days. The bringing to light of various financial scandals turned business confidence for the worse. Rail miles constructed fell, although pig iron production increased slightly during the year.

The Panic of 1873 burst the post-Civil War speculative bubble, and as a financial crisis, triggered an economic depression in Europe and North America. The reversal of investor optimism was global, as was the crisis, although London was largely spared by the crisis. English investors, however, did suffer a strain from the American crisis.

The Coinage Act of 1873 also contributed to the American downturn by immediately depressing the price of silver, which hurt mining interests. The financial dislocations in the United States were muted by actions of the New York Clearinghouse Association. With the Panic of 1873, the downturn started in October 1873 and would last 65 months (until March 1879), hence its name as the Long Depression. Business conditions weakened. The Long Depression was a worldwide price phenomena and economic recession, beginning in 1873 and running through 1879. Real gross output during this period would fall 22 percent.

Figure 4.4
Pig Iron Production in the United States
(Millions of Tons)

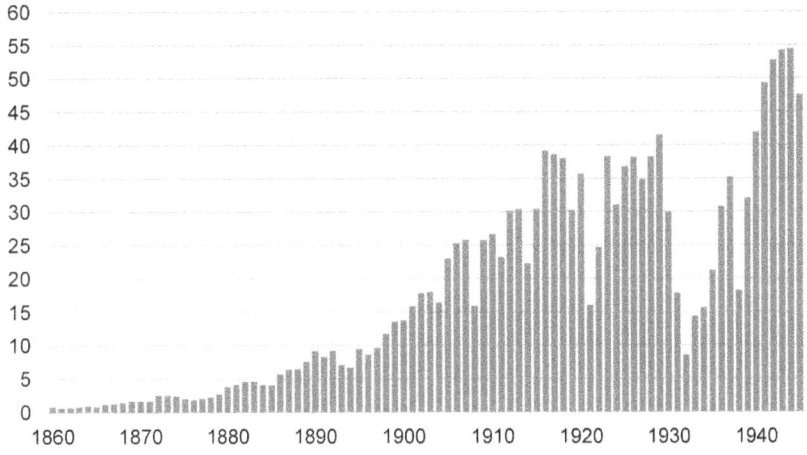

Source: American Iron and Steel Institute

Industry was affected, as new railroad construction collapsed to 2,117 miles in 1874 and 1,606 miles in 1875. This led to a severe decline in production at iron foundries and mills, as well as other supplier industries. Pig iron shipments would fall to 1.869 million tons in 1876, and only slowly recover. Prices of a variety of iron and steel products collapsed and would remain low for years. Railroad construction would remain depressed until 1878. Pessimism prevailed and failures mounted. The Erie Railroad and others would go into receivership, and freight wars among competing railroads would emerge during this downturn. Industries supplying this sector declined as well.

Stagnation in industry and trade became the rule. Business was depressed for six years, one of the darkest periods in U.S. business cycle history. This is the longest period of economic contraction recognized by the NBER, and some economists view the Long Depression as the entire period from 1873 to 1896. Inactivity in industry and trade was prolonged and would be marked by failures and bankruptcies among banks and businesses. Over-capacity in many lines of business was a result of this worldwide depression. This downswing was experienced in all major industrial nations and was largely industrial in character.

In 1876, liquidation was very thorough. Bank clearings fell, as did pig iron production and most other measures of activity. Social strife emerged, and 1876 featured a tightly contested election that extended into March 1877, fostering uncertainty. In the end, Rutherford B. Hayes was elected president over Samuel Tilden after a deadlock and the Compromise of 1877. The frauds that characterized both parties were so large that to this date, it is uncertain whether Tilden or Hayes was actually elected president.

Rising unemployment, deflation, and wage cuts of the era led to labor turmoil, such as the Great Railroad Strike of 1877 and the "Molly Maguires" in the anthracite coal district. Railroad strikes necessitated military force. Agricultural activity generally expanded during the depression, but with low prices. The decline in crop prices led to bankruptcy and to the Granger movement in challenging the railroads. Many states would assume regulation of the railroads. It also led to silver agitation (or "easy money") in Congress and eventually the Silver Purchase Act of 1878 (aka the Bland-Allison Act) was passed. This act required the Treasury to buy a set amount of silver every year at a ratio of 16-to-one with gold. This marked the first success for the free silver forces, but it was only a partial victory. Agitation for free coinage of silver would continue for another 25 years.

Signs of improvement in some areas began to emerge in 1877 and 1878. Rail construction increased, as did pig iron production. Strikes were still common, and failures remained high. The stock market was still unsteady and inactive. Bank clearings, however, began improving.

By 1879, conditions were emerging for recovery. On January 1st, the United States returned to the gold standard with the Specie Payment Resumption Act, which had passed the year before. Some economists attribute this to the end of the Long Depression. The gold standard was popular with bankers, industry, and savers but was unpopular with farmers and debtors.

Activity in the first half of 1878 had stabilized for some sectors and would give way to improvement in trade and overall revival along business lines in 1879. Railroads were reorganized on a sounder footing, and renewed construction would lead to an upswing. Money was easy, and agriculture was aided by large crops and high prices. After five-and-one-half years of depression, prosperity returned. Aided by crop pressures in Europe, commodity, and other prices advanced, as did stock prices. These European crop failures occurred during a favorable season for American farmers, which facilitated exports to high levels and to high prices. The renewed prosperity among farmers aided the grain-carrying railroads and increased the demand for all types of commodities.

The Long Depression also introduced a period of deflationary pressures that lasted until 1893. Some of this was caused by stagnation of real activity but also because of productivity-enhancing technological innovation.

Some manufacturing industries did not contract during the downswing, and some even expanded modestly. Out of the Long Depression, new industries would emerge. Although steel production had increased 16-fold from 1865 to 1872, it would continue to expand, as diffusion of the Bessemer process increased as new applications emerged, and steel would be an industry propelling economic growth for decades. The period also witnessed the introduction of chemistry to a variety of applications in industry.

Cycle 19: Gold Resumption Prosperity and the Crisis/Depression of 1884

At the end of 1878, it was apparent that the Long Depression was slowly disappearing, and general revival was on the horizon. The federal government assured convertibility of its paper money at par and re-established a gold standard. With the return to the gold standard, the recovery fully emerged in 1879. The recovery and expansion of activity would last 36 months, rising nearly 32 percent to peak in March 1882. It would be accompanied by rising prosperity. Cycle 19 was another major cycle.

There was a rapid expansion of industry and trade, construction, and speculation. It was also a good year for agriculture. Still a leading industry, railroad building revived, increasing to 4,809 miles in 1879, to 6,711 miles in 1880, to 9,841 miles in 1881, and to 11,569 miles in 1882. It led to rapid expansion of supplier industries. Iron and steel benefited. Pig iron production advanced from 2.30 million tons in 1878 to 4.62 million tons in 1882. There was enormous output of manufactured goods, and mills were soon in full operation. Mining expanded as well. There was greater activity in foreign trade and in building construction. Prosperity quickly diffused throughout the economy. Confidence was high, consolidations were in progress, and new industries were started.

The upswing featured increasing issues of new securities, advances in bond prices, along with equity prices; however, there were intermittent reversals. Speculation increased. Prices for steel and many commodities also rose. Money was in demand, and rates began to gradually increase.

In 1880, Senator James A. Garfield, a Republican, was elected president. He was assassinated in July 1881 and succeeded by Chester Allen Arthur. Optimism began to wane later in 1881, and the pace of expansion slowed. A rate war broke out among railroads and was settled in early-1882. Fundamental conditions began to decline and would soon become unsatisfactory.

Activity continued into 1882, but the pace eased further, as railroad construction reached its peak. The transition between prosperity and depression was said to be slow. Profits declined, as did security issues. Export demand fell off. Money tightened, and a steadily increasing depression in industry and trade ensued. Coal was emerging as a major fuel for heating, largely supplanting wood, and it was also fueling a revolution in industry. Production exceeded 100 million tons for the first time in 1882 and would continue a long ascent (interrupted by hiccups here and there) until the 1920s.

Railroad construction declined to 6,745 miles in 1883 and 3,923 in 1884. Production was curtailed in many industries and grew worse in 1883, a year of declining business volumes. Particularly, iron, steel, and mining were affected. For example, raw steel production fell from 1.95 million tons in 1882 to 1.74 million tons in 1884. Steel prices declined sharply and would remain low for years. Postal receipts declined. Wages and commodity prices fell, and unemployment increased, as stagnation in industry and trade would last until early 1885. Excess inventories put pressure on prices. In this cycle, railroad construction would bottom out at 2,975 miles in 1885. Agriculture featured low prices with mixed crops. There were many failures during this downturn, and banks were reluctant to make new loans. The downturn started in March 1882 and would last 38 months, reaching a trough in May 1885. Real gross output during this period would fall 21 percent. Business activity and prices would both decline, and uncertainty increased.

In the last phase of the depression in 1884, money tightened further, and there were many notable failures of railroads and other companies. This led to panic, with subsequent bank and broker failures. A bank panic emerged in New York, when the brokerage firm of Grant and Ward failed, as did Marine National Bank. Other prominent failures occurred. The panic did not last long but has been referred to as the Crisis of 1884. A fear emerged that the United States Treasury would resort to payment in silver. Confidence was shaken, and failures spread to other states. Bond and stock prices declined, as did crop prices. Depressed prices pushed the New York Clearing House to extend credit to failing banks, averting even more financial loss. There was a coal strike in the fall, and with growing pessimism (melancholy was a word used to describe sentiments), Grover Cleveland, governor of New York and a Democrat, was elected president.

Figure 4.5

Cycle 19: Gold Resumption and the Crisis/Depression of 1884
Index of Real Gross Output where 2017 = 100

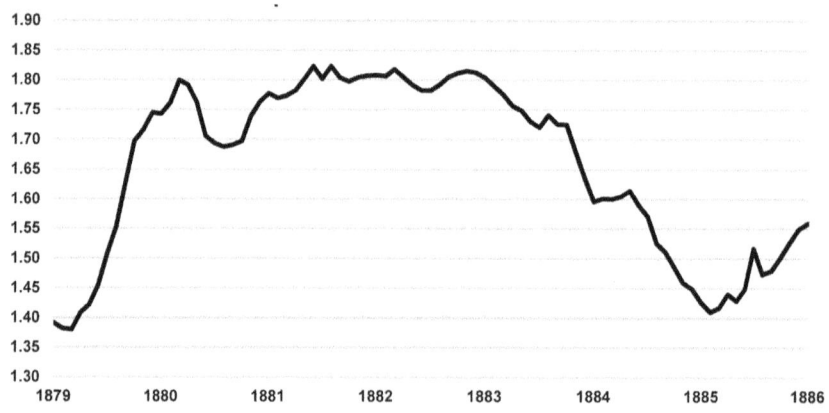

The depression was felt in other nations, although the timing in Great Britain was later. Among the five major economies, the depression was more industrial in character. This was compounded by rumors of war in Europe. The depression in some of these nations lagged until 1886 and 1887.

New rail construction in 1885 declined further. Overall business inventories had become very depleted, and with economic 'dullness' in the early months of 1885, a general business recovery emerged in May 1885. Cleveland's term was thus marked, nearly from the beginning, by improvement, especially in the iron and steel industries. Steel was a new material and gained during the year. As prospects for business improved, so did the prospects for railroad investment, and construction would rebound. Money rates had dropped, and there was considerable issue of new stocks and bonds.

Cycle 19 witnessed a big increase in immigration, a wave that would last until World War I. This wave of immigration would be marked by increasing urbanization.

Cycle 20: Recovery and Railroad Prosperity I

After an extensive period of price deflation, Cycle 20 started shortly after the start of the Cleveland Administration in May 1885. The recovery was slow at first, but with good prospects and expanded investment in railroads and building construction, the recovery gathered steam. It was marked by improvement in manufacturing, especially in iron and steel. Steel prices began their upward movement that would last until early-1887. Railroad construction rebounded, from 2,975 miles in 1885 to 8,018 miles in 1886. It lifted the rest of the economy as well. Steel production jumped from 1.92 million tons to 2.87 million tons and would improve even further in 1887. Money was easy, bond prices moved higher, and the stock market revived. Silver agitation emerged again.

The upswing gathered strength with the revival of railroad construction, iron and steel, other industries, and mining, as well as improvement in foreign trade. Agriculture prices and crops were mixed, and the sector improved. Banks expanded loans and investment. The year 1886 was marked by a peak in bond prices but also by labor troubles, a major railroad strike, and the Haymarket massacre in Chicago.

Railroad building and business activity revived, with 1887 as the record — 12,876 miles — in the history of the nation for number of miles of new track constructed. By the peak of the cycle, there was widespread activity with higher prices, speculation, and a boom in Western real estate. Production in nearly all sectors of the economy improved. Pig iron production reached 6.42 million tons and steel 3.73 million tons in 1887. The volume of foreign trade also increased. The upswing of the cycle, however, was of short duration, lasting only 22 months, with a 46.6 percent gain in real gross output. Investment opportunities in rail became exhausted. Federal government debt reduction resulted in a contraction of national bank notes. Money tightened, and stock prices peaked early in 1887, as did bond prices and security listings. Business activity peaked in March, and a 13-month downturn emerged, one in which real gross output would fall 20.5 percent.

With easier money, stock prices reached bottom and improved, and a trough was reached in April 1888. It was a mild recession. Investments in railroads and buildings weakened during this period, the former more so than the latter. Rail construction fell by half, from 12,876 miles in 1887 to 6,900 in 1888. In 1889, it would fall further. Although textiles remained prosperous, the iron and steel industry was depressed. Mines and factories were idled. An unfavorable balance of trade emerged. There was a decline in overall production and generally declining prices. Business failures increased. With the downswing in business activity, labor strikes were more limited, and reorganizations in railroads were completed. The depression affected voter sentiments, and Senator Benjamin Harrison, a Republican and grandson of President William Henry Harrison, was elected to the presidency in 1888, defeating the Democratic incumbent, Grover Cleveland.

The Interstate Commerce Act of 1887 was passed to regulate monopolistic practices of the railroad industry. The Act was the first of many Progressive policy initiatives and required that railroad rates be "reasonable and just," but did not empower the government to fix specific rates. The Act established the Interstate Commerce Commission (ICC) and was the first major step towards regulation of economic exchange.

Cycle 20 witnessed the emergence of trusts in a variety of industries. This was a new form of corporate organization that owned the assets of multiple firms in the same line of business. Larger and larger companies were forming, and the trend would gather strength in the 1890s.

A month prior to the trough, the Great Blizzard of 1888 paralyzed the East Coast from the Mid-Atlantic to Maine. Railroads were shut down, and people were confined to their homes for up to a week in some areas. Telegraph lines were disabled, and the storm was a disaster for cities like New York and Philadelphia. The New York Stock Exchange was closed for two days. Nearly 500 people died from hypothermia and other causes fostered by the March storm, one of the most severe blizzards in American history. This storm likely delayed the upswing.

Cycle 21: Railroad Prosperity II and the Panic of 1890

As with the prior administration, a recovery (and prosperity) emerged near the start of the Harrison Administration, with the trough in the cycle pegged to April 1888 by the NBER. Business activity made tremendous gains. Improvements in railroad construction led to supply constraints in iron and steel, especially in steel rails. Rail construction advanced from 5,162 miles in 1889 to 5,427 miles in 1890. This aided iron and steel and coal mining. Building construction revived as well, and good crops came at a time when crops overseas were poor. Foreign trade improved, as did shipping. Prosperity spread to mining and other industries.

The advent of trust and investment companies facilitated the promotion, underwriting, and speculation of companies, especially mining companies in North America and South America. Speculative investments were made in Argentina, where a land "boom" mania emerged, along with that for infrastructure improvements.

The upswing in Cycle 21 witnessed the advent of electric street railways, strong growth of the steel industry, and advanced communications (telegraph, telephone, etc.). Advancements in kerosene lighting favored the oil market but would find competition from electrical lighting. Many new enterprises were started. The year marked an expansion in equity markets. The upswing would last 27 months and would be accompanied by a 39.8 percent gain in real gross output. This cycle marked the beginning of the world's first period of globalization, which would end in 1914.

Employment and wages gained, as activity in agriculture, mining, manufacturing, and trade all rose. Steel production rose from 3.24 million tons in 1888 to 4.78 million tons in 1890. As a new material of choice in construction and manufacturing, the steel industry would experience strong growth during the next several decades. American oil production exceeded 100,000 barrels per day for the first time in 1890. Optimism emerged. Real estate speculation was active, particularly in the West, which made money more stringent in the East. Money gradually tightened, and financial strain emerged, the result of overseas events. In addition, 1889-1890 saw a nationwide influenza pandemic. This affected output.

The Panic of 1890 started in Great Britain (also known as the Baring Crisis) and spread to the United States, causing a short panic in New York. It was precipitated in London, as Barings Bank was on the edge of bankruptcy due to risky Argentine investments. Its near collapse and troubles caused financial distrust and tight money.

Important London banks combined to guarantee creditors of the firm against loss. This caused London-based investors to pull back on their foreign investment commitments. Money here became even tighter, as funds were withdrawn back to London. Bond prices and then stock prices declined, as did confidence. Business pessimism and caution were widespread, and Great Britain was laid low in 1891.

Figure 4.6
Raw Steel Production in the United States
(Millions of Tons)

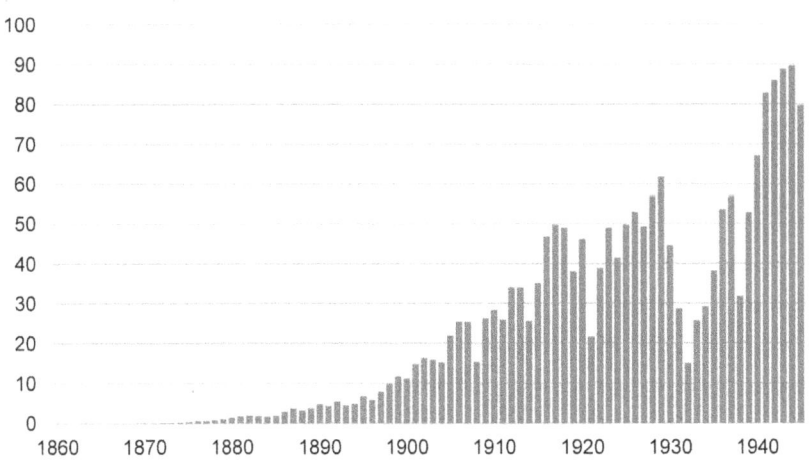

Source: American Iron and Steel Institute

Silver production soared during the 1880s, pushing the price of silver down to 20-to-one by 1890. In response to silver agitation from miners and farmers, the Sherman Silver Purchase Act was passed, which increased the amount of silver the government was required to purchase on an annual basis.

The business cycle peak occurred in July 1890 and resulted in subsequent liquidation. The downswing was short, lasting only 10 months with a trough reached in May 1891. Real gross output would fall 15.8 percent. Production of woolen goods and anthracite coal were adversely affected. Rail construction eased, affecting iron and steel and other industries as well. Steel production fell to 4.3 million tons in 1891. Crops were also poor and accompanied by the highest prices in a decade. Business failures increased and bank reserves decreased.

Stock prices bottomed out and then improved, and interest rates declined. Gradually improvement in business emerged although the recovery lagged in the South. International monetary disturbances are largely to blame for this recession, and it is possible that the upswing would have been longer if not for this foreign crisis.

In response to the rise of trusts in many industries and the concentration of capital, the Sherman Antitrust Act of 1890 was the federal government's first attempt at antitrust law to proscribe the rule of free competition among those engaged in commerce. The Sherman Act broadly prohibited 1) agreements and 2) conduct that restrict interstate commerce and competition in the marketplace. Other policy developments included the McKinley Tariff Act and the Sherman Silver Purchase Act. Both would eventually prove unpopular and affected business confidence. Immigration gained during this cycle, and combined with the legislation, influenced the downswing.

By this time, the opening of the West was no longer a dominant stimulant to economic growth. Rather, the United States had emerged as a major industrial nation.

Cycle 22: The Panic of 1893

Confidence gradually restored, and depressed business activity bottomed out in May 1891. A moderate improvement in business and industry emerged as tight money eased, and Cycle 22 was underway. The year was favored by good crops, which fostered more confidence.

The upswing in business activity gathered strength in 1892, and there was a significant expansion of manufacturing, particularly iron and steel. Indeed, steel production would quickly rebound, reaching a new high of 5.49 million tons in 1892. Foreign trade improved, as did most equities and bank clearings. On the other hand, railroad construction was muted during this upswing, a reflection of the unwillingness of foreigners to invest in the United States. Cotton and wheat production were soft. Silver agitation continued, as did social unrest. The year was marked by labor unrest, culminating in the Homestead riots at Carnegie's mills. Immigration increased. Business suffered in the wake of low prices for agricultural products, which caused a rather bad year for farming.

The Republican-dominated Congress and the Harrison Administration enacted the McKinley Tariff in 1890, and by boosting spending, turned the Federal budget surplus into deficit. Both were unpopular. Former president Grover Cleveland won his party's nomination and defeated President Harrison in the 1892 presidential election, making Cleveland the only president ever elected to discontinuous terms. Signs of the economic expansion reaching maturity were evident at the time.

The upswing lasted only 20 months, with business activity peaking in January 1893. The overextension of credit to several railroads, the failure of the Philadelphia & Reading in February, and withdrawal of European investment led to a stock market and banking collapse. This Panic was also precipitated, in part, by a run on the gold supply. In addition, declining wheat prices were a factor. Another factor was America's bimetallic policy. Silver advocates had succeeded in passing the Sherman Silver Purchase Act in 1890, which attempted to keep silver on a monetary basis with gold at a ratio different from relative market values at the time. Silver inflation emerged. Federal gold reserves were depleted as was public confidence, which reached its ebb when the British government closed the mints in India to the free coinage of silver in May 1893. A panic broke out. Monetary uncertainty quickly spread to banking and industry, and with the failure of the Chemical National Bank in Chicago in May 1893, and National Cordage in the same month, the panic became nationwide. Credit conditions became stringent, and coal, pig-iron, and industry in general came to a standstill. Steel production fell back to 4.5 million tons. Railroad construction collapsed, falling from 5,427 miles in 1894 to 1,420 in 1895. Indeed, several prominent railroads — the Erie, Northern Pacific, and Union Pacific — fell into receivership. At one point, as measured by track mileage, one-third of the railroads went into bankruptcy. The easing of exports was another factor.

The Free-Coinage Bill was passed by the Senate but defeated in the House. This created uncertainty during 1892, especially among foreign investors who doubted the willingness and ability of the nation to redeem obligations at par in gold. There were fears the United States was abandoning the gold standard in favor of silver. In addition, litigation over railroad combinations put additional burdens on sentiments. Business was worried, and working capital pared back.

As a result, Cleveland inherited an already weakening economy, and in his second term, the United States sank into one of its most severe economic depressions in history. The Sherman Silver Purchase Act had eroded confidence in the stability of the currency and was at the heart of the nation's economic troubles. The crisis largely revolved around the money question, and the president called Congress into special session and, over considerable opposition from Southern and Western members of his own party, forced the repeal of the act. This was to convince the world that American money was sound, and the nation ready to meet its obligations. Cleveland's effort to stop silver monetization led to a schism in the Democratic party, ending his role as party leader. He would be America's last "hard money" president.

Figure 4.7
Cycle 22: The Panic of 1893
Index of Real Gross Output where 2017 = 100

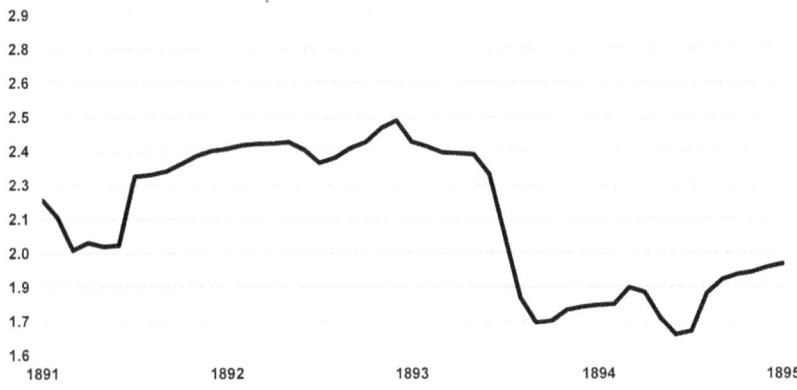

The depression was already gathering strength, and the downturn became severe and deep. Mining and manufacturing production fell, and agriculture was affected by low prices and crop failures. In addition to an agricultural depression, there was agitation for "free silver" and the emergence of labor troubles.

Uncertainty was high. Money was very tight, and stock prices collapsed, as did bond prices. There were hundreds of bank closures and many business failures, in addition to many railroads in receivership. The downswing lasted 17 months and ended in June 1984. It was marked by a 32.8 percent decline in real gross output, making this depression one of the worst in American history. Liquidation was widespread, and business confidence declined further. By mid-1894, severe stagnation was the order of the day, and there was widespread unemployment, railroad and industrial strikes, plus social unrest. Mills were shut down, and great poverty existed in the cities. A bituminous coal strike idled many steel mills and factories. The Pullman strike occurred at this time as well. Even hunger was widespread. A march by unemployed workers — Coxey's Army — was to protest the unemployment caused by the

Panic of 1893 and to lobby for the government to create jobs, which would involve building roads and other public improvements. The thinking was that workers paid in paper currency would expand the currency in circulation, which was consistent with populist thought of the day. These strikes likely delayed recovery. The year was deemed the worst since the end of the Civil War.

Gradually, money became easy, and bond prices moved higher. Lower tariffs certainly helped, as did the repeal of the Silver Act. Hope revived, as would business, as evidence of business improvement across many sectors emerged. Thus, Cycle 22 came to an end in June 1894. Some economic historians argue that the financial panic of 1893 led to an economic depression lasting five years.

The Panic of 1893 led to the Free Silver Movement, which attempted to replace the gold standard. Cycle 22 was also marked by high immigration.

Cycle 23: Revival of 1895 and the Silver Campaign Depression

Business conditions recovered gradually from the trough of Cycle 22 in June 1894, but the beginning of 1895 was still marked by gloom. It was not until late 1895 that the effects of the crisis finally dissipated. In the meantime, a boom in the iron and steel industry emerged. Pig iron production rose from 6.66 million tons in 1894 to 9.45 million tons the next year. Steel production rose from 4.90 million tons to 6.79 million tons in 1895. Building construction expanded, and freight volumes rose considerably.

There were good crops, although prices tended to be low. Money turned easy, and equity and bond prices improved. The upswing would not last long, only 18 months, with activity peaking in December 1895. Real gross output would gain 38.9 percent during this period. What precipitated the end of the upswing was diplomatic difficulties, with Great Britain over the boundary between British Guiana and Venezuela in 1895. The difficulties would not be resolved until early 1896, but the dispute shocked business interests. Various Congressional resolutions threatened hostilities with Spain over Cuba.

A mirror image of the upswing, the downturn would last 18 months, with real gross output declining 16.7 percent over the period. This featured a return to depression, and some economists view this cycle, and the one before, as one long generally depressed cycle following the Panic of 1893, that had a short spurt of growth mid-cycle, a "double-dip" recession. Some economists compare this cycle to that of the unsatisfactory upswing of 1933-37. I maintain the NBER classification of the cycle. Foreign holdings were liquidated, money rates firmed and tightened, and equity and bond prices declined. Building construction peaked early and then declined and was followed by falling orders for railroad and other equipment. Iron production dropped off, and business activity across many other sectors declined. Unemployment increased as did business failures. Most notable of these was the Baltimore and Ohio. There were difficulties in agriculture, although foreign trade was mixed. There was a marked decline in commodities and other prices.

In 1895, a panic would occur as Treasury gold reserves were drawn down. The nation faced default. Our last "hard money" president, President Grover Cleveland, was unable to convince Congress to issue new bonds that could be sold in exchange for gold. Julius Pierpont (J.P.) Morgan, who was vilified in the press, demanded a meeting with President Cleveland and was granted one. In this meeting Morgan put forth a plan for the United States to sell 3.5 million ounces of gold to the British. His plan was successful. It would not be the only time that Morgan came to the rescue of the nation.

The uncertainty of the presidential election of 1896 provided another barrier to improvement, and a brief panic ensued, as the presidential election would determine the fate of America's finances.

Money rates rose during the year, and equity markets remained dull. Business sentiments were greatly unsettled by the free silver campaign. Silver reserves dropped as former Congressman William Jennings Bryan was nominated the Democratic candidate on a platform of abandoning the gold standard. Former Ohio governor William McKinley, a Republican, championed the gold standard, and his election would put an end to the silver agitation and resulted in a victory for the gold standard. The nomination of Bryan affected business sentiments, but with his defeat, a rebound in equities occurred.

The depressed economy yielded to revival, despite a severe bituminous coal strike. The cyclical trough was reached in June 1897, several months after the start of the new administration. The pace of failures eased, and commodity prices bottomed out. Foreign trade became active, and money became easier, with advances in equity and bond prices. The year was marked by good crops, but also the lowest prices since the Civil War for some crops.

In the background of Cycle 23 was a Cuban independence movement that gained momentum. Revolts had been occurring for some years in Cuba against Spanish colonial rule, but American public opinion was changing and would lead to political controversy over recognition of Cuban independence.

Cycle 24: "Splendid Little War" Prosperity and Mild Post-War Recession

The upturn phase of Cycle 24 started a few months after the start of the McKinley Administration, in June 1897. This would last 24 months, with real gross output expanding 44.5 percent during the upswing phase of the cycle, as soft business activity gave way to revival and improvement. Money became easier, and there was a marked rise in equity and bond prices. Bank clearings improved, and failures declined. Commodity prices stabilized after three decades of general decline. Pig iron, steel, and coal production all rebounded sharply. In addition to improving industry, trade, and commerce, there were excellent wheat and cotton crops accompanied by large grain exports. In 1897, the Dingley Tariff was enacted. It raised rates but ended anxiety among manufacturers.

In 1898, the revival of activity strengthened, and prosperity emerged, spreading to railroads, agriculture, retail, industry, and business in general. Export demand improved. Mining and manufacturing reached new highs. Money was easy.

The start of the year would be marked by the February explosion that sank the U.S. battleship Maine in Havana Harbor. The clamor for war with Spain gained momentum, and in April, war was declared. The Spanish-American War was underway. Secretary of State John Hay later referred to it as a "splendid little war," as it was short (10 weeks) and one-sided with many quick victories. By August, peace was declared. The United States acquired The Philippines, Guam, and Puerto Rico as territories. Cuba gained its independence. The peace treaty signed in December provided additional support for the revival of business.

A boom in the iron and steel industries was underway that would largely last (with a hiccup in 1900) until the next cycle. Production of other construction materials gained as well, as did building construction. Expansion of business activity continued into 1899 and was accompanied by large crops and goods prices, rising commodity prices, rising stock and bond prices, speculation, and a large issuance of new securities. Demand for materials was intense. The upturn ended in June 1899, as money tightened and as construction projects were completed. New construction contracts were checked by high prices, and construction activity fell. Stock and bond prices slipped, and a panic emerged. This was largely a financial phenomenon. The outbreak of the Boer War added to uncertainty. A minor cycle, the downswing would last 18 months, ending in December 1900, and would feature a 12.2 percent peak-to-trough decline in business activity. Strikes in copper and anthracite coal occurred, and other labor troubles were present. Bank clearings eased, as did production in many industries. The recession was mild. Indeed, evidence of it does not show up in some annual economic time series.

The Gold Standard Act was passed, formally establishing the gold standard. Money turned easier, and bond and equity prices improved. President McKinley was re-elected, and it was clear that the nation was safe from Bryan free silver policy. This fostered improved business confidence and would give way to easier money, rising bond and equity prices, and a revival of business activity.

Cycle 24 saw the formation of many industrial combinations as many industries consolidated. In addition, immigration was at high levels. The Kingdom of Hawaii was overthrown in 1894, and a provisional republic was put in place from 1894-98. In 1898, the United States annexed the Republic of Hawaii. The year 1899 would mark the start of a bear market in bonds that would last until 1920.

Cycle 25: Merger Prosperity and the Rich Man's Panic of 1903

In combination with improved business confidence, a fall in prices marked the trough of the mild post-war recession, and consumption revived almost immediately from the December 1900 trough. The upswing in Cycle 25 would last 21 months and would see real gross output gain 20.6 percent. This was another mild cycle.

Business activity would expand significantly, with many records for production.

Despite a strike in 1901, steel production would rise from 11.2 million tons in 1900 to 16.4 million in 1902, and pig iron production from 13.8 million tons to 17.8 million. Money was easy, with higher bond and equity prices. Bank clearings improved. Indeed, there was a rise in railroad security prices after a panic set off by a fight over control of the Northern Pacific, which, would create the Northern Securities Company. Security listings gained, and there were gains in the volume of business in many lines.

As the new century took hold, large business interests with huge combinations and trusts became the order of the day. The United States Steel trust brought together by J.P. Morgan in 1901 was the largest. The year 1901 was marked by a severe drought. In September 1901, President McKinley was assassinated in Buffalo, and Vice President Theodore R. Roosevelt took office. A progressive, he would be a bane to these trusts and large banks. A partial panic occurred during the year, but equities soon advanced again. Northern Securities was sued by the Federal government under the Sherman Antitrust Act, resulting in its dissolution in 1904 when the Supreme Court ruled in favor of the government's case. However, business confidence was compromised. It was comprised further with the beginning of a long "trust busting" campaign by the new administration. This fostered fear and distrust in the business sector, and investment and business activity would languish within a year. Labor troubles added to the discomfort of business.

Prosperity continued into 1902 with higher volumes of business activity. The year marked good harvests. Several bank consolidations occurred, and new issues continued at high levels. A serious anthracite coal strike occurred, the effects of which would linger through the winter, even including a "coal famine" in 1903. J.P. Morgan helped President Roosevelt settle the coal strike by persuading the mine owners to consent to arbitration.

Financial strains began to emerge. Money gradually tightened and became stringent. Bond prices declined. Confidence was shaken by anti-trust agitation and persecution of trusts. Equity markets were unstable, and liquidation in stock occurred in the closing months of the year. Although agriculture did well in 1902, Cycle 25's peak occurred in September with a downswing lasting 23 months to

August 1904 and a peak-to-trough decline in real gross output of 11.3 percent. Steel production declined, but pig iron gained slightly. Both would decline in 1904. Other industrial and commercial activity declined, as did commodity prices. Building construction declined. Unemployment increased, and there were labor troubles. U.S. Shipbuilding and other firms went into receivership. Money remained tight, and bond and equity prices reached lows as what is known as the Rich Man's Panic (as reported by contemporary newspapers) was played out. This occurred as the volume of new capital issues floated was so great that the market for them became saturated during a period when trust busting became more aggressive. Banks had lent heavily against bonds and stocks as collateral, and both banks and insurance companies had invested in new securities to a very large extent. Liquidation took hold, and the steel boom, which commenced in 1899, was at an end. The downturn even affected United States Steel, which needed to reduce wages.

In mid-1904, money became easier with rising bond and equity prices. Soft business activity gave way to revival by the fall, and lower costs made new building construction possible. Industrial production would soon

reach new highs, and overseas orders would stimulate the iron and steel industries. Agriculture had a good year with large crops and high prices. In November 1904, President Roosevelt was re-elected. Overseas, the Russo-Japanese war started. Cycle 25 featured high immigration levels.

Cycle 26: Corporate Prosperity and the Panic of 1907

Preceded by rising bond and stock prices, and aided by very good corn and cotton crops, the revival in industry, trade, and commerce gathered strength in the fall of 1904, and in 1905, momentum was even stronger. The upswing would be marked by higher railroad construction (from 3,842 miles in 1904 to 5,623 in 1906), rising commodity prices, prosperous steel production (rising from 15.2 million tons in 1904 to 25.4 million in 1906), expanding foreign trade, and continuing extension of business activity. So much so, there were logistical congestion and constraints. Wages advanced. These years also featured good crops and good prices for those crops. Also known as the Roosevelt Prosperity, the upswing would last 33 months, with real gross output rising 37.0 percent from August 1904 to May 1907. The upswing was plagued by the anthracite coal and other labor difficulties These years were also marked by anti-railroad political agitation and the rise of trust-busting investigations and lawsuits (railroads, sugar, meat, etc.), as well as new reform initiatives. It was after all, the Progressive Era, and the stance of the Administration would foster business uncertainty. In 1905, confidence was shaken by the Life Insurance and Traction exposures of the year.

Expansion of business activity continued in 1906 and into early 1907. Prosperity was briefly halted by the San Francisco earthquake. There were large gains in foreign trade and excellent harvests. Commodity prices continued to rise, and transportation challenges continued. However, by early 1907, it was apparent that industry and commerce were slowing, and in March, a weakening of the real economy occurred, followed by a panic, as the weak economy exposed over-leveraged industrial firms and banks. Construction contracts fell off. Foreign trade was easing, and there were some minor overseas panics. Bond and stock prices reached peaks and then declined. Money became tight and even stringent. Credit conditions in the fall of 1907 were more difficult than in prior years, as funds were needed for rebuilding San Francisco, which added to tightness in markets. Speculation had heightened in the year before, and credit was stringent abroad, as well as across the nation. As real gross output turned, banks found their cash reserves low. They were obliged to curtail credit and boost interest rates. The reversal was quick and dramatic. Trust companies were the latest financial innovation, and a prominent but over-leveraged Knickerbocker Trust Company failed in October 1907. Within a day, almost all trust companies were subject to runs, and a contagious panic spread.

Agriculture was still a leading sector of the economy, and seasonal needs for money fostered instability within the system. Correspondent bank relationships were fully developed. Small country banks would find themselves with surpluses of funds at times of the year, and they deposited excess reserves with city banks, their correspondent banks. In turn, these city banks had correspondent (and seasonal) relationships with large banks in New York. The New York banks provided loans for the purchase of stocks. The flow of money was reversed when country banks called for a return of their funds to provide loans to farmers for seed and machinery. At this point, the New York banks would call in money they loaned for speculative purposes. As a result, each fall witnessed generally stringent credit conditions with an adverse effect on commerce and industry.

On some occasions, unforeseen events emerged, leading to "credit crunches" as speculators and investors needed to sell securities to raise funds to repay loans. This would put further pressure on stock prices and the further calling in of loans. This is precisely what happened in 1907. It seemed to come without warning and was particularly disconcerting to investors and business leaders alike.

The Panic of 1907, also called the Knickerbocker Crisis, was a three-week collapse of the equity market that caused several financial institutions to close their doors. Banks suspended payments. The stock market collapsed, and bond prices dropped further. This was followed by other financial institutions. In addition, financial difficulties of United Copper led to a run on Mercantile National Bank, the financier of the venture. Many banks across the nation refused to convert deposits into gold specie or currency. Banks eventually met the situation by issuing clearinghouse certificates in various cities. These certificates served as a kind of emergency currency, standing midway between promissory notes secured by collateral and asset currency. The certificates had been used before, most notably in 1860, 1873, 1884, 1890, and 1893.

Figure 4.8
Cycle 26: Corporate Prosperity and the Panic of 1907
Index of Real Gross Output where 2017 = 100

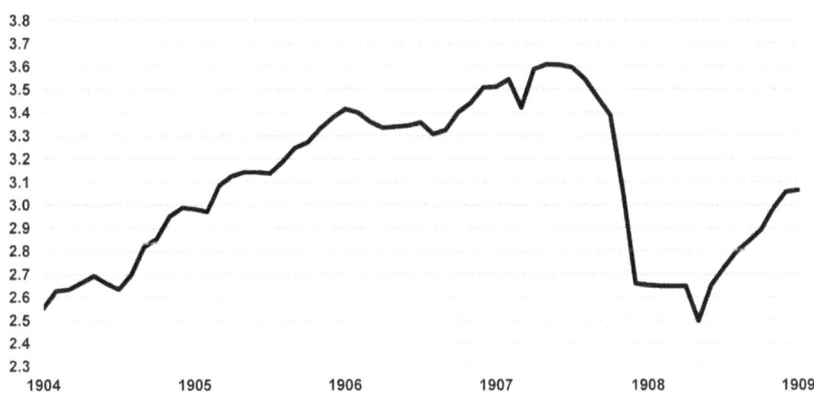

In New York, the leadership of J.P. Morgan was paramount in the effort to stem the panic. As the panic got underway, Morgan acted to restore order and formed a committee to determine which institutions could be saved after the panic, and which would have to be sacrificed. He discontinued the disorganization and restored discipline, making it possible for markets to work again. Think of it as triage in a hospital emergency room. Morgan summoned leading bankers and financial experts to his home, where they set up shop in his library. Over the course of three weeks, Morgan and his associates labored to channel money from the strong institutions to the weaker ones, in an effort to keep them afloat. They saved the country from a severe financial crisis. Only years earlier, he had been vilified by the Administration, and now he was viewed as a savior.

Legislation that was averse to the trusts and railroads added to business uncertainty. By the end of the year, the nation had fallen from prosperity into depression. Economic disturbances emanating from the Panic were widespread and made an already stagnated economy turn downward. As the banking panic emerged, equity prices collapsed, and the contagion spread further to the real economy, resulting in a 13-month downswing, and a 30.8 percent decline in business activity. Business was paralyzed, and the Panic led to a severe downturn in business activity. Steel production fell from 25.4 million tons in 1907 to 15.4 million in 1908. Pig iron and textiles production fell as well, as did railroad miles constructed.

The downswing was accompanied by severe unemployment and many failures. Social unrest followed and money remained tight. The Interstate Commerce Commission had been regulating railroads for many years, and railroads claimed that they were forbidden to earn adequate rates. Several railroads went into receivership. Weakness spread to other industries. New construction dropped to low levels. A constriction of foreign business occurred, and foreign trade ebbed.

The first signs of recovery were given by the stock exchange. By 1908, equity and bond prices started to move higher, and money became less tight. The downturn reached a low point in June 1908, giving place to improvement. A temporary currency bill was passed to meet the depressed conditions. The Aldrich-Vreeland Act of 1908 enabled national banks to issue notes freely during a crisis and eventually, the Federal Reserve Act of 1913 would improve upon these provisions.

The Panic of 1907 was quick and severe and was the first global financial crisis of the century. Financial markets in Great Britain, Germany, Japan, Egypt, Chile, and other nations were affected. The depression was an international depression, although Americans in general did not think of it as such, for they were mainly concerned that it was fostered by a financial panic so serious that it was apparent to many that the monetary and banking systems needed reform. It led to Congress passing the Federal Reserve Act of 1913, establishing regional Federal Reserve Banks, whose purpose was to provide elasticity to the banking system and serve as a lender of last resort. That is, a central bank that could provide funds to the banking sector in periods of crises, panic, and instability.

The downturn associated with the Panic of 1907 was so severe that economists stopped using the term panic to describe downturns and switched to using the word depression. Despite the downturn, immigration reached new records in this cycle but also fell off in wake of the Panic.

Cycle 27: Recovery and Mild Panic of 1910-11

An advance in equity and bond prices, as well as security issues signaled the recovery that emerged in June 1908. As the year progressed, there was sustained improvement in business activity. Crops were good as well. In November 1908, William Howard Taft (former Secretary of War) was elected 27th president, securing continuation of Republican administration and policy. This eased uncertainty. Money rates continued at a low level.

The upswing continued into 1909 and was accompanied by a marked rise in prices. Agriculture was mixed, but steel production jumped to 26.4 million tons and would finally surpass that of pig iron production. Railroad mileage expanded. American oil production exceeded 500,000 barrels per day for the first time in 1909. The loss of kerosene for lighting by the spread of electric lighting was more than offset by increased demand for gasoline being used in automobiles, a new growth industry. Despite these gains, coal would remain a leading fuel for heating and for industry. Immigration rose further. Money became tighter, and bond and equity prices declined. The financial situation became unsound. Eventually business activity was checked, and a peak was reached in January 1910. This ended a 19-month upswing, which had seen a 45.7 percent gain in real gross output.

The fallout from the Sherman Antitrust Act saw major companies dissolved, including Standard Oil and American Tobacco. This fostered uncertainty. Railroad "baiting" continued, and other anti-trust suits against companies were initiated. There were copper and railroad strikes in the Northwest. The Payne-Aldrich Tariff Act was passed in response to a call from President Taft for lower tariffs. The bill failed to significantly decrease tariff rates and caused him to lose the support of the progressive wing of the Republican party. All combined to dampen business sentiments and foster a mild panic among investors. Money was tight, and bond and equity prices softened.

In 1910, a group of bankers met at Jekyll Island to create a blueprint for an American central bank. The plans would be debated and passed in Congress in 1913 and would provide for the creation of the Federal Reserve, both a government agency and a private bank. Reflecting American distrust of large organizations, the "Fed" is a network of 12 regional banks, each owned by private banks in the district. Through time, policy would become more centralized in Washington, DC.

The 1910 mid-term elections resulted in Democrat success. Government delays in trust and railroad rate questions added to uncertainty. Investment conditions were affected by Supreme Court decisions and reorganization of large corporations under the Sherman Anti-Trust Act, which added to business uncertainty.

In 1910, the railroads granted advances in wages to workers as part of the settlement of successful strikes ordered by the Federal Arbitration Board. Management of the railroads believed that their higher operating costs would be mitigated through increased traffic rates. The new Interstate Commerce Commission, however, declined to allow higher rates. As a result, railroads curtailed construction, from 4,122 miles in 1910 to 2,997 in 1912. This also dampened business sentiment, adding to the downswing that had set in and that would last 24 months, bottoming out in January 1912 and marked by a mild 11.9 decline in real gross output.

Early on during the recession, steel production expanded but would eventually succumb to the depressed economic conditions. Pig iron production was adversely affected, and industrial and commercial activity faltered. Foreign trade continued its momentum at first, but that fell off as well. Deflationary forces were in play. Agriculture was mixed (the result of drought), but immigration eased. This was a mild but longer than average recession.

Eventually, money eased, and steady but slow rises in equity and bond prices occurred, as a recovery emerged. In addition, railroads made quick adjustments to meet new business conditions.

Cycle 28: Progressive Era and the War Recession

Although the Roosevelt Administration would be considered progressive in its policies, Cycle 28 would be called the Progressive Era. More anti-trust suits (gunpowder, sugar, etc.) were forthcoming. It would be a major cycle.

As money became easier, equity and bond prices moved up, and a revival in business activity emerged in January 1912. With a good farming season, accompanied by poor harvests in Europe, foreign trade and the nation further recovered. Improvement across business was marked by easy money, which turned tighter later in the year as commodity prices rose, and many labor disputes emerged. Strikes in anthracite mining were notable, as it was a common source for residential and commercial heating. The stock market turned dull, and bond prices declined. The year was marked by the Titanic disaster, and flooding in the Mississippi early in the year, war in the Balkans, and the presidential election.

Former President Roosevelt lost the presidential nomination of the Republican Party to incumbent president William Howard Taft and therefore ran as a third-party candidate for the Progressive Party (often referred to as the "Bull Moose Party"). This split the Republican vote, and New Jersey governor (and former president of Princeton University) Woodrow Wilson, a Democrat, was elected president, taking only 42 percent of the popular vote but a very large majority of the Electoral College votes. His administration was even more progressive than Roosevelt's and would be the high-water mark of progressivism for decades. A fourth candidate was Eugene V. Debs of the Socialist Party.

Tariff discussions and investigation of corporations unsettled business sentiments, and an incoming progressive administration fostered further uncertainty among the business community. Money tightened, and stock prices slumped, as did bond prices. Thus, the upswing lasted only 12 months, ending in January 1913. Real gross output would increase 17.2 percent in this upswing.

The length of the downturn would be twice that of the upturn, a full 23 months, with real gross output declining 16.0 percent to December 1914. Business conditions continued to grow steadily worse throughout the year and into 1914. Money stringency and credit contraction characterized 1913. Much of the financial strains resulted from the Balkan wars. This monetary stringency led to a steady contraction of business activity.

A severe downswing emerged with extensive unemployment and many business failures. The Revenue Act of 1913 (also known as the Underwood Tariff) reduced rates and helped offset downward momentum. Commodity prices eased, but a temporary boom would emerge with the war in Europe. Foreign trade, however, declined. The downward phase would be marked by extensive progressive legislation, which further contributed to uncertainty.

Overseas, Great Britain suffered a short-lived financial crisis in mid-1914, as alarm spread across Europe after the assassination of

Archduke Ferdinand, heir to the throne of Austria-Hungary. Fears of war mounted, leading to volatility in exchange rates and in the equity markets. There were panics in Vienna, Berlin, Paris and London. The latter was the center for international finance. Equity prices collapsed, and the contagion spread to New York. Bank rates were raised. War concerns extended the decline of 1913 into 1914. Liquidation continued.

Figure 4.9

Cycle 28: Progressive Era and the War Recession
Index of Real Gross Output where 2017 = 100

The outbreak of the World War (or Great War as it was first known) threw commerce and industry completely out of long-standing, domestic-oriented supply, resulting in changes in business methods and a greater focus outside the United States. The outbreak of hostilities resulted in slumping bond prices and a stock market collapse and would paralyze world money markets. A three-day bank holiday was put in place, and the New York Stock Exchange closed for four months. The American financial system met the shock with no formal government aid. Emergency measures employed in Paris and London were not employed here. As in 1873, 1893, and 1907, clearinghouse certificates were used among banks in New York, and the situation was liquid and solvent. Virtually all the world's financial markets closed their doors. This would foster panic and deepen the depression. Factory operations were restricted, and unemployment increased, as did the number of failures.

The war, however, would eventually provide opportunities for American industry and lead to an end to the downturn. Orders from Europe would soon be pouring into American industry, unleashing a boom period. This, along with good crops, provided evidence of pending improvement in business. Matters soon began to adjust themselves to the new business environment, and the downturn ended.

Eventually, money loosened, and bond yields eased. Monetary conditions became easier. The financial system remained resilient, and a large expansion of credit would soon emerge, leading to wartime inflation.

This cycle also saw the Income Tax Amendment, as well as the Trade Commission Act and the Clayton Antitrust Act. These sought to prevent unfair methods of competition in commerce and anti-competitive practices, such as price-fixing, cartels, monopolies, and trusts. All of these were major hallmarks of the Progressive Era. Additional suits against trusts were made during this cycle.

The World War would halt immigration, although it would later slowly revive. On a positive note, the Panama Canal was opened.

Cycle 28 witnessed the establishment of the Federal Reserve System. For many years, it was apparent that the banking system of the United States was inadequate to meet the financial needs of the nation. This was especially apparent in the Panic of 1907. The greatest defect was on the matter of bank reserves, more specifically the lack of centralized reserves that would combine the power of the nation's banks to withstand the stress of financial crises. In the years between 1907 and 1913, the National Monetary Commission was formed and comprised of top bankers and government officials. The Commission traveled to Europe to examine central banking overseas. The Federal Reserve System was created in December 1913, when President Woodrow Wilson signed the Federal Reserve Act into law. The Act created 12 Federal Reserve Banks and thus 12 reservoirs (or pools) of reserves for district banks to draw upon in times of need. The Act also created an elastic currency, the Federal Reserve notes. The Act facilitated financing of foreign trade by allowing member banks of the system to deal in foreign acceptances and establish foreign branches. The inauguration of the Federal Reserve System in November 1914 restored the monetary situation to a more normal footing. It was the cooperation of banks, clearinghouses, stock exchanges, and the Treasury which met this first shock of the war. The establishment of the Federal Reserve also made panics less likely. In the years after its establishment, only two major panics likely occurred. These were associated with the Great Depression and the Great Financial Crisis.

Cycle 29: War Prosperity and the 1918-19 Influenza Pandemic

The World War resulted in a revival of American business activity, beginning in industries manufacturing rails, ships, munitions, and other war materials. There was an enormous increase in exports. With Russian grain exports blockaded, demand for American wheat soared. Great Britain, France, and the Allies stepped up their purchases of American farm products and manufactured goods. As the British blockade tightened, exports to the neutral Scandinavian nations particularly increased.

Unemployment gradually disappeared, although the South lagged in the recovery. Cycle 29 would feature an upswing lasting 44 months, with real gross output rising 55.1 percent from December 1914 to the peak in August 1918. It would be characterized as war prosperity, or a war boom.

American turned to the production of materials, which was facilitated by easy credit. There was a great quickening of industry, and by year-end in 1915, any industrial slack had disappeared. Labor and capital were being fully utilized.

Prices, at first, rose slowly but accelerated in what would be a long bout of inflation. The rapid rise of prices took the nation by surprise.

Money became easy, and equity prices gained during 1915 and 1916. Bond prices improved. Bank loans expanded, as did stock speculation. Aided by war orders and grain exports, these years were marked by rapid gains in business activity and expanding trade, especially foreign trade. Steel production would rise from 25.6 million tons in 1914 to 49.8 million in 1916. It would remain at those levels through 1918. Similar gains occurred in pig iron. Nearly all lines of business participated in the boom, and new production records were set. A great wave of industrial expansion occurred. Large harvests and record crops would characterize these years. Domestic trade began to revive. Bank clearings expanded by one-third in 1916 alone. Wage advances were evident in virtually every branch of business, and labor shared in the prosperity. Profits of industrial corporations were very good in 1915-17, although in 1918, higher taxes would cut into them.

Inflation intensified. Overall prices had gained 1.0 percent in both 1914 and 1915, but in 1916, averaged 17.4 percent. More was to come, and overall prices advanced 18.0 percent in 1917 and 14.6 percent in 1918. Consumer prices advanced 51.0 percent between 1914 and 1918, likely the highest four-year gain in American economic history.

In 1915, the Supreme Court would uphold U.S. Steel Corporation, marking the end of the first period of progressive legislation and regulation. Government policy became more favorable to business. The year would see the sinking of the Lusitania, which engendered a change in American sentiments away from neutrality and towards war preparation.

The year 1916 would mark military intervention in Mexico and President Wilson's reelection. The Shipping Act established the Shipping Board as an emergency agency to increase the number of U.S. ships supporting war efforts. The Federal Farm Loan Act was passed with the intent to increase credit to rural family farmers. It would aid agricultural production for the war effort but would also contribute to the weakness of the sector in the 1920s.

Both equities and bonds advanced in 1916. Advances in stock prices slowed and temporarily tightened, likely in anticipation of slower growth ahead. When it became evident that the war would last longer, a rally occurred. Bonds gained slightly at the end of the year. In December, President Wilson sent his first peace note to the belligerents, resulting in a market set-back. The index of the top 40 stocks closed 1916 lower than the start.

Business activity would continue to expand into 1917 when Germany announced unrestricted submarine warfare. The United States would declare war in April, and the Compulsory Military Service Act would soon be passed. Government soon began the task of concentrating the nation's industrial power on branches of industry essential for war needs. Business in such lines was very active. Other branches, however, suffered from priority rulings, which gave precedence to war needs in regard to transportation and raw, materials. Industry was reorganized, but there were shortages of fuel and labor, as well as freight congestion at ports. Commodity and other prices would continue to rise, and the government would assume control of the railroads and introduce a price-fixing policy. Food controls were enacted. Coal, electricity, bread, and other products would be rationed.

The traditional American policy of financing war was by war loans. The scale of need for the World War made this inadequate, and a mix of higher taxes and borrowing from the people instead of the banks was pursued to the highest extent possible. The Federal Reserve engaged in orthodox central banking principles (keeping the rediscount rates above the market rate) and performed well during the war. The Fed was supportive and reduced the reserve requirements in 1917. An important factor was the rationing of credit, especially for industries deemed non-essential. No attempt was made to fix wages.

There was a clear understanding of economic fundamentals and the perverse effects of price controls. The use of price fixing was thus cautious and limited to select commodities. Some industries (grain, flour and fuel) had administrative boards that were trusted by the industries. The notable exception was the Fuel Administration and its price fixing in bituminous coal, which led to the shutting down of high-quality mines in favor of low-quality mines with high ash content. The problem was quickly identified and remedied.

Figure 4.10
Coal Production in the United States (Millions of Tons)

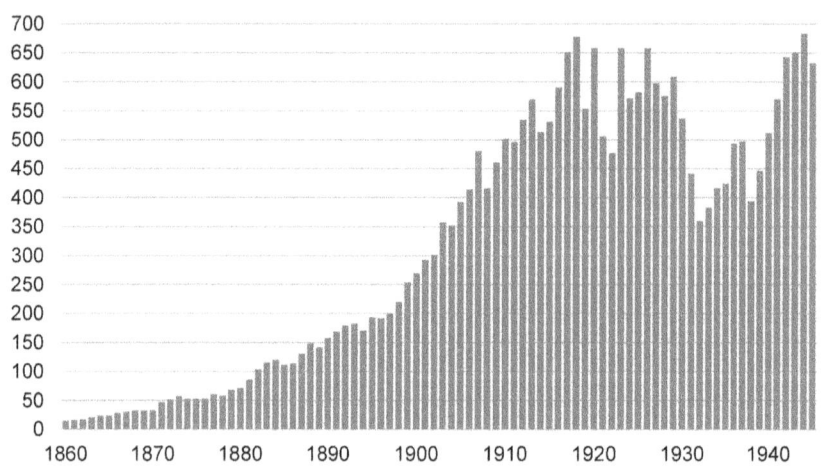

Source: *Statistical Abstract of the United States*

The bond market was monopolized by government issues. Liberty Loans were introduced, and money tightened. Bank loans expanded, but bond prices fell as did equity prices. An embargo on gold exports was put in place. Large harvests occurred, and farmers received high prices. This encouraged more planting and speculation, and farmland increased.

By 1918, extensive conscription was underway, and the movement of American troops to Europe progressed rapidly. Although crops were largely excellent, strict conservation of food and fuel and some government price controls remained in place. That said, they were largely ineffective, and inflation accelerated further, even as the government took control over major products and operated the railroads, which had faced congestion that year. Labor troubles emerged. Labor shortages resulted in wages rising sharply. The Pitman Act authorizing the sale of silver was passed. Money became very tight, and the issue of new securities restricted.

There were some problems in the war effort. One issue was the use of cost-plus contracts, which resulted in higher prices. There was some concern about war profiteering, but heavy taxes on profits eroded some of this.

Figure 4.11

Cycle 29: War Prosperity and the 1918-19 Influenza Pandemic Index of Real Gross Output where 2017 = 100

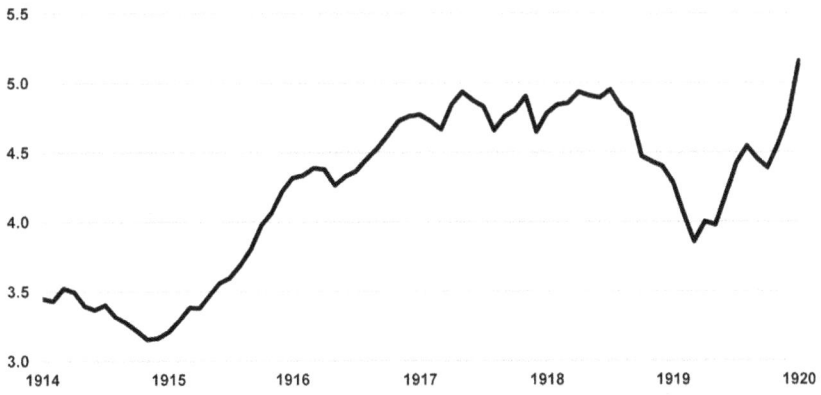

Business activity continued to expand until August 1918, when the downturn started. It would be short but sharp, lasting only seven months but witnessing a 21.2 percent decline in real business activity. This downturn was largely fostered by the outbreak of the influenza pandemic.

During the 19th century and before, there were numerous localized outbreaks of yellow fever, typhoid fever, cholera, etc., in the United States. Health officials (at least some of the older doctors) in 1918 were used to dealing with them.[10] This pandemic marked the first nationwide outbreak. Originating in either China or the United States, the "Spanish Flu" pandemic started in January 1918 and ended in December 1920, infecting 500 million people, about one-third of the world's population at the time. The death toll is estimated between 50 million to 100 million (including 675,000 in United States), making it one of the deadliest pandemics in human history. Most influenzas are U-shaped in affecting populations, either the young or elderly. The 1918-19 influenza epidemic was particularly nasty, with a higher-than-expected mortality rate for young adults aged 20-29 years. The conditions of the Great War (overcrowding and global troop movement) and lack of vaccines and treatments helped spread the pandemic. To maintain morale, censors minimized early reports of illness and mortality. Spain was neutral and had a free press, and it was in Spain where the first reports emerged, hence the misleading "Spanish Flu" name for the pandemic. The 1918-19 influenza pandemic consisted of three waves in the United States: first wave in spring 1918, the second and most deadly wave in fall 1918, and a tertiary wave in spring 1919. Although nationwide, clusters were on the East Coast and Midwest, and largely correlated with military bases and troop movements.

The NBER dates this recession from August 1918 to March 1919, a seven-month recession. The Allies experienced military reverses in March-July 1918. This created uncertainty. At this time, the War

---

[10] In 2020, health professionals were not used to dealing with these outbreaks.

Finance Corporation was organized. July 1918 was a critical month, as the Allies finally gained momentum, but labor troubles began on the home front. The severe influenza epidemic hampered industry in July through December during the second and most deadly wave.

The Administration seized control of shipping in August, with controls on trading modified or removed in December after the Armistice was signed on November 11th. A striking feature of the downturn was the post-war inflation. Consumer prices continued to rise into January 1919, eased for a month, then began climbing again.

By September 1918 it was clear the German position was hopeless, and on November 11th the armistice was signed. The downturn was brief, preceded by advancing interest rates and declines in bond prices, stock prices, and new issues.

During November and December, the majority of war orders were cancelled. Military production soon wound down. It was, however, not a cause of the downturn, which began in August of that year, when the second wave of the pandemic surged. The winding down, however, would play a role in 1919. Uncertainty increased as the pandemic spread. Production of consumer-oriented goods and services, catalog sales, construction volumes, and producer durables would all fall, largely in line with the pandemic. Factory employment fell, and the limited measures of unemployment that existed rose. The downturn would end in March 1919 after the influenza pandemic had largely played out, money eased, and as war restrictions were eased. A liquidation of bank credit took place as businesses reduced borrowing or paid off existing loans.

Although government control of prices ended with 1918, commodity and other prices continued to rise. Labor troubles and steel, coal, and other strikes continued through 1919. Most notable was the Boston Police Strike. A large number of Republicans from around the country admired the skill with which, as governor of Massachusetts, Calvin Coolidge put down the strike. He was nominated as Warren Harding's vice president nominee in the

1920 election and would succeed Harding after his untimely death three years later. Unemployment rose, as soldiers began returning home in 1919. The year would be marked by the "Red Summer" of 1919, when fears of Bolshevism mounted. In addition, race riots and lynchings swept the nation.

With the passage of the Sixteenth Amendment in 1913, the initial top rate on income taxes (only for the wealthy) was 7 percent. In four years, the top rate was 77 percent. Meanwhile, inflation pushed more earners into the top tax bracket, since the progressive tax brackets were not adjusted for changes in the cost of living. This was the first instance of bracket creep and would play a role in fostering uncertainty and hampering investment during Cycle 29.

Immigration would rise after the cessation of hostilities. Eventually, the pandemic ran its course. Uncertainty eased, and confidence improved with the end of the war. Economic activity resumed, setting the stage for an upswing of business activity. Major banks continued to provide loans to our Allies in order to give them time to set their houses in order.

Cycle 30: The Forgotten Depression

After the recovery from influenza-induced downswing of 1918-19 started in March 1919, commodity prices turned, and orders began to advance again. Commerce and industry would expand sharply in this cycle, reaching new highs.

Prices, wages, foreign trade, bank credit, and other indicators of business reached new levels of activity. Federal spending did well into 1919, and easy money policy by the Federal Reserve continued as well. Labor troubles and strikes were many during 1919. There was a national steel strike, a citywide strike in Seattle, and a strike by the Boston police. Unemployment rose amid the return of nearly four million men from military service.

The year was a sharp reaction from the restrictions imposed by the war. Equities advanced. Stock markets speculation reached new heights. Bank credit expanded. Encouraged by low interest rates, speculation steadily increased. In keeping the rediscount rate below the market rate, the Federal Reserve permitted the expansion to move faster than it would have otherwise. Speculation in farmland and other real estate reached new highs.

There had been a shortage of housing during the war, and rents rose rapidly during 1919 and 1920. New construction, which had been largely restricted to industrial and war projects, soon was geared towards residential building. Automobile factories soon had a six-month order backlog. Production rose from 943,000 in 1918, to 1.65 million in 1919, and 1.91 million in 1920. A wave of extravagance swept the country. The year 1920 would mark the year in which the United States clearly emerged as the world largest economy, a distinction it has held since then.

The business community widely expected the price inflation during the war to reverse as it had in the past, but no deflation occurred, and in fact, consumer prices rose 14.6 percent in 1919 and 15.6 percent in 1920. Commodity prices rose at a swifter rate than anytime during the war and, in 1919 and 1920, was accompanied by a rapid rise in wages.

Business and consumer optimism increased. There was a great rebound in business activity, and prosperity was quickly reached as the recovery gathered momentum. Still, by 1920, the economic situation became unbalanced. The railroad systems were under severe strain during the war. Traffic was dislocated, and maintenance work was delayed, resulting in post-war strains. Furthermore, railway wages were high and efficiency low.

Rising costs in industry characterized 1919 and 1920, resulting in declining profits. Mining, railroads, and public utilities were particularly affected. As the outlook of profits diminished, creditors became nervous, and a reaction occurred.

Emerging strains in the credit situation resulted in a general rise in commercial paper rates. Banks became over-extended and soon restricted credit. As a result, money tightened, and bond prices fell. Money rates reached very high levels. The stock market fell, and commodity prices followed. The inevitable fall in business activity soon occurred. James Grant (2014) referred to this as the "Forgotten Depression." The upswing lasted only 10 months, with real gross output rising 33.6 percent from March 1919 to January 1920. The New York Federal Reserve bank rate was increased to limit the effects of inflation, and interest rates rose in the United Kingdom and elsewhere.

With the ending of war orders, overtime work ceased, and the war bonus system was abandoned. Labor soon became restless. Strikes continued and occurred in almost every branch of industry. In November, a great steel strike involving over 365,000 workers took place. This was the year of the "Red Summer," as well as other social unrest. Pig iron and steel production suffered during the year but would soon rebound. American oil production, however, exceeded 1.0 million barrels per day for the first time in 1919.

In 1920, over-expansion was unprecedented, as was inflation. The upward trend in prices, however, was checked almost over-night, and as typical in a downturn, prices declined at a violent pace. Commodity prices broke first, and then all prices began to yield. From a 15.6 percent rise in consumer prices in 1920, deflation emerged. Consumer prices would fall 10.5 percent in 1921, the most deflationary year in American history. Prices would fall by 6.1 percent in 1922. There were widespread wage reductions, and labor difficulties arose, as labor was unwilling to accept reduced wages. A general weakness in business activity occurred. Steel production fell from 46.2 million tons in 1920 to 21.6 million in just one year. Coal mining, and the textile industries in particular, suffered during the downturn. The downturn was marked by widespread inventory accumulation. Companies that had stocked up on raw materials and other inventories when the inflation was in place soon found themselves with materials worth only half as much. The value of inventories shrank, and liquidity decreased. Cancellation of contracts became widespread. Factories closed down, and questions of solvency emerged. The unemployment rate expanded from 2.3 percent in 1919 to 11.9 percent in 1921. In the latter year, the cotton crop would fail. Failures began to increase.

Figure 4.12

Cycle 30: The Forgotten Depression

Index of Real Gross Output where 2017 = 100

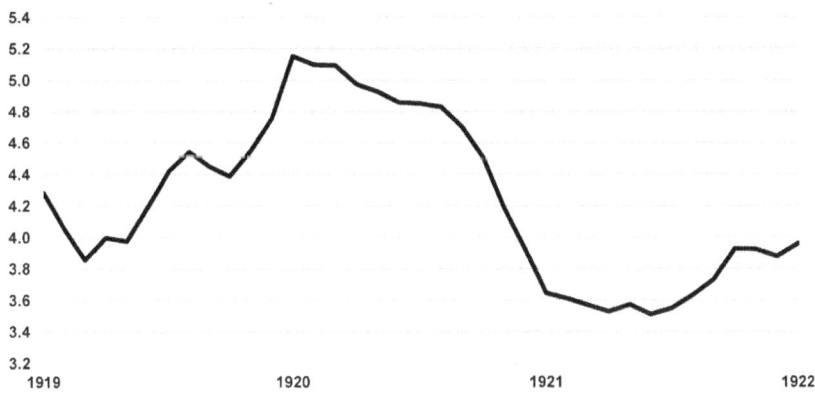

The World War led to an expansion of agriculture. Credit flowed to this sector amid rising prices for cotton, wheat, and other crops, and subsequently, land prices. Aided by rising prices, agriculture used the wartime earnings to increase mortgage levels. Farmers became over-extended, and with the end of the war, crops in Europe would rebound. The boom was soon followed by the inevitable bust, with a collapse in prices in the early-1920s that would characterize the decade. The damage was compounded by debt. Indeed, farm prices fell over 40 percent in 1921 alone, ushering in what would be a difficult decade for the sector. It would be the start of a decade of the agriculture sector depressed by the loss of export markets. In addition, the advent of the automobile resulted in the large-scale decline in oats output, as there was a reduced need for horses in transportation.

The period from wartime inflation to post-war deflation was short and forceful. Orders were cancelled, and the decline in activity came quickly. Money became extremely tight, and equity and bond prices declined sharply. As the value of assets used as collateral declined, the number of bank failures rose, from 65 in 1919, to 155 in 1920, and 506 in 1921. These were largely small, rural banks, often exposed to the agriculture sector where the fallout from the debt overhang, and falling prices engendered a long period of decline.

Industrial stagnation and unemployment would reach its worst in 1921. Failures continued to mount as prices declined, and with weakness in Europe, foreign trade was depressed. The New York Federal Reserve bank rate was reduced three times. Further reduction in bank discount rates occurred, as did wage reductions. The British bank rate was reduced as well, but the year saw hyperinflation and the collapse of the German mark.

The history of U.S. banking shows a preference or bias for small banks. A distrust of big banks led to a massive expansion of small banks. In 1896, there were 12,112 banks. Nearly all operated in one state and most were one branch banks serving one community. The number of banks would peak at 30,736 in 1922 and over the course of the next 100 years, fall to about 4,000 amid consolidation with the growth of multi-state banking.

The federal government balanced the budget, and the Federal Reserve began purchasing government securities. By mid-1921, as money began to ease, equities and bond prices recovered, heralding the end of the downturn. As the banking situation improved, money rates became easy. Commercial paper rates declined. The tide also turned, as consumers began adopting newer appliances like refrigerators, washing machines, and radios, all fostered by the revolution in electricity that had some four decades earlier.

No stimulus was administered, and by the end of 1921, a strong recovery in business activity was underway bringing employment gains with it. The downturn largely cured itself. Business leaders and bankers were thorough in cleaning up the weak spots and in making the needed adjustments in prices, costs, inventories, and volumes of activity. Costs rapidly readjusted as did wages.

The downswing lasted longer than the upswing, a full 18 months compared to 10 months. Commencing in January 1920, a trough in the downturn would be reached in July 1921. During that time, real gross output declined 31.9 percent. The downturn was short but extremely painful. Some economic historians feel that Cycle 29 and this cycle were one extended cycle. I go with the NBER timing, of viewing both as individual cycles.

This depression was not unique to the United States. A severe depression occurred in Great Britain and elsewhere in Europe, as economies adjusted to the post-war realities. The experiences and policy responses, however, differed among nations. Great Britain also went through an inflationary boom, and its deflation was also sharp. France did not really participate in the 1919-20 boom and experienced only a mild decline, while Germany experienced little gains at first and avoided declining activity. However, the hyperinflation would soon change that, resulting in widespread economic disruption.

Cycle 30 was overlaid by the Red Scare, a widespread fear of far-left extremism, including Bolshevism and anarchism. The Russian Revolution, anarchist bombings, and labor strikes added to this fear. At its height in 1919–20, concerns over the effects of radical political agitation in American society and alleged spread of communism and anarchism in the American labor movement fueled a general sense of concern and uncertainty. The Wall Street bombing of September 1920 would result in tighter immigration, culminating in the Immigration Restriction Act of 1921.

The year 1919 would mark the founding of the General Motors Acceptance Corp., which democratized and advanced consumer credit. In 1920, the Prohibition Amendment became effective, and the Woman's Suffrage Amendment was ratified. The Transportation Act provided for the return of the railroads to private control. William G. Harding, a Republican senator from Ohio promised a return to "normalcy" and was elected president in a landslide. After the Great War, and the influenza epidemic and its associated recession, there was a change in American society. The old and familiar were cast aside, and there was a passion for living, setting the stage for the Roaring Twenties.

Cycle 31: Recovery, the Roaring 20s, and the 1923-24 Recession

With easier money and reduction in bank rediscount rates, bond prices gained and rose rapidly. With the cleaning up of credit and cost readjustments among business, business activity and employment began to rally.

The 1920s are known as the "Roaring Twenties" as widespread market participation surged. A new industry of brokerages let small investors buy equities with borrowed funds. Investors put down a fraction of the price, typically 10 percent, with the stocks serving as collateral. The mutual fund industry, for example, would emerge in 1924, providing smaller investors with even more opportunities to invest. Investment trusts were a new and popular means of investment for ordinary men and women. Borrowed money poured into equity markets, and stock prices soared during the decade.

The first signs of recovery emerged in 1921 in the housing sector, and a general upturn in business activity would follow. A recovery in industry, commerce, and trade emerged in July 1921 and would last 22 months, with the next peak occurring in May 1923. This was a period of unprecedented growth, with real business activity advancing 65.3 percent. The 1920s were an economically strong decade. Unemployment remained low. Modern economic analysis found that the actual unemployment rate during the 1920s was below the natural rate for two-thirds of the years after 1920. It was a decade where most Americans purchased automobiles, radios, telephones, and other appliances that we continue to purchase today. Productivity gains allowed people to work fewer hours, and the five-day workweek emerged in the 1920s.

The upturn was not based on government policy to promote economic activity. There was no deficit financing. Rather, there were Federal budget surpluses every year, and the government debt was gradually wound down. Sound government financial and Fed monetary policies generated business confidence.

The year 1922 would be one of marked improvement. Gains were evident in almost every branch of industry and commerce. Building contracts reached new highs and were led by investment in new industries. Stock prices advanced and credit conditions improved. The condition of the banking sector was strong.

The recovery was steady in Cycle 31, but the gains in business activity were breathtaking, especially in industry. In two years, steel production more than doubled, from 21.6 million tons in 1921 to 49.0 million tons in 1923; pig iron production increased from 16.0 million tons to 38.4 million tons in the same period. Money was easy, and a boom in construction and the automobile industries emerged. Automobile production more than doubled as well, rising from 1.5 million units in 1921 to 3.6 million in 1923. Truck production advanced from 148,000 units to 409,000 units. The automobile industry became a leading sector of the economy, forever changing American society. It would bring about the demise of the interurban trolley system. The great wave of railroad construction had clearly come to an end, and railroads began to give up branch lines, or saw their revenue slowly dwindling due to competition from the automobile in personal mobility and from trucking in goods transportation. Production of consumer durables and investment goods was a central feature of 1920s prosperity. Residential and business construction also drove the boom. Mass production was applied to industry, with the result of a decade of cost reductions and deflation. One factor in the business revival was a large spurt in applying new technologies to industry. Most notable was the electrification of industrial systems.

In 1923, American oil production reached 2.0 million barrels per day, and in 1924, natural gas production would exceed 3.0 billion cubic feet per day. Electricity generation expanded sharply, and widespread adoption and connection to electrical grids by the typical household allowed a plethora of new low-cost appliances and radios.

One factor in the upswing, as in all revivals of business activity, was an easing of the money market and expansion of bank credit. The Federal Reserve banks had reduced their rediscount rates in 1921. The New York Federal Reserve bank rate was reduced again in mid-1922. The Fed also conducted its first large-scale open market operations with a sharp increase in purchases of government securities. It would be an artificially generated expansion of bank credit, coming after four years of war and four more years of economic imbalances caused by the war.

With wage reductions, labor difficulties continued into 1922 and 1923 and included railroad, building trade, and coal strikes. A rail strike in September 1922 affected about one-half of rail traffic and was accompanied by sporadic violence. The coal strike was so severe that Ford Motor closed temporarily due to a coal shortage. To protect factories and farms, the Fordney–McCumber Tariff of 1922 (aka Tariff Act of 1922) raised American tariffs on many imported goods. Stocks and bonds reached new peaks, but labor troubles in coal and railroads were amiss, resulting in strikes.

There were further reductions in farm prices, and agriculture was under pressure. It was still an important industry (nearly as large as manufacturing in terms of value), and protective tariffs hampered exports, as the sector continued to struggle. In 1924, the sector got some relief as the Canadian wheat crop was poor, and our harvests were good. However, this relief would not last.

Figure 4.13

Automobile Production in the United States (Thousands of Units)

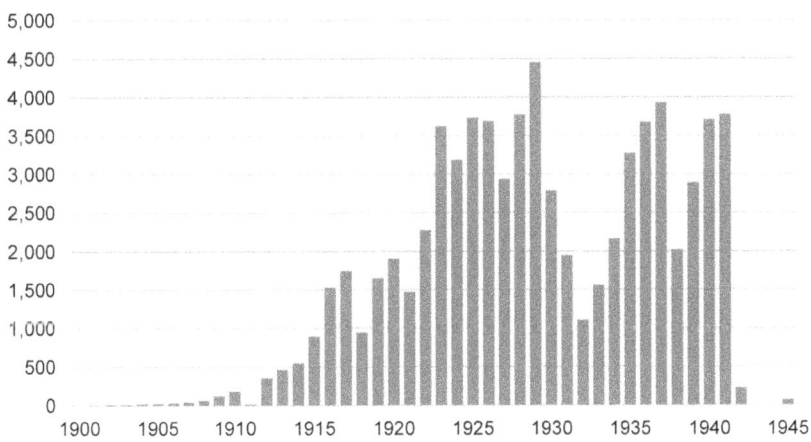

Source: Statistical Abstract of the United States

Industrial production reached new records. This was accompanied by sharp rises in many prices and corresponding expansion of bank credit, along with renewed speculation. By 1923, general increases in wages and prices emerged, and the Federal Reserve continued to sell large volumes of securities, but shortly intervened by raising discount rates.

The higher rates provided a sharp check to the rise in prices and to business activity in general. Industrial production began to recede. The downturn began in May 1923 and would last 14 months, ending in July 1924, with a 19.0 percent decline in real gross output. This 'dullness' was largely concentrated within industry. Banks liquidated over-extended loans, and industrial companies readjusted inventories. Commodity prices gradually declined, money became easier, and equity and bond prices revived, as did business activity later in the year. Although deep, the downturn was brief, and its business and financial consequences were not serious. It was largely a hiccup in what was a long period of very dynamic growth and has largely been forgotten even by students of the business cycle. Indeed, building construction reached a new record, despite 'dullness' in other sectors.

Harding created the Bureau of the Budget (now the Office of Management and Budget) and initiated the Washington Disarmament Conference of 1921-22, a first attempt at arms-control. In 1923, President Harding died and was succeeded by Vice President Calvin Coolidge. In response to the downturn, the Revenue Act of 1924, also known as the Mellon Tax Bill, cut federal tax rates, and established what would eventually be the United States Tax Court. It was the sweeping income tax reform proposed by Treasury Secretary Andrew Mellon and signed by President Coolidge, which helped the economy recover. It reduced top income tax rates from 70 percent to 25 percent, and it offset some of the ill effects of the Tariff Act of 1922. Along with efforts at controlling spending, the tax cuts would result in years of budget surpluses.

Overseas, France occupied the Ruhr and there was a severe earthquake in Japan. This cycle witnessed the collapse of the German mark.

Cycle 32: Coolidge Prosperity and the 1926-27 Recession

Also referred to as the New Era prosperity, the recovery from the mild recession ending July 1924 resulted in an upswing lasting 26 months, with real business activity rising 36.6 percent through October 1926. Money was easy, and the New York Federal Reserve reduced its bank rate. Equity and bond prices rose. A gradual rise in the second half of 1924 saw higher commodity prices and foreign trade. Prosperity quickly returned with marked expansion of business activity.

The year 1925 was a year of expansion and general prosperity. Building construction reached new highs, and there was active real estate speculation, especially in Florida. Money rates were low and aided the recovery of business.

Another anthracite coal strike occurred in 1925. The Dawes plan laid the foundation for loans to Europe (with reforms) and resulting heavy purchases in the United States was a favorable development. As a result, the year was marked by increased foreign trade, firm commodity prices, and improving equity and bond prices. Agriculture continued to lag in this economy.

The rise of consumer credit marked this decade. A rise in incomes made many more households eligible to borrow, and amidst rising prosperity, consumers took greater risks. This led to a cycle of improving incomes and credit, increasing purchases of appliances, rising production, expanding employment, and further improving incomes. The cycle witnessed a large increase in installment buying. It also witnessed the emergence of chain stores and advertising campaigns.

The upturn was the beginning of a five-year period of nearly unbroken prosperity. The nation roughly doubled the number of automobiles in operation, as well as miles of paved roads and highways. Business and financial sections of major cities were largely rebuilt, suburbs spread, and one of the greatest construction booms was underway.

Although agriculture and the textile industry remained depressed, railroad and automotive orders stimulated the steel industry. Production would rise from 41.4 million tons in 1924 to 61.7 million in 1929. Pig iron production would feature similar gains. Automobile production rose from 3.2 million units in 1924 to 4.5 million units in 1929, and truck production followed suit.

The Teapot Dome scandal was a bribery scandal involving the Harding administration from 1921 to 1923. Several of Harding's cabinet officials were involved in the scandal. President Coolidge was not connected. Prosperity was widespread. With favorable economic tailwinds, President Coolidge easily won the presidency in his own right during the presidential election of 1924, taking a majority of the popular vote against two opponents — Democrat John W. Davis and Progressive Robert La Follette — while hardly mentioning either by name.

Prosperity lasted so long and spread throughout most sectors (sans agriculture) that many business leaders, and consumers generally believed that the United States had reached a new era, in which long-standing problems in the economy were solved. Cycle 32 was a period of large speculative activity in equities and real estate. Large security offerings were placed, and a real estate boom and inflation marked 1925. Indeed, the years 1925 through 1927 would see widespread stock speculation.

In 1925-26, there was a long anthracite coal strike. The Federal Reserve continued to sell securities. The land boom in Florida was one of the greatest speculative booms in American history up to that time, but the real estate bubble finally burst, and there was uncertainty concerning its collapse. A destructive hurricane only added to the state's woes. With the increased production in California fields, oil prices collapsed. Along with the stock market, brokers' loans surged, and margin debt reached record levels by March 1926. The New York Federal Reserve increased its bank rate twice during 1926, and money became tighter. The first was followed by liquidation.

Several industries turned dull. Commencing in October 1926, the downturn lasted only 13 months, with a 38.7 percent decline in real gross output. It was largely an interlude in what was a long period of unbroken prosperity. In 1927, there were strikes in the coalfields, as well as disastrous flooding along the Mississippi, but the downswing paralleled Ford Motor's closing of its automobile plant for six months, while a model change (from Model T to Model A) was made. This involved laying off 60,000 workers and fostered ripple effects among both upstream and downstream industries. This minor downturn is considered by some economists to not be sufficiently important to be considered the end of a cycle, but I go with the NBER timing of these cycles. Wage reduction occurred, and activity in many business lines declined.

With the absence of export trade, the agricultural sector remained weak. Producers of raw materials similarly suffered.

In response to the downturn, the New York Federal Reserve lowered its bank rate. Moreover, the Federal Reserve banks made very large purchases of securities and bills. The Federal Reserve had been created to provide elasticity during a financial crisis and also to finance seasonal needs for cash. It was not created for the purpose of financing a stock market boom, which it did in much of the period from 1922 through 1928, with rediscount rates generally held below the market rate and with its newfound tool of open market purchases. The easy money stance resulted in expanding bank credit into other uses besides commerce, most notably real estate mortgages and installment finance paper. It fostered a rapid rise in stock prices.

Demand for Ford's new Model A in 1927 quickly outpaced production, leading to increased hiring, and stabilizing economic activity. The downward cycle reversed, and the brief recession of 1926-27 ended in November 1927.

Andrew Mellon was Treasury Secretary from March 1921 into February 1932. He served in three Administrations: Harding, Coolidge, and Hoover. One of his achievements was the Revenue Act of 1926, which reduced the top marginal rate to 25 percent, raised the personal exemption for federal income taxes, abolished the gift tax, reduced the estate tax rate, and repealed a provision that had required public disclosure of federal income tax returns. Instead of increasing Federal debt, tax revenues expanded in subsequent years, and with Coolidge's budget austerity, the public debt would fall over 21 percent. Moreover, productive activity would expand over 20 percent from 1925 to 1929.

Overseas, several European nations restructured their debts. Great Britain returned to the gold standard during this cycle, but at the prewar level of $4.85 per pound sterling that made British industry non-competitive. British coal strikes and a general strike marked the cycle, and the English bank rate was reduced in order to strengthen the weakened economic activity.

Cycle 33: Bull Market Boom, Stock Market Crash, and the Great Depression

Stock prices responded well to Federal Reserve purchases of government securities during 1922-27. Stock prices more than doubled, and the rising prices would feed speculation and generate a psychological boom atmosphere. This would come to define the 1920s. Excessive money fostered speculation in every field, not just the stock market. Real estate speculation was rampant.

With reduced interest rates, the New Era prosperity soon returned after November 1927, and a period of over-expansion of credit and wild speculation ensued, which led to the so-called "Bull Market Boom" of the 1920s. Some economic historians feel that the New Era prosperity of Cycle 32 and this cycle were one extended cycle. I go with the NBER timing of both as individual cycles.

All indicators of commerce, trade, and industry expanded during the upswing. Mail order catalog sales (the Amazon of the day) increased, and automobile production rose from 2.9 million units in 1927, to 3.8 million in 1928, and would peak at 4.5 million in 1929. Steel orders rose, and production would rise from 49.3 million tons in 1927 to a new peak of 61.7 million in 1929. Pig iron experienced gains of similar magnitude, and both oil and gas production rose. By 1929, overcapacity began to emerge, most notably in textiles, automobiles, and tires.

There were few major strikes during the upswing, and inflation was largely nonexistent. Government policy remained favorable. Unlike the tax reduction bills of 1921, 1924, and 1926, which focused on individual tax rates, the Tax Reduction Act of 1927 was focused on corporate taxes. In 1928, with President Coolidge declining to run for another term, Commerce Secretary (and Republican) Herbert Hoover ran, and was elected. Optimism followed the election of Hoover.

The upswing was fueled by stock market and other speculation, inflated by anticipatory buying based on hope that prices would continue to rise, a classic bubble situation. Between early 1927 and October 1929, share prices would more than double. Indeed, stock market prices rose every year between 1921 and 1929. A wider segment of the population would own shares, and stock market euphoria reached new highs. The rise in prices and lure profits caught the imagination of the American public. The New Era philosophy had a hypnotic hold on society. The boom was unprecedented, large, speculative, and unsustainable. It may have reflected confidence in growth but was clearly unsound. As in an earlier new era of 1896-1903, this boom was characterized by a great consolidation movement. The 1920s also saw the rapid growth (and multiplication) of investment trusts.

Commercial banks became more cautious through increased margin requirements and reduced loan values. To a certain extent, markets reacted and found new sources from which to draw funds. One major source was brokers' loans "for account of others."

Extensive bond issues were forthcoming, as were other security issues. The stock market speculation was also fueled by large-scale expansion of speculative credit. The Federal Reserve was concerned about the stock market boom and sought to restrain speculation, in a way that would not halt economic expansion. In a reverse of policy, the New York Federal Reserve would raise its discount rate from 3 to 5 percent, while selling government securities in 1928. In 1929, the Federal Reserve Board would warn against further expansion of credit for speculative purposes, and money rates rose. As brokers' loans further gained, the Federal Reserve would raise interest rates higher, with the discount rate reaching 6 percent by August. The upswing lasted 21 months, with real business activity peaking in August 1929, well before the stock market crash. In American business cycle history, the "real economy" often turns well before equity markets.

The long bull market in stocks was unprecedented. The Dow Jones Industrial Average increased six-fold from August 1921 to September 1929. Soon after prices peaked, Yale economist Irving Fisher proclaimed, "stock prices have reached 'what looks like a permanently high plateau.'" Although a leading contributor to economics, Fisher's quote has unfortunately and unfairly become part of his legacy. The boom ended in a bust, as booms always do. To the end, some financial leaders continued to encourage investors to purchase equities. Most notable was Charles E. Mitchell, president of the National City Bank (now Citigroup) and a director of the Federal Reserve Bank of New York.

By 1929, excessive speculation in the stock market became a problem not only for the United States but also the whole world. The rise in interest rates reversed the flow of funds between the United States and Europe, creating strains in Europe.

With higher interest rates, money tightened somewhat. Commerce, trade, and industrial activity slowed, peaked, and then began to ease. As industrial activity peaked in June, other sectors soon followed, with employment holding up until September. Bond prices had been declining for some time, and the flow of security issues turned as well. A recession was developing, and in October, equity markets reacted and would collapse severely, via the Stock

Market Crash of 1929. The avalanche of selling began on October 24th and share prices would fall 13 percent in one day. A coalition of bankers attempted to restore confidence by publicly purchasing blocks of shares at high prices. The effort failed. Investors began selling madly. Share prices plummeted. They would fall 20 percent during the next year, and by 1932 would fall (as measured by the Dow Jones Industrial Average) to under 10 percent of its 1929 peak. This resulted in a large-scale loss of confidence among business and consumers. The liquidation was prolonged and severe, resulting in little faith in the stock and banks for a generation. The 1929 high wasn't regained until 1954.

Figure 4.14
Cycle 33: Bull Market Boom, Stock Market Crash, and the Great Depression

Index of Real Gross Output where 2017 = 100

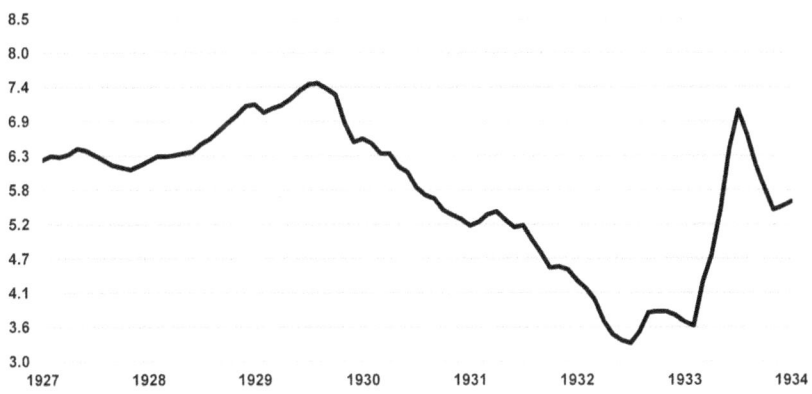

As in 1907, a bankers' committee was formed to prevent further demoralization of the market. The New York Federal Reserve purchased treasuries and lowered its discount rate first to 5 percent and then to 4½ percent. With the shock to business sentiments, the downturn gathered strength in the fall, resulting in a drastic contraction of industry. The Federal Reserve was a fairly new institution and could have alleviated the downturn with more aggressive lowering of interest rates. Instead, it kept interest rates too high, too long.

Initially, the Administration called for a conference for stabilization of industry. President Hoover insisted that businesses holdup wage and prices. In prior downswings, wages and prices adjusted quickly, resulting in a clearing of labor markets, with employment soon returning to prior levels. In this case, businesses could not afford to retain high wages. Rising and sustained unemployment was the result.

Banking panic and a collapse in the money supply took place. Industrial production, trade and commerce, employment, and prices would all fall substantially. The downturn and depression would last 43 months, nearly four years, and featured a 42.7 percent peak-to-trough decline in real gross output. It would be called the Great Depression and was the longest and deepest in American history. It was a steady and continuous decline, a long grinding descent of productive activity. The Smoot-Hawley tariff, business uncertainty, and other factors also contributed to this extremely deep depression.

In 1930, signs of slight stabilization appeared, but the Smoot-Hawley Tariff of 1930 was of enormous controversy at the time of its passage and remains one of the worst tariffs in American history. The tariff grew out of the campaign promises of Herbert Hoover during the 1928 presidential election. Smoot-Hawley raised average tariff rates from the already high rates prevailing under the Fordney-McCumber Tariff of 1922 and pushed average tariffs to over 41 percent. It was an oppressive piece of legislation. The 15-month long debate in Congress fostered considerable uncertainty, and its enactment would lead to other nations enacting protective tariffs as well, further contributing to the downswing and worsening of the depression. The depression in Europe affected American trade, as did currency devaluations and rising tariff barriers, which worsened the downturn.

Agriculture fell to its worst level since 1921. The wheat carryover had doubled in the three prior years, and the new Farm Board's action likely intensified the overhang in the following crop year. American industry was further curtailed. Uncertainty and fear caused consumers to reduce purchases of big-ticket items, like automobiles, that were typically bought with credit. Firms saw demand decline, so they slowed production and furloughed workers. Unemployment rose, and the contraction that had begun in the summer of 1929 deepened. Mail order houses cut prices, and the year 1930 would mark the start of three years of severe deflation, immensely hurting debtors and distressed banks that loaned the money. Widespread bankruptcies of non-bank companies weakened banks and hindered credit flows, resulting in many bank closures which seemed to rise as the downturn grew. During the 1920s, bank failures averaged over 588 per year, rising through mid-decade and then easing by 1928. Most of these were small, rural one-branch banks, as multi-branch banking was prohibited in much of the nation. The problems in agriculture fostered these failures, as did the collapse of the value of assets and collateral for loans. In addition, inter-state banking did not exist. Many of the banks were outside the national banking system, or if in the system, fearful of borrowing from (or discouraged by) the Fed. This resulted in a tenuous banking system, one fragile and open to widespread failure. In 1930, the number of bank failures would double to 1,352, 2,294 in 1931, and 1,446 in 1932, when the decline in business activity appeared to be reaching a trough. Among mounting bank failures in late 1930, the Bank of the United States (an unfortunate name for a bank) failed, and there were widespread bank runs. Several Wall Street stock exchange houses failed. The New York Federal Reserve would reduce rates to 2 percent, but despite low money rates, credit was tight, extremely tight. Bank failures mounted, and in 1933, amid a banking crisis, 4,004 would fail. During these four years, the number of banks (again mostly small) was reduced by over 42 percent. The losses to depositors were large, and the effect on those borrowing from the banks was important as well.

Unlike previous crises, moreover, there was a failure of cooperation in Wall Street and between government and finance. Clearinghouses had worked in prior crises but were not pursued in this one. There was also a failure between London, Paris, and New York. The collapse of Credit-Anstalt in 1931 brought about growing difficulties in Austria and Germany. There was an unsuccessful international effort at containing the emerging contagion. France delayed too long, and the pressure on banks in Germany increased. Great Britain abandoned the gold standard, as did other nations. A foreign run on the gold of the United States occurred. The crisis was international.

Bank credit evaporated during 1931-32. With the liquidation of bank credit, many interior banks were unable to lend to good customers. There were severe losses on security loans and on real estate loans. Depositors were fearful of individual banks and began to take cash out of the banks and hoard it. This exacerbated the situation and would result in a number of bank runs.

The collapse of borrowing and the fall in the value of assets taken as collateral by the banks creates losses for the banks, who seek to contain such losses. Banks are thus forced to contract credit, call-in loans, or suspend operations. This forces their customers (and others) to contract investment and curtail (or suspend) operations. In turn, this reduces the demand for their suppliers, and so on. Bank failures provide a mechanism that amplifies a downturn and makes it widespread. This is precisely what happened after 1929.

Agricultural prices fell by half by 1932, and a general deflation arose. Consumer prices were stable in 1929 and fell 2.3 percent in 1930, accelerating to a 9.0 percent decline in 1931, a 9.9 percent decline in 1932, and a 5.1 percent decline in 1933. Deflation hurts debtors and adds to bank, business, and consumer failures.

In 1930, total rail track mileage operated by railroads would reach a peak and then begin a long-term decline, as automobiles and trucking (and later air travel) would capture market share away from railroads in both passenger and freight markets. The downturn was most severe among the industrial sectors, especially durable goods. Automobile production would fall from 4.5 million units in 1929, to 2.8 million in 1930, 1.9 million in 1931, and would bottom out at 1.1 million in 1932, before rebounding to 1.6 million in 1933. Truck production followed a similar downward path. Steel production fell from 61.7 million tons in 1929 to a low of 15.1 million tons in 1932, before rebounding in 1933. Pig iron followed suit. Oil and gas production eased. Housing activity collapsed, and there was a steep fall in business investment and commercial construction. Indeed, business investment would fall to essentially zero by 1933, as business confidence buckled.

Unemployment was the most obvious symptom of the depression. The unemployment rate rose from 3.2 percent during 1929, to 5.9 percent in 1930, 22.7 percent in 1932 and averaged 23.4 percent in 1933, affecting about one in every four workers. As in other downturns, unemployment was concentrated among producers of goods, especially durable goods. As the depression deepened, more people became homeless, resulting in shanty towns that were soon called "Hoovervilles." Social unrest mounted, resulting in the Veterans' Bonus Expeditionary Force marching on Washington to demand early bonus payments. Encamped in the Anacostia Flats, it was dispersed by force.

Fiscal policy was expansionary during the first two years of the depression as government expenditures for goods and services continued to rise. However, fiscal policy was also contractionary, as taxes increased relative to economic output. The increase in tariff rates only added to this. As an emergency measure, the Reconstruction Finance Corporation (RFC) was created to prop up banks, life insurance companies, savings and loans, farm-mortgage associations, and railroads. The measure enjoyed limited success. In 1932, the Emergency Relief Act provided loans to states and for public works. The year also saw the passage of the first Glass-Steagall Act, which authorized the substitution of government securities for commercial paper as collateral for Federal Reserve notes and also permitted the Federal Reserve to resume purchases of government securities.

The Democrats would gain further strength in both houses of Congress during the 1930 mid-term elections. For the 1932 presidential election, both parties actually adopted conservative economic platforms. In mid-1932 stock prices, farm prices, and industrial production rallied. Still, the tide turned once again for the worse.

The state of the economy and nation was so bad that the Democrats took all of Congress in 1932. The downturn associated with the Great Depression would come to an end in March 1933, the month of the bank crisis and the start of a new administration, as New York's Democratic governor Franklin D. Roosevelt (FDR) had won the 1932 election in a landslide, after promising a New Deal. The downturn would be extended due to the long delay between the election and the start of the new administration. There was failure of cooperation between President-elect Roosevelt and President Hoover, which worsened the situation. Rumors that the incoming administration was going to take the nation off the gold standard contributed further to hoarding and worsened the banking situation. Efforts to persuade the president-elect to deny these rumors were unsuccessful. The government was largely paralyzed during this period.

Improving expectations due to a new administration, however, were a key factor at the trough. A renewed "run" on banks occurred in January 1933, and the move to restrict or suspend banks (i.e., bank holiday) moved rapidly. The four interim months saw the Depression reach its worst depths, and by inauguration day, four-fifths of the banks were closed. As banks began failing in large numbers in early 1933, President Hoover drafted an emergency banking bill.

This was ignored by Congress. Five days after the March 4th inauguration, Congress passed the Emergency Banking Act of 1933. It included almost identical language to Hoover's bill. With a new Administration and new hope, the recovery began in 1933.

In 1922, the number of U.S. banks peaked at 30,736, and as late as 1928 there were 26,401 banks. The 1920s depression in agriculture had particularly affected rural banks. With the Great Depression, the number fell to 14,771 banks in 1933.

The new administration started with virtually every bank in the nation closed. The control of the banking situation passed from the banks and the Federal Reserve to Washington. The Great Depression marked a sea of change on how government policy dealt with downswings. Previously, government policy response was minimal and fearful that public support in the form of transfer payment would foster idleness or be used to buy votes by big-city political machines. During the 19th century, a wide variety of civic, religious, and other leaders formed voluntary (and usually local) groups to take the lead in providing relief. The Great Depression overwhelmed many of these efforts, and the underlying progressivism of the Roosevelt Administration resulted in a large-scale expansion of government involvement. From this time, with each subsequent downturn, the government generally took on a more active and primary role, and voluntary organizations, a secondary role.

In addition, social priorities would change in the United States. Price and economic stability based on hard currency took second place, as employment and economic revival took first place.

The Great Depression was truly international in scope. It was nearly universal. Many nations retaliated against Smooth-Hawley, but the financial contagion spread, leading to bank failures across developed nations and widespread political and social unrest. Great Britain abandoned the gold standard in 1931, as did many other nations. The Great Depression would take unemployment to over 15 percent in Great Britain. The depression was severe in France and in Germany. In Germany, it would lead to the rise of Adolph Hitler and the Nazi party.

Cycle 34: Slow Recovery, Experimentation, and FDR's Depression

A trough in the business cycle was reached at the same time the new administration started. The nation was tired of the three-and-a-half-year depression and was ready for change. New hope was in the air. The reopening of the banks was handled well by the new administration. Hoarded money poured into the banks, as the banks that were reopened were believed to be sound. The panic was over.

Early on, beer production was relegalized. Breweries reopened, upgraded capital, hired workers, and purchased barley malt, kegs, glass bottles, and delivery trucks. In a similar manner, other industries began the step towards recovery. The recovery began in March 1933 and would last 50 months, with real gross output improving 63.9 percent through May 1937, the next business cycle peak. The previous peak of business activity, however, would not be reached in this upswing. It would be reached in September 1939. Some observers look at the 1930s as being one entire downturn. As always, I go with the NBER timing of business cycles. The 1929 peak would not be reached until late-1939, as war preparations were underway.

Much has been written about President's Roosevelt's first one hundred days and the New Deal. The banking holiday and the introduction of deposit insurance to strengthen banks would bring the wave of bank failures to an end. Some 4,004 banks would fail in 1933. Despite some change in reporting for the statistics collected, only 448 banks would fail during 1934-1940. This was the major factor in ending the Great Depression. World trade and U.S. exports bottomed out in 1933 and began a slow recovery, as did business investment. That being said, recovery was still painstakingly slow.

With a slow and uneven recovery, unemployment remained a problem. After reaching a peak of 23.4 percent in 1933, the unemployment rate stubbornly and slowly moved down, reaching 19.1 percent in 1934, 17.6 percent in 1935, 14.2 percent in 1936, and 12.2 percent in 1937.

Figure 4.15
Cycle 34: Slow Recovery, Experimentation, and FDR's Depression
Index of Real Gross Output where 2017 = 100

During the first 100 days of the Roosevelt Administration, the Banking Act of 1933 was passed and signed into law. It created the Federal Deposit Insurance Corporation (FIDC) to insure bank deposits as a way of reassuring depositors and preventing banks runs and panics. The Glass-Steagall Act separated commercial banking and investment banking. It limited the underwriting of bonds by commercial banks and forbade loans by banks to its own officers. The Securities Act of 1933 required that investors receive financial and other significant information concerning securities being offered for public sale and prohibited deceit, misrepresentations, and other fraud in the sale of securities.

The Securities Exchange Act of 1934 created the Securities and Exchange Commission (SEC), which was given broad authority over all aspects of the securities industry. This includes the power to register, regulate, and oversee brokerage firms, transfer agents, and clearing agencies, as well as the nation's various securities exchanges. The Banking Act of 1935 restructured the Federal Reserve and its relationship with the Treasury and Comptroller of the Currency.

Other New Deal measures followed. The Civilian Conservation Corps was created to supply jobs to some three million young men. The Civil Works Administration would employ another four million to build bridges, roads and schools, and the Works Progress Administration (WPA) would build other public works.

The National Industrial Recovery Act (NIRA) would create the National Recovery Administration (NRA) and authorize industrial and trade associations to establish codes, fix prices and wages, and restrict production. Industries most enthusiastic with the idea were largely those seeking to preserve the high tariffs. Labor unions saw an opportunity to seek a shorter work week and enforce minimum wages. This legislation would delay the price and other market adjustments needed for recovery and would feature limited success before being ruled unconstitutional in 1935. In essence, this government agency took over the private sector through management oversight. This was precisely what Adam Smith argued against in 1776. The NRA led to a multiplication of new rules for business, resting not on law, but on arbitrary decisions of administrative bodies, which were subject to change. It did not lead to economic recovery as expected and likely pushed recovery back further, due to the distortions it created. A failure, the burden of the NRA fell hardest on small business and on machinery and other capital goods industries. It fell hardest on the South, as well as on Blacks. In the 1920s, the Black unemployment rate was actually lower than that for Whites. This was at a time when Jim Crow laws were at their worst, and the Ku Klux Klan at its height of power. Starting in the 1930s the Black unemployment rate would consistently exceed (to the present) that for Whites.

The Agricultural Adjustment Administration (AAA) sought to control agricultural prices by impeding farm output. The Tennessee

Valley Authority (TVA) was created to develop a major impoverished region. The National Labor Relations Act (NLRA) gave workers the ability to join a union and for collective bargaining. It created the National Labor Relations Board (NLRB) to supervise union elections (and certify them) and investigate unfair employer practices. The Social Security Act of 1935 created the Social Security program, as well as insurance against unemployment. The Revenue Act of 1935 raised taxes on incomes over $50,000 (about one million dollars in today dollars) and raised corporate, estate, and gift taxes. Other New Deal measures — too many to mention — were enacted. Although some measures were good and necessary, in the aggregate, price fixing and government largesse lengthened the Great Depression by creating tax and regulatory burdens on the economy while fostering uncertainty.

In April 1933, President Roosevelt abandoned the gold standard. There was no pressure nor shortness of gold. The abandonment represented bad faith on the part of the government. It became unlawful to own or hold gold coins, gold bullion, or gold certificates. By the end of the year, the administration would embark on a new program for the control of commodity prices by varying the purity of gold. The US dollar was effectively devalued. The Gold Reserve Act of 1934 put this into law. Silver interests saw their opportunity, and the Silver Purchase Act of 1934 was passed and signed into law. It authorized purchases of silver at home and abroad and permitted Treasury to issue silver certificates. It would lead to a major crisis in China, which was on a silver standard. In 1935, the Supreme Court would uphold the abrogation of gold clauses in private contracts. This added to uncertainty in business and finance.

This plethora of "bold persistent experimentation" of regulatory and other measures under the New Deal often changed the operating environment for business, frequently in conflicting ways and regularly reversed. This makes for "regime uncertainty" and challenges in business planning. This put a damper on business.

The New Deal would have unintended consequences. Added to this were proposals to punish the wealthy with the Wealth Tax of 1935 and a move to tax retained corporate earnings in 1936, while the president continued to rail against businessmen. The Administration, at times, seemed to relish intimidating business. The Labor Relations Act of 1935, better known as the Wagner Act, altered the balance of power in American labor relations by giving labor new bargaining leverage.

Moreover, tax policy would work against recovery. During the Coolidge Administration, the top tax rate was 25 percent. Under Presidents Hoover and Roosevelt, it would rise to the 60 percent and then the 80 percent range. By 1934, American tax rates were the highest in the world. The New Deal tax policy was more concerned with redistribution than with raising revenue. Moreover, Louisiana Senator Long's "Share the Wealth" program pushed the senator onto the national scene. The potential for a 1936 challenge for the nomination frightened the Administration and rises in income tax rate were proposed. Although an inheritance tax was rejected, the Revenue Act of 1935 did raise estate and income taxes radically. Combined state and local taxes (New York being the highest) raised the estate tax to 72 percent and the federal income tax to 83 percent. The Act was popularly known as the "Soak the Rich" tax. These dangerously high rates dampen entrepreneurship. The Undistributed Profits Tax of 1936 was designed to force the distribution of corporate profits by dividends. The law in particular affected capital-intensive industries. All of this dampened business confidence and investment.

The recovery from the Great Depression would be weak and uneven, the result of the inconsistent, changing, and sometimes vindictive policy and the uncertainty it fostered among the business community and consumers as well. All of the various tax, industrial, agricultural, trade, monetary and other measures, many of which were contradictory, weighed on business. Adding to this was the utterances by the president that were hostile to business. Business confidence was low, investment lagged, and many measures of economic activity would not be reached until the 1940s.

After the U.S. Supreme Court in the famous *Schechter* case, ruled in 1935 the National Industrial Recovery Act (NIRA) was unconstitutional, the stock market rose and was followed by business activity improving at a steady expanding pace. Production of capital and durable goods moved upward, and capital spending plans began to be made.

The Administration shifted to focusing on social issues and in 1936, President Roosevelt was re-elected. However, political developments would emerge that were antithetical to business and financial confidence. During the presidential election, Republican candidate Governor Alfred Landon of Kansas made a speech that was interpreted as favoring a higher protective tariff. The Undistributed Profits Tax of 1936 was passed and signed into law. It was designed to force the distribution of corporate profits by dividends. In 1937, the president would attempt to pack the Supreme Court. By 1937, the Wagner Act had resulted in large-scale unionization efforts and in a series of strikes, most notably in Detroit and Cleveland.

Steel production would rise from 15.1 million tons in 1932 to 25.7 million in 1933, 29.2 million in 1934, 38.2 million in 1935, and 53.5 million in 1936, a level still off from 1929. Pig iron shipments followed a similar pattern. Automobiles were emerging as the leading industry, and factory sales would nearly quadruple from 1.1 million in 1932 to 3.9 million in 1937, a new record, despite a large strike that year. Oil production bottomed out in 1932 as well and would exceed 3.0 million barrels per day for the first time in 1936, rising even further throughout this cycle. Natural gas production would feature a similar pattern.

The stock market crashed in late 1937. Businesses blamed the New Deal series of government-financed infrastructure work projects and uncertainty. The Administration blamed a "capital strike" (lack of investment) on the part of businesses, while New Dealers blamed cuts in program funding. The sources of the downturn were clearly domestic, as no other major nation experienced a recession. Monetary policy was tightened, as banks had accumulated large excess reserves, and the Federal Reserve viewed these as inflationary. Indeed, inflation as measured by consumer prices, more than doubled from 1.5 percent in 1936 to 3.1 percent in 1937. To reduce the risk of inflation, the Fed increased reserve requirements in August 1936 and announced further increases in 1937. The banks were largely holding excess reserves as a precaution against possible bank panics and runs. The increase in reserve requirements caused the money stock to contract and security yields to increase. In addition, the Federal Reserve raised margin requirements to a high level.

Fiscal policy was more restrictive. Higher taxes from the Revenue Act of 1935 hit those higher-income households who supply savings, and thus capital, needed for investment and economic growth. An excess profits tax was imposed in mid-1936, which led to reduced business investment. The Social Security payroll taxes on employers rose from one percent in 1936 to three percent in 1937, and veterans' bonus payments that started in mid-1936 ended in 1937. An attempt was made to balance the budget after the New Deal spending. Another factor was diminished profits and policy uncertainty, which along with higher payroll costs (from Social Security taxes) and union inroads in key industries, affected productivity and increased costs that outpaced selling prices. As a result, firms cut back on their plans for business investment. Business leaders avoided long-term commitments of capital. The year 1937 was marked by major and violent strikes at Ford Motor, Republic Steel, and other industrial firms. Thus, the upswing would be cut short by a recession during 1937-38.

Preceded by a violent break in the stock market, the downturn was one of the worst in American business cycle history. It was short, lasting 13 months, but real business activity would fall 28.4 percent between May 1937 (the peak) and June 1938 (the trough). The number of unemployed doubled during the downturn. The winter of 1937-38 was particularly bleak. It was referred to as the Depression of 1936-37, or as Roosevelt's Depression. Unemployment would rise from 12.2 percent in 1937 to 18.4 percent in 1938 and would remain above 10 percent through 1941. Steel production would fall from 56.6 million tons in 1937 to 31.8 million the next year. Pig iron and automobile production would fall as well, and oil and gas production output eased. The Undistributed Profits Tax was repealed early in 1938, which aided recovery of business investment, but it would be increased military production leading up to World War II during 1938-1940 that spurred economic recovery.

The downturn resulted in Republican gains in Congress during the mid-term elections of 1938. Beginning with that election, there was clear evidence for an ebbing tide for the Democrats and for the New Deal. The 1937-38 downturn would mark the last of the New Deal legislation. The Wages and Hours Act, also known as the Fair Labor Standards Act, was the first act in the United States prescribing nationwide compulsory federal regulation of wages and hours. The law, applying to all industries engaged in interstate commerce, established a minimum wage of 25 cents per hour for the first year, to be increased to 40 cents within seven years.

The New Deal was viewed as an economic policy to promote employment, and the historic and statistical records show that it was a failure. The unemployment rate in 1940 averaged 14 percent. Through excessive regulation and taxation, New Deal policies slowed technological progress when it hindered business investment. By the onset of World War II, the American capital stock had grown obsolete. For example, the *American Machinist* reported that 70 percent of the nation's metal working equipment was older than 10 years in 1940. A large body of technological knowledge (e.g., television) was not taken up, there was unused capacity in labor (as measured by unemployment), and there was still a great amount of idle capital. There was considerable slack heading into the imminent war.

The two downturns associated with the 1930s were so severe and widespread that economists stopped using the term depression to describe downturns and switched to using the word recession. During this cycle in 1936, noted British economist John Maynard Keynes would publish *The General Theory of Employment, Interest, and Money*, which sought to provide a reason for prolonged unemployment and supported a remedy for recession based on more active government policy.

The Great Depression had seen the rise of economic nationalism, the "beggar thy neighbor" trade policies of the 1930s. The international situation in the second half of the 1930s turned worse. The rise of Mussolini and fascism in the 1920s, along with the Great Depression, would lead to the rise of Hitler and National Socialism in Germany. A breakdown in international cooperation resulted. Italy's 1935 invasion of Ethiopia exhibited the weakness of Great Britain and France. Although the latter would begin rearmament programs, these were slow, and that weakness emboldened Hitler and Germany, the latter still smarting over the provisions of the peace treaty after the World War decades earlier. Hitler reoccupied the Rhineland without opposition in 1936, and the Berlin-Rome Axis was formed. The latter would be joined by Tokyo. In Asia, an increasingly aggressive Japan would invade China. In 1936, Hitler began mass production of military planes, some of which were used in the Spanish Civil War. At the same time, pacifism was the norm among the peoples and governments of Great Britain, France, and the United States. Appeasement seemed to be the order of the day. In 1938, Hitler invaded and annexed Austria. Czechoslovakia would be next, and in 1939 Hitler made demands on Poland. The inevitable war began on September 1st and would define the next cycle. America was unprepared.

Cycle 35: War Prosperity and Transition to a Consumer Economy

The upswing began in June 1938, before the mid-term congressional elections. Activity would be propelled by increased production of military goods. The 1929 peak of real business activity would finally be met (September 1939) in this upswing. Recovery and expansion would last 80 months, with real gross output rising 147.2 percent during the upswing. This would be the longest upswing in American business cycle history to date, just beating the previous record of 79 months during Cycle 1.

The upswing was preceded by a rise in the stock markets in 1939 and in 1940 by improving Republican prospects for the congressional elections. It was further aided by Republican gain in the election. In 1940, President Roosevelt ran for a third term and was re-elected, primarily as people were afraid to "swap horses" in the midst of a deteriorating world situation. His Republican opponent Wendell L. Willkie, an attorney and corporate executive, also ran an ineffective campaign.

The Great Depression would continue to define the economy early on in this cycle, but the transition to war would characterize 1940 and 1941. During the interwar years, the American people were disillusioned by the World War and were against war and militarism in general, as well as manufacturers of arms and munitions, the so-called "merchants of death." Senate hearings were held on the subject, and a series of Neutrality Acts was passed in the 1930s. Public opinion was for neutrality, so the nation was unprepared for what was to come. Germany's conquest of France left Great Britain with inadequate financial resources, and with the push of the Roosevelt Administration, the American Lend-Lease System provided support.

Attitude towards rearmament changed in 1940 due to events in Europe, and the nation began to rearm. Changes in procurement (cost-plus and negotiated payments), changes in tax law, and government financing of investment in plants and equipment fostered a build-up. The Defense Plant Corporation (DPC) would play a very large role, building plants and leasing them to industries. The DPC would own over 90 percent of synthetic rubber and magnesium capacity, over 70 percent of aircraft capacity, and nearly 60 percent of aluminum capacity. The industries in the lease contracts were given the option of buying the plant and equipment once the war was over. Other government corporations — Reconstruction Finance Corporation, War Shipping Administration, Defense Supply Corporation, Metals Reserve Company, and Rubber Reserve Company — funded expansion elsewhere. The Home Owners Loans Corporation, Federal Land Banks, and United States Maritime Commission were also involved.

To prepare for war, the president enlisted the help of business leaders for a variety of mobilization committees, boards, and agencies. Within two years, more than 10,000 business leaders would be recruited into positions in the federal government. The focus of these leaders was on cutting the "red tape" and getting the job done. This would lead to the building of the "arsenal of democracy" and a strong upswing in business activity, as war production skyrocketed.

Although the government focused on winning the war, the administration did see it as a means of furthering its New Deal program of redistributing wealth. An attempt was made to limit incomes to $25,000. It failed. The administration resisted changes to New Deal legislation which would have boosted efficiency. The WPA, for example, continued until 1943, after 11 million had been conscripted. The 40-hour workweek was maintained. Price controls were imposed in 1941 and 1942, and they would not be abandoned until 1946. Government pressure for unionization continued.

The upswing would see an easing of unemployment, from 16.4 percent in 1939 to 14.0 percent in 1940, and 10.9 percent in 1941. After Pearl Harbor and the declaration of war, a war-command economy emerged amid patriotic fervor. With the draft pulling in more than 12 million potential workers into the armed forces, as well as large gains in draft-exempt employment, unemployment virtually disappeared, with the unemployment rate falling to 1.3 percent during 1944. Labor force participation rose sharply for women, teenagers, and older Americans.

Figure 4.16

Cycle 35: War Prosperity and Transition to a Consumer Economy
Index of Real Gross Output where 2017 = 100

After falling during the second half of the 1930s, stock prices actually bottomed during April 1942, just before America's victory over Japan in the Battle of Midway. A bull market emerged, with prices soaring 158 percent through mid-1946.

Everyone that desired to work was working. Due to price controls and rationing, conditions for consumers were actually much worse than the official data suggests. Workers worked harder and longer hours, often at inconvenient times, and with greater physical risk. Shortages and other inconveniences were the norm, and real consumer spending would fall during the war. Still, national solidarity was sustained. Workers faced unprecedented earnings and were able to save and build up household balances. That said, there were labor difficulties during the war. Union membership had grown through the 1930s and World War II, peaking at almost a third of the nation's workforce by 1946. A major coal strike occurred in 1942 in what was one of the coldest winters on record. Despite organized labor's no-strike pledge during the war, production workdays were lost due to illegal wildcat strikes that occurred in subsequent years.

During the war, the U.S. government largely displaced private sector business investment. Expansion of war production facilities was equivalent to over 55 percent of capital formation. Investment went towards aircraft, shipbuilding, chemicals, iron and steel, aluminum, and other non-ferrous metals, machine tools and other machinery, electrical equipment, petroleum products, military and other vehicles, and of course, munitions. It was one of the largest expansions of capital investment in history, but because of the dearth of investment in the private sector, private capital stock actually fell. As would be expected, not all of government investment was efficient, and large-scale waste occurred.

Automobile production would fall from 3.78 million in 1941 to only about one thousand vehicles during 1943 and 1944. Truck production would average about 800,000 units per year for the duration, but both gave way to the massive gains in ship, tank, aircraft, and other armament production that would characterize the war years. Military aircraft production would rise from 1,800 planes in 1938 to over 95,000 in 1944. Merchant vessels completed would rise from 24 (181,000 gross tons) in 1938 to 1,661 (12.5 million tons) in 1944. The so-called Liberty ship was a class of cargo ship built in the United States during World War II. Adopted for its simple, low-cost construction, these ships were mass-produced on an unprecedented scale, and came to symbolize U.S. wartime industrial output.

War production was extensive. Krug (1945) reported that over 295,000 aircraft, 64,000 landing vessels, 6,500 other naval ships, 5,400 cargo ships, 86,000 tanks, 315,000 pieces of field artillery and mortars, 17.4 million rifles and other firearms, 41.4 billion rounds of ammunition, and other munitions were produced.

The war effort would pull other industries along. Steel production, for example, would more than double from 31.8 million tons in 1938 to 89.6 million tons in 1944, and with victory in sight, would ease to 79.7 million in 1945. Oil production would rise from 3.3 million BPD (barrels per day) in 1938 to 4.7 million BPD in 1945.

Federal employment would rise from 1.0 million in 1940 to 3.5 million in 1945. Increases in national military expenditures resulted in taxation changes. The first Revenue Act of 1940 provided slight increases in a surtax on the higher income brackets, and a second Revenue Act of 1940 provided for an excess profits tax for corporations. The Current Tax Payment Act of 1943 introduced withholding taxes on individuals. Tax rates on higher incomes would reach 91 percent.

In World War II, greater reliance was made on short-term borrowing, with heavy borrowing from commercial banks and the Federal Reserve banks. The debt was largely unfunded and was aided by artificial manipulation of interest rates by the Federal Reserve. This would crowd out private business investment, and the government began making working capital advances to industries scaling-up for production. Commercial banks could lend to the government without limits, and the government would use these monies in financing war industries. Price fixing was done by the Office of Price Administration (OPA) and was relied upon more than in World War I.

Beginning in 1942, the Federal Reserve helped the U.S. Treasury to finance war debt by pegging interest rates on short-term Treasury bills (T-bills) at a fixed interest rate and capping rates on longer-term Treasury securities. This "yield curve control" would last in one form or another, until the Treasury–Federal Reserve Accord in 1951.

In 1944, at Bretton Woods, New Hampshire, the Allies met to discuss and lay out a plan for the post-war global economic regime. The United States would exchange dollars for gold at a rate of $35 per ounce. Making the dollar convertible into gold and pegging the other currencies to dollars at a fixed rate was meant to provide stability into international trade and commerce. The hope was to avoid the competitive currency depreciations and rampant tariff increases that had worsened the Great Depression in the 1930s and helped to precipitate World War II. Bretton Woods would lead to the creation of the International Monetary Fund (IMF) and the International Bank for Reconstruction and Development (IBRD), commonly known as the World Bank. The former was to be concerned with limiting variation in exchange rates, and the latter was to be primarily an investment institution. This gold exchange standard would characterize economic progress until the 1970s.

In 1944, President Roosevelt ran for an unprecedented fourth term and was re-elected. Also, it was apparent that the Allies would be victorious, and as a result, production of armaments and munitions began to ease. War production was ramped down and would virtually cease. Real gross output would peak in February 1945. Unions began to reassert themselves, and with partial lifting of restrictions, minimum wages would rise. In addition, credit was tight. The inevitable post-war downturn would last eight months, with business activity falling 16.4 percent from its peak by October. That said, the foundations for real prosperity had been laid and would soon return. The unemployment rate was largely unaffected as demobilization occurred, and a transition to a peacetime economy proceeded. Various policies enacted to aid returning servicemen helped spur the automobile and housing markets, helping to end the downturn.

The period reflected little Federal Reserve independence, which had an agreement with Treasury. The main function was to foster low interest rates to service the large Treasury debt incurred during the war. There was explosive growth in the monetary base and a tripling of the Federal Reserve's balance sheet from 1942 to 1945. Combined with supply-demand imbalances (e.g., little consumer durables production relative to demand), and large household savings, money growth would result in an explosive rise of inflation after the war. It would take several years after the war for the Fed to achieve independence.

This cycle ended with the death of President Roosevelt in April 1945. He was succeeded by Vice President Harry S. Truman, who had been on the job less than three months. Truman would lead through the end of the war.

CHAPTER 5

Post-World War II to the Present

"Long distances used to be a moat that both insulated and isolated people from workers on the other side of the world. But every day, technology narrows that moat inch by inch. Every person in the world is on the verge of becoming both a coworker and a competitor to every one of us ... Technological change is going to reach out and sooner or later change something fundamental in your business world."

—Andy Grove

Introduction

In a war-devastated world, the United States at the end of 1945 was the sole great power survivor, accounting for nearly half of the world's manufacturing. The system of war-time controls was gradually abandoned as the economy moved to a peace-time footing. The controls, however, were retained longer than after World War I, likely to block another speculative boom and post-war recession.

This period would be marked by continued expansion of population, from 140 million in 1945 to 330 million in 2020. After 1965, the composition of immigration would change, with fewer entrants from Europe, and more from Latin America and Asia.

The post-World War II period was marked by increasing government involvement in the economy from both a fiscal and regulatory perspective. It also marked a robust, modern consumer-oriented economy, with post-war cycles featuring a more active role of consumer spending.

At war's end, the United States was the preeminent economy. Talk of an "American Century" was common. Through the mid-1960s, the economy experienced relatively stable economic growth (with intermittent downturns) with minimal inflation. The economic environment was favorable.

This period is noted by the link between the state of the housing market and the health of the wider economy. During the post-World War II period, residential investment represented a small share of GDP (about 4.6 percent on average), but it has typically varied more wildly than other sectors. Moreover, falling residential investment typically acted as an early-warning indicator, accounting for about a quarter of output shortfalls on the eve of a recession. The housing market has generally been both a reliable predictor of downturns and frequently a cause of recessions. Significant housing troubles likely preceded nine of the 12 recessions since the end of World War II.

The Federal Reserve started this period with an agreement with the Treasury to peg interest rates and not pursue monetary control. Gradually the Fed would achieve independence. The Federal Reserve's involvement in response to financial panics and economic downturns also heightened through this period. The year 1946 would mark the start of a second bear bond market that would last until 1981. As an active tool, monetary was generally subordinate to fiscal policy in the period up to the 1980s.

In 1946, Congress passed the Employment Act of 1946, requiring the federal government "to promote maximum employment, production and purchasing power." For a period in the 1950s and into the mid-1960s, full employment and economic growth appeared to be possible but would be tested in the 1970s by inflation and a stagnating economy.

In 1977, Congress amended the Federal Reserve Act, directing the Federal Reserve to "increase production, so as to promote effectively the goals of maximum employment, stable prices and moderate long-term interest rates." In response to the inflation of the 1970s and mid-decade recession, the Full Employment and Balanced Growth Act of 1978 (commonly referred to as the "Humphrey-Hawkins Act") was passed, making the federal government responsible for achieving full employment and price stability, among other goals. The first two — maximum sustainable employment and price stability — are commonly referred to as the Fed's "dual mandate." This legislation would have profound effects during this period.

Unlike the years prior to World War II, business cycles in the post-war period became increasingly influenced by economic policy measures, as policymakers attempted to stabilize and "fine-tune" the economy. Post-war policy, especially during the 1950s and 1960s, can be characterized as one of Keynesian demand management, with a focus on full employment as the trauma of the 1930s influenced priorities. Indeed, these two decades would be the high watermark of a Keynesian approach to fiscal policy. Stabilization policies moved into the mainstream, and by the late-1960s, many economists began to think that the business cycle could be eliminated. However, a key question followed: was did demand management policies end up stabilizing or destabilizing the economy?

The 1940s through 1980s witnessed the Cold War, which can be dated to 1947, when Soviet representatives walked out of a conference that would result in the Marshall Plan. This was followed by the takeover of many Eastern European governments in 1948, the Berlin crisis in 1948, the communist takeover of China in 1949, and a Soviet nuclear test. These developments would lead to the formation of NATO in 1949. Geopolitical tensions and uncertainty were in the background. The Cold War would occasionally erupt in hostilities, including the Korean War (1950-53) and the Vietnam War (1964-75).

The international currency regime for the post-war period until the early 1970s was one of fixed but adjustable exchange rates, as envisioned under the Bretton Woods agreement. The gold exchange policy for the dollar provided the foundation for post-war growth. The International Monetary Fund (IMF) would play a large role in this currency regime.

Figure 5.1
Real Gross Output of the United States: 1940-1923
Index of Real Gross Output where 2017 = 100

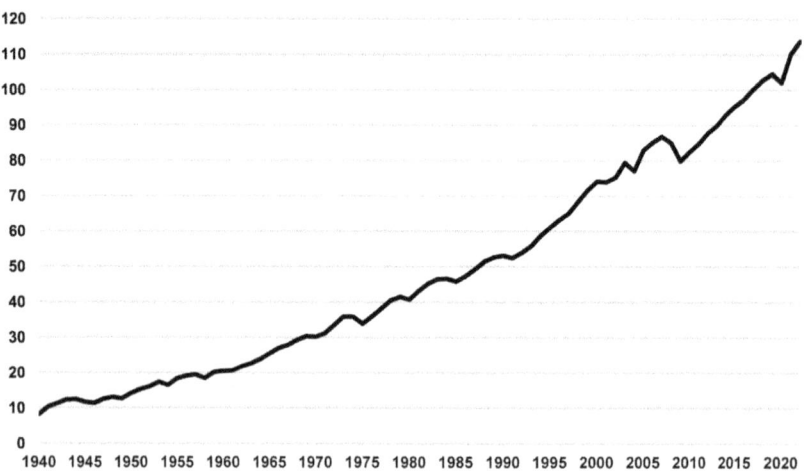

The "beggar-thy-neighbor" trade policies of the 1930s worsened the Great Depression for most nations. The idea that more open markets promote innovation, competition, and growth took hold after the war, and nations pursued them, first in the General Agreement on Tariffs and Trade (GATT), founded in 1948, and then after the GATT was transformed into the World Trade Organization (WTO) in 1995. This rules-based system (and its international institutions) contributed to post-war prosperity.

For the early post-war period to the early-1960s, business cycles were relatively short. Business and consumer optimism would be a feature of this early period. In addition, the presence of automatic stabilizers (progressive income tax rates, unemployment compensation, deposit insurance, social welfare programs, etc.) were credited by economists for recessions being milder. A secular rise in inflation and unemployment would mark this early period.

The annals of American commerce and industry (and the data on real gross output) from World War II to the present include five major downswings which developed in the following years, namely 1957, 1973, 1981, 2007, and 2020. The elapsed time between the major downswings averaged 13 years. Minor downswings occurred in 1945, 1948, 1953, 1960, 1969, 1980, 1990, and 2001.

As John Calverley has pointed out, the nine- to 10-year business cycle pattern first observed by Clement Juglar and confirmed by Joseph Schumpeter, broke down in the 1950s likely because of stop-go fiscal policy. It also broke down in the 1970s when the massive oil shock of 1974 upset the pattern. Excluding these two decades, some of the upswings during the period were the longest in American business cycle history, with particularly long upswings in the 1960s, 1980s, 1990s, and 2010s.

Beyond business cycles, this was an important period for the United States. The 1940s witnessed a devastating world war. Peace largely reigned, providing opportunities to focus on domestic problems. As an "unfinished nation" the Civil Rights era and its accomplishments cemented the ideals of the American Revolution.

Cycle 36: Transition to Consumer Economy and Brief Recession of 1949

The consensus among economists was that the expansion of activity during the war was temporary, and that the economy would quickly return to the depressed and deflationary conditions of the 1930s once demobilization occurred, as millions of returning servicemen would face massive unemployment. This turned out to be a false scenario. Accumulated savings by households during the war, along with pent-up demand for all kinds of goods that were not available during the war years, would lead to economic prosperity, not the depression that many economists expected. With solid improvement apparent, real gross output grew until November 1948, a 37-month upswing and a 28 percent gain in business activity.

Removal of price controls in 1945 and 1946 improved business confidence. Businesses converted to a peacetime footing, as factories changed from producing military goods and munitions to consumer and investment goods. Households were eager to purchase automobiles and appliances when these goods became available, and they were able to use their savings for these purchases. Automobile production would rise from about 70,000 in 1945 to 2.15 million in 1946, 3.56 million in 1947, and 3.91 million in 1948. Production would rise through the years (and even during the next recession) to a new peak of 6.67 million units in 1950, when another war would intervene. Truck, appliance, and steel production followed suit, as would oil and natural gas production. Residential construction, which was limited during the war, rose sharply, as development of the suburbs expanded. For consumers, 1946 was a prosperous year.

Post-war prosperity was also led by a surge in business investment and the productive activity resulting from that investment. Financing was easy, and the Revenue Act of 1945, which lowered the top corporate income tax rate and repealed the excess profits tax, led to rising profits and the internal ability to fund capital expenditures. Removal of price controls in 1945 and 1946 led to improved business confidence and encouraged business investment. The command-and-control war economy was dismantled. Federal government employment would fall from 3.5 million in 1945 to 2.7 million a year later.

Figure 5.2

Cycle 36: Transition to Consumer Economy and Brief Recession of 1949

Index of Real Gross Output where 2017 = 100

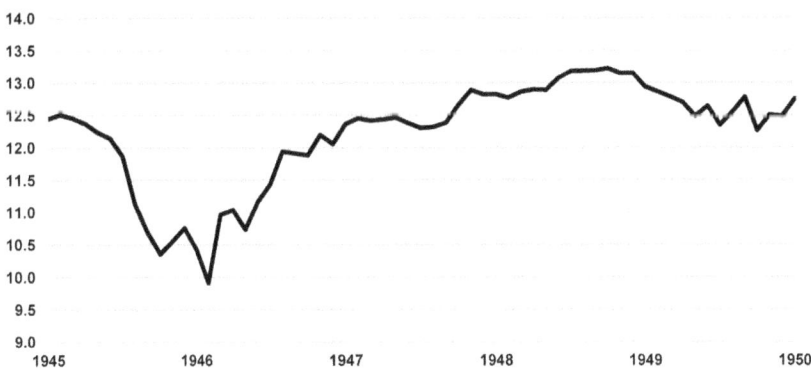

Rising union strength didn't bring labor peace. After World War II, there was a series of notable strikes which crippled major industries, as workers pushed for wage increases after wartime price and wage controls ended. In January 1946, a steel strike involving 800,000 workers became the largest in American history. It was followed by a coal strike in April and a rail strike in May. President Truman seized the railroads in an attempt to contain the issue, but the national railroad system was shut down for several days. Other strikes included workers at meatpackers, automobile companies, electrical equipment manufacturers, and even Hollywood film crews. These helped swing popular and political opinion against organized labor, and the 1946 mid-term Congressional elections gave Republicans control of both houses for the first time since 1930. The result was the passage of the Taft-Hartley Act in 1947, which extended and modified the 1935 Wagner Act. It prohibited certain union practices and required disclosure of certain financial and political activities by unions. By curbing the activities and power of labor unions, it fostered improved business confidence, leading to additional business investment. Union membership as a share of the total employment would peak and begin a long-term decline. However, work stoppages remained frequent. There were 270 of them, involving more than 1,000 workers in 1947, rising to a peak of 470 five years later.

The economy absorbed the millions of returning servicemen as the teenagers, women, and older workers staffing the war industries left the labor force. Also, many of those returning veterans took advantage of the GI Bill and went off to college. Unemployment would tick up to 4.4 percent in 1946, but as industry, commerce and trade improved, it would ease to 3.5 percent in 1947, a level likely below the natural rate of unemployment. The civilian labor force in two years would rise by 6.3 million people to 60.2 million in 1947. The year 1947 featured two consecutive quarters of declining real GDP. This is an unofficial definition of recession, but the year would feature no recession.

The Employment Act of 1946 would lay the responsibility of stability of inflation and unemployment onto the federal government. This was a contradiction. The nation has been scarred by the 1930s, and with a bias in fighting unemployment, an unintended consequence was that it allowed inflation as a permanent feature of the economy. The act created the Council of Economic Advisers (CEA) and the Joint Economic Committee (JEC) for Congress. It also would lead to the establishment of Keynesian economic thinking for a generation and to the development of a plethora of economic statistics.

After the war, there was a severe shortage of housing. Conversion from military production to consumer goods production took time, and many consumer goods were hard to find. As a result, prices soared when wartime price controls ended. The lifting of price controls, supply shortages, and pent-up demand for appliances, automobiles, and other products caused the CPI inflation rate to soar. Inflation remained an issue. as demand generally exceeded the ability to supply (conversion does not occur overnight), and would rise from 2.3 percent in 1945, to 8.3 percent in 1946, and 14.4 percent in 1947, before "easing" to 8.1 percent in 1948. Farm prices, in particular, rose sharply. Wages also increased once controls were lifted. During these last two years, overall industrial production rebounded sharply and ran close to capacity. Rising business activity helped to bring down inflation by boosting supplies of consumer goods. The years 1946-48 had imbalances arising from the war's near-cessation of consumer durables production. Eventually, pent-up demand would subside.

It was the first major bout with inflation in over 25 years. Concerned about inflation, the Federal Reserve began to allow short-term interest rates to rise, while maintaining the peg (as per agreement with Treasury, so-called yield curve control) on long-term rates. The Fed ended the wartime peg on short-term Treasury rates, letting markets set them. Monetary policy at the time was focused on the supply, rather than the price, of money and credit. The yield curve flattened, credit tightened, and a brief recession followed. In early 1948, the Fed raised the reserve requirements to absorb some of the excess reserves in the banking system. The monetary base continued to slowly rise, but a decline in the money multiplier caused nominal money stock to decline, apparently leading to recessionary conditions.

The labor strikes, along with rising inflation, caused stock prices to fall 30 percent through June 1949. The bull market in equities resumed during the 1950s.

With a period of Federal Reserve monetary tightening and the announcement of President Harry Truman's "Fair Deal," uncertainty arose. A recession was the result. Real business activity peaked in November 1948, and a 12-month economic downturn ensued, ending in October 1949. Real gross output during this period would fall 7.3 percent. The downturn has often been referred to as a post-war recession.

A tax cut in 1948 also helped to stabilize household incomes and consumer spending. Business activity and prices would both decline, with consumer prices down 1.2 percent for the year. With returning veterans reentering the workforce, unemployment began to rise, and the unemployment rate would nearly double from 3.8 percent in 1948 to 5.9 percent in 1949. Economic forecasters of the time expected a much worse recession, perhaps influenced by their experiences of the 1930s. With prosperous times leading up to the election, President Truman was elected to serve as president in November 1948, in what was a close race.

By the late-1940s, the Federal government once again was running modest budget surpluses. Business was on a peacetime footing. With the recession, inflation moderated, and by 1949, consumer prices actually declined (by 1.2 percent) and would rise by 1.3 percent in 1950.

Cycle 37: Korean War Prosperity and Post-War Recession

The downturn in Cycle 36 came to an end in October 1948 after inventories were drawn down. Indeed, by early 1949 it was apparent that inventory liquidation had been excessive, and there was a need to build inventories. This would resume in 1950 and be heralded in mid-1949 by rising equities. An expansion of activity began, and the upswing was aided, as military production began to increase after the start of the Korean War in June 1950. The upswing would last 45 months, ending in July 1953, when military production eased with the cessation of hostilities. Real gross output would rise by over 44 percent in the period.

In October 1950, Chinese troops crossed the Yalu River to assist North Korea and engaged U.S. troops, who had crossed the 38th Parallel and were approaching the Yalu River. The war would not be over soon. The war fostered panic buying by American consumers, centered largely in sugar, coffee, automobiles, and appliances.

Figure 5.3
Cycle 37: Korean War Prosperity and Post-War Recession
Index of Real Gross Output where 2017 = 100

With the war, steel production would rise from 78.0 million tons in 1949 to 105.2 million in 1951. Production would ease in 1952 but rise again to 111.6 million tons in 1953, before falling again during the post-war recession. In April 1952, President Truman ordered the U.S. Army to seize the nation's steel mills to avert a strike. When the presidential order was ruled unconstitutional by the Supreme Court in June, an eight-week strike again led to wage and steel price increases. The president also had to temporarily seize the railroads because of an impending strike during the Korean War.

Production of automobiles fell from 6.67 million in 1950 to 4.32 million in 1952 but would rise afterwards, as the hostilities wound down. Oil production would rise from 5.0 million BPD in 1949 to a new record of 6.5 million BPD in 1953. The Korean War led to a decline in the unemployment rate, from 5.9 percent in 1949 to 2.9 percent in 1953.

The Korean War created new inflationary pressures. Annual inflation rose to 7.9 percent in 1951, as the war led to a boom in commodity prices and accelerated inflation. Moreover, consumers rushed to purchase items deemed likely to be rationed (as in WWII), leading to a supply shock, as supply could not keep up with demand. The Federal Reserve initially expanded the money supply and credit but eventually wanted to raise interest rates. The Fed was committed to support the bond market by purchasing all government securities. Controversy arose between the Federal Reserve and the Treasury. This resulted in more independence for the Fed and an agreement in early 1951 to check credit expansion without the use of direct controls. The Federal Reserve had been concerned about inflation and abandoned the agreement with Treasury to peg long-term interest rates, and in early 1953, raised the discount rate. The Fed tightened monetary policy to curb inflation in 1952, which increased pessimism about the economy and suppressed demand in interest-sensitive sectors.

Business activity continued to expand into 1953, but by summer, it was clear that the pace had slowed down. With the easing of hostilities in Korea, military production declined, and a business cycle peak was reached in July 1953. This actually coincided with the truce and cessation of the fighting. In addition, some economists believed that the boom in consumer durable goods purchases had run its course.

A brief and somewhat mild 10-month recession ensued, with a trough reached in May 1954, accompanied by an 8.5 percent decline in real gross output. Production of automobiles would fall from 6.1 million units in 1953 to 5.6 million in 1954. Truck, tire, steel, and pig iron production would also fall. Oil and natural gas production, however, would continue to expand during the recession. The reduction of production led to a decline in business investment and liquidation of inventories that lasted into early 1954. The 10-month recession was followed by a period of low inflation and even deflation during 1955. Unemployment would rise from 2.9 percent in 1953 to 5.5 percent in 1954. The Fed eased credit to forestall recession but was too late. Perhaps anticipating a mild recession, the stock market remained relatively strong. A tax cut in 1953-54 also helped to stabilize households' income and consumer spending.

The 1952 presidential race led to the election of General Dwight D. Eisenhower, a Republican. This led to a revival of business confidence and a shift in fiscal and monetary policy that would characterize the decade.

Cycle 38: Golden Age of American Prosperity and Recession of 1958

The post-Korean War recession ended in May 1954, and with the liquidation of inventories, productive business activity increased rapidly in 1955. This was followed by rising incomes and consumer spending, especially on durable goods. The upswing would last 39 months, ending in August 1957. Real gross output would rise 19.4 percent during this period. Cycle 39 would mark a golden age of American prosperity. Consumers were eagerly building new homes and purchasing automobiles, appliances, and other consumer durables, the most notable of which was the television. The latter fostered whole new industries. There would be a revival of optimism about the future. In 1956, President Eisenhower was easily re-elected. Economists of different perspectives would look back to the 1950s (for different reasons) as sort of a golden age for the American economy.

Figure 5.4

Cycle 38: Golden Age of American Prosperity and Recession of 1958

Index of Real Gross Output where 2017 = 100

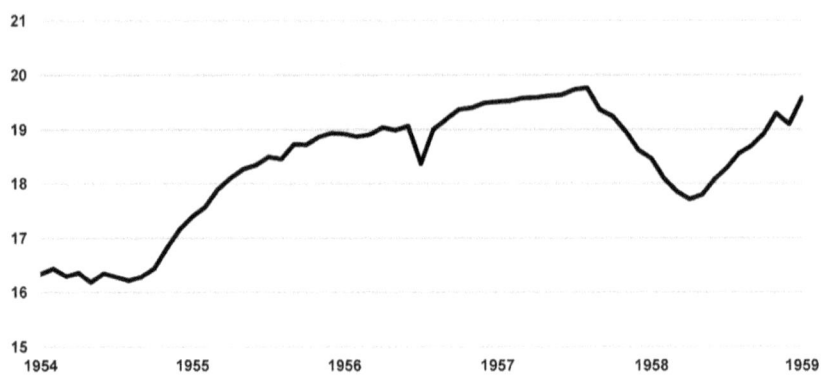

Real business activity grew rapidly during the upswing. It was particularly strong in 1955. Oil production went from 6.3 million BPD in 1954 to 7.2 million BPD in 1957. Natural gas production featured similar gains. Automobile production would rise from 5.6 million units in 1954 to 7.9 million units in 1955. The large jump was fostered by major changes in automotive design. The 1955 models were quite different and exciting. In addition, three-year automotive loans were introduced. Production would ease in 1956 and partially rebound in 1957. Truck production followed suit. Steel production would rise from 88.3 million tons to 117.0 million tons in one year. A three-week long strike by steelworkers in 1956 achieved large settlements in wage increases, better pay for weekend work, and supplemental unemployment benefits. Production began to ease in 1957, as inventory accumulation fostered liquidation in the second half of 1957. Nonetheless, steel production remained above 110 million tons. Business investment jumped and would lead to expansion of machinery and other capital goods industries.

After the post-war recession, deflationary forces were in play. From September 1954 through August 1955, the Consumer Price

Index (CPI) registered 12 consecutive monthly negative year-earlier comparisons. This was a deflationary period that later Fed chairs would fear, but it was a period in which commerce moved forward. Under a gold exchange standard, prices did fall in times of peace and even prosperity. Inflation would begin to exert itself, and after the negative 0.4 percent decline in prices in 1954, would reach 3.3 percent in 1957. Unemployment would fall from 5.5 percent in 1954 to 4.1 percent in 1956.

Monetary growth peaked in 1955. As inflation accelerated, the Fed tightened monetary policy to curb inflation, short-term interest rates rose, and eventually the tightened monetary conditions during the two years preceding 1957 helped to foster an economic downturn.

The business cycle peak occurred in August 1957. The recession was short, lasting eight months, but it was severe, with real gross output falling 10.4 percent peak to trough. It was the most severe since the 1930s. The trough was reached in April 1958. Automobile production would fall from 6.1 million in 1957 to 4.3 million in 1958, the worst years since 1948. Steel production would fall from 112.7 million tons in 1957 to 85.2 million tons in 1958. The recession was marked by large inventory liquidation, as well as a decline in business investment shifts in exports. Exports surged early in 1957 in response to the Suez Crisis and closure of the canal, which disrupted global oil trade. This was reversed with the reopening of the canal. The spread of the "Asian flu" also led to a slowdown in production. This recession has also been referred to as the Eisenhower Recession.

Unemployment rose from 4.1 percent in 1956 to 6.8 percent in 1958, higher than the previous recession. With the recession, inflation would fall to 2.8 percent in 1958. For the next five decades, inflation would only ease during recessions, not turning to deflation, as it had through much of the nation's history. This deep recession without a significant decline in inflation led many economists to question the compatibility of full employment and price stability.

The recession was short because the Fed took a series of steps to boost monetary (or credit) growth, including three cuts in the discount rate and two reductions in reserve requirements. In addition, the government relaxed mortgage rules, lengthened unemployment benefits, and accelerated highway and other construction projects.

This cycle marked the passage of the Federal Aid Highway Act of 1956, which authorized the construction of a 41,000-mile network of interstate highways that would span the nation. Under the terms of the law, the federal government would pay 90 percent of the cost of expressway construction. The resulting development of this interstate highway network would lower logistical costs and aid in productivity growth for the nation.

Cycle 39: End of 1950s and Mild Recession of 1960-61

A strong economic recovery emerged, ending the 1950s on a solid note. With the end of inventory liquidation in 1958 and a need to rebuild stocks, productive activity would gain. With rising employment and incomes, consumer spending for non-durable goods and services increased as well. As interest rates declined, housing activity increased. The upswing, however, would be relatively short, only 24 months. During the upswing, real gross output would rise 16.3 percent.

Automobile production would rise from 4.26 million units in 1958 to 6.68 million units in 1960, below the previous peak in 1955. Truck production moved in a similar pattern. Oil production rebounded to 7.2 million BPD in 1960, and natural gas production reached a new record of 35 billion cubic feet (BCF) per day. Production of consumer durable goods gained as well. New consumer and business services also gained traction.

During the upswing in 1959, foreign imports of steel into the United States began to exceed exports for the first time. Despite such vulnerability, a half-million steelworkers went on strike in July, bringing the steel industry to a halt. The strike yielded small wage and fringe benefit increases and some cost-of-living provisions. The steel strike of 1959 was the beginning of a decades-long relative decline in the fortunes of the American steel industry. Steel production would rebound from 85.3 million tons in 1958 to 99.3 million tons in 1960, well below the previous peak. The strike was so severe it would cause a flattening and easing of real gross output.

Inventories across industries that had been depleted during the strike were rebuilt rapidly by early-1960 and then accumulation slowed. As a result, productive activity could not be sustained. Consumer durable goods production also weakened.

In addition, a backlog of deferred demand was largely met, and with higher mortgage interest rates, housing construction fell back, from 1.54 million units in 1959, to 1.26 million in 1960. In 1960, Congress passed legislation to create the real estate investment trust (REIT) as a means to facilitate lending. It would also foster speculation in the decades to come.

During the upswing, unemployment fell from 6.8 percent in 1958 to 5.5 percent in 1959 and 1960. Inflation more than doubled from 0.7 percent in 1959 to 1.7 percent in 1960. The Fed tightened monetary policy, once again in hopes of mitigating inflation, and raised interest rates. The peak of business activity was reached in April 1960. This fourth post-war recession was primarily monetary in cause, and would be short, only 10 months, and mild, with a 3.4 percent decline in real output. Real gross output started falling during the second quarter and would continue into early-1961. Most major industries drew down inventories. Noteworthy is that this recession did not feature two consecutive quarters of declining real GDP. Although the recession was mild, the peak unemployment rate almost reached that of the prior severe recession. The weakened economic conditions would lead to the election of Senator John F. Kennedy (Democrat) in 1960 in a close election with Vice President Richard Nixon.

Figure 5.5
Raw Steel Production in the United States
(Millions of Tons)

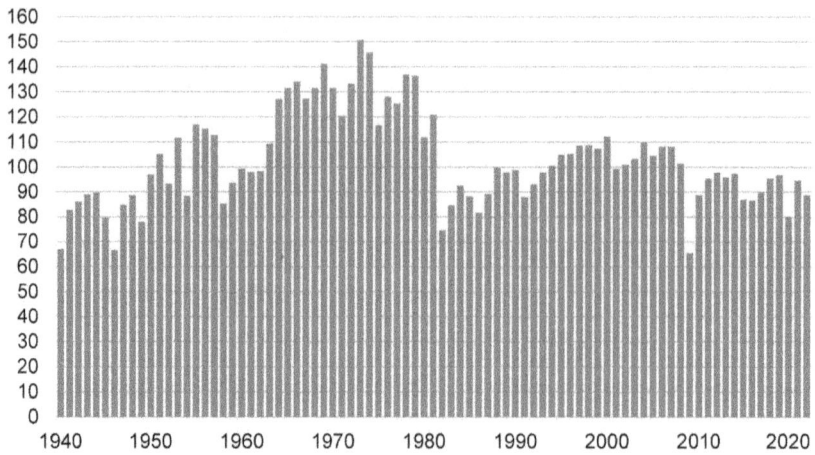

Source: American Iron and Steel Institute

The recession ended in February 1961, just in time for a new administration. Newly elected President Kennedy started with a 12-point stimulus plan that included a higher minimum wage, unemployment benefits, and widened social security benefits. The recession of 1960-61 preceded a long period of growth in American business cycle history, lasting nearly nine years.

Cycle 40: The Go-Go 1960s, Heyday of Keynesian Economics, the Rise of Inflation, and Recession of 1970

The upswing of Cycle 40 would, at 106 months, be the longest-to-date in American economic history. It would start in February 1961 and last until December 1969, with real gross output rising 53.5 percent during this period. The record upswing would, however, be eclipsed by upswings in the 1990s and 2010s. Some economists and historians would look back to the 1960s as the "golden age" of American prosperity. Still, problems existed and would set the stage for even worse problems in subsequent years. The most notable problem was inflation.

Figure 5.6

Cycles 39 and 40: The Go-Go 1960s

Index of Real Gross Output where 2017 = 100

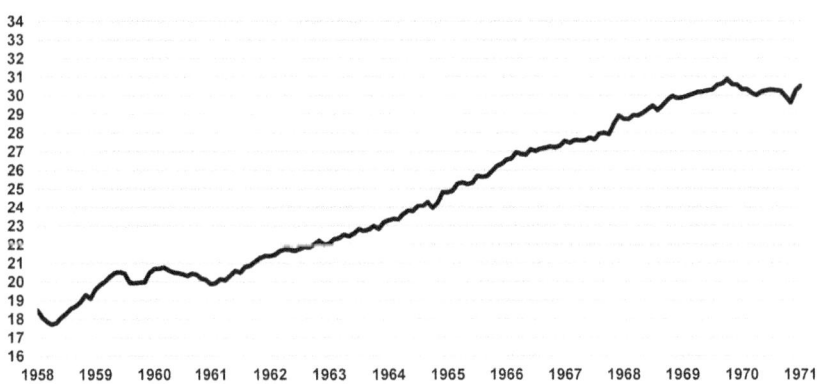

The 1960s have been referred to as the "Go-Go" years, a cultural artifact of the Baby Boomers. The latter — those born between 1946 and 1964 — represented the largest demographic cohort to date. Their progress in life can be characterized as a "pig in a python" as they aged. In the 1940s, the rapid rise in their births strained hospital capacity. In the 1950s and 1960s, their entry into schools strained local school districts, leading to sustained construction of educational facilities, starting with elementary, middle, and senior high schools and then, eventually, colleges and universities. Whole industries would follow their development, and a youth culture would emerge. Demographic change is a strong determinant of long-term economic growth.

With Americans continuing to move to the suburbs, housing construction would average 1.42 million units per year during the decade of the 1960s. Automobile production would rise to 5.5 million units in 1961 and would then average over 8.0 million units per year through 1969. The advent of color television would result in a round of upgrades and purchases, with fairly rapid diffusion.

Unemployment rates would remain persistently elevated, gradually falling from 6.7 percent in 1961 to 5.2 percent in 1964 and would fall beneath 4.0 percent in 1966. From there, they would fall to 3.5 percent by the end of the decade. On the other hand, inflation, which would average 1.0 percent per year in 1961-62, would gradually rise throughout the decade, ending at 5.5 percent in 1969. In the first five years of the upswing, inflation remained low. Policy makers at the Federal Reserve and in the various administrations became complacent.

It is convenient to divide the decade into two periods. The first is the period from 1961 to 1966. These years were accompanied by relatively stimulative monetary and fiscal policies. In 1963, President Kennedy was assassinated and succeeded by Vice President Lyndon B. Johnson. The Revenue Act of 1964 was a tax cut act proposed by President Kennedy, passed by Congress, and signed into law by President Johnson. The act cut federal income taxes by approximately twenty percent across the board, with the top federal income tax rate falling from 91 percent to 70 percent on incomes over $100,000 (about $880,000 in 2022 dollars) for individual filers. The act also reduced the corporate tax from 52 percent to 48 percent and created a minimum standard deduction. An investment tax credit and more liberal depreciation allowances were also enacted. These stimulated the economy and triggered the 1960s economic boom. They have been referred to as the Kennedy tax cuts by both Keynesians and supply-siders.

In addition, President Johnson embarked on his Great Society programs, which boosted Federal expenditures two-fold. The president wanted to complete FDR's New Deal and pushed through a number of programs, including Medicare and Medicaid, Head

Start, and the Mass Transit Act. At the same time, the United States boosted military spending for the war in Vietnam, and military production began to gear up. It is questionable if the economy needed this stimulus, and the new spending caused increased inflation. Economic growth was strong, but inflation heated up, rising from 1.3 percent in 1964, to 1.6 percent in 1965, and 2.9 percent in 1966. It would rise further as the decade went on, and with the Federal Reserve accommodating this spending, would lead to a vicious cycle of expanding money supply and spiraling prices, wages, and rising interest rates.

Real gross output grew a tepid 0.5 percent in 1961 but would average 5.6 percent per year in the years 1962 through 1966. Military production gained, as did production of automobiles, appliances, consumer electronics, and other consumer durables. New consumer non-durable goods proliferated, as did new services. Leisure and hospitality, food service, air travel, and other consumer services expanded, as did advertising, accounting, management consulting, and other business services. By 1963, natural gas production would exceed 40 billion BCF per day, and by 1966, oil production reached over 8.0 million BPD. Business and consumer optimism prevailed. In January 1966, the Dow Jones Industrial Average, a composite of the prices of 30 top U.S. industrial stocks, topped 1,000 for the first time. By late-1965, the Federal Reserve was concerned about an overheating economy and allowed short-term interest rates to rise. In 1966, economic growth slowed, a so-called growth recession, that lasted from the second quarter into the second quarter of 1967.

Production of many consumer durable goods eased but was offset by advances in non-durable goods production and the output of services. The growth recession soon led to resumed expansion, aided by military spending during the Vietnam War and the further expansion of the Great Society programs. This led to the second period, which comprises the remainder of the decade, the years 1967 through 1969. President Johnson's economic advisors issued a warning that federal financing of both a war and the social welfare programs would foster economic pressures. Their advice was to support a tax increase to "cool off" the economy. The Administration enacted a temporary income tax surcharge that took effect in 1968. It was a failure, as inflation would rise from 3.1 percent in 1967, to 4.2 percent in 1968, and to 5.5 percent in 1969. The tax surcharge would thwart growth, with real gross output averaging only 4.0 percent per year during 1967-69. By 1968, oil production would exceed 9.0 million BPD, and natural gas production would exceed 50 billion BCF per day. After 1968, military production would begin to ease, as military involvement in Vietnam peaked. A presidential election would see former Vice President (under President Eisenhower) Richard M. Nixon elected in 1968.

By the late 1960s, as inflation began to accelerate, the holders of dollars feared the loss of the currency's purchasing power. At the same time, U.S. trade balances were deteriorating, in part due to competition in manufactured goods from West Germany and Japan. Protectionist sentiments in the country were growing, and the Nixon Administration, Congressional leaders, and many business leaders believed that the link to gold overvalued the dollar, making U.S. imports inexpensive and exports dear. This would eventually lead to uncoupling the dollar with its gold link to devalue the dollar in relation to other currencies. It was thought that this would boost American exports. In the next decade, inflation would get much worse, and would be known as the Great Inflation of the 1970s.

Cycle 40 would feature the high-water mark for Keynesian macroeconomic policy. While attending Harvard as an undergraduate, President Kennedy would have been exposed to Keynesian economic principles, and he appointed several Keynesian economists (John Kenneth Galbraith, Walter Heller, James Tobin, etc.) in advisory roles, both in his campaign and in his administration.

The period since 1940 would mark explosive growth in plastic resins, synthetic materials that began to supplant metals, glass, paper, and other materials in a variety of building and construction, automotive, packaging, and other applications. The success of this industry was symbolized (although that wasn't the intent of the quote) in the 1967 movie, *The Graduate,* where young Benjamin Braddock's father's friend Mr. McGuire advises him, "I want to say one word to you. Just one word…Are you listening?…plastics." Figure 5.7 illustrates the growth of this industry, rising nearly eight-fold in the 1940s (from a very low base), nearly three-fold in the 1950s, and more than doubling in the 1960s.

Figure 5.7
Plastics Resins Production in the United States
(Billions of Pounds)

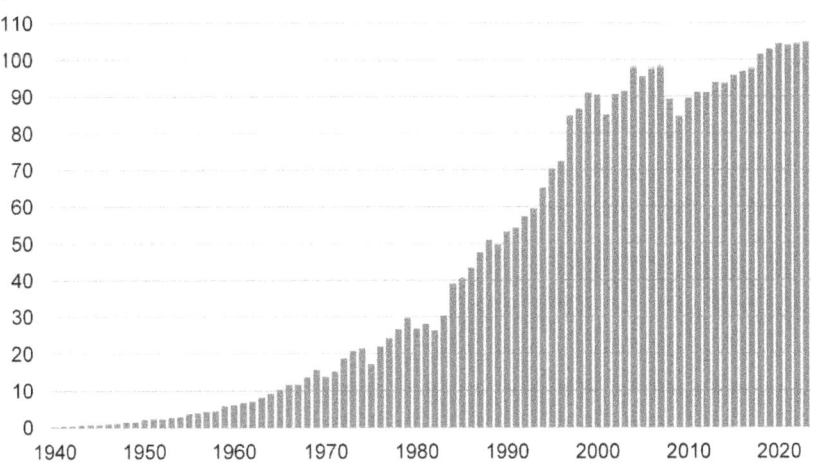

Sources: Census Bureau, United States International Trade Commission, author's estimates

At the end of the cycle's upswing, inflation was rising, likely a result of increased deficits. A push to balance the budget deficit from the Vietnam War in 1969 to surplus, accompanied by the Fed 's restrictive monetary policy (i.e., raising interest rates) to control inflation, ended the upswing. The tightening would result in a mild recession. The business cycle peak occurred in December 1969 and would last 11 months. The decline in real gross output would be 2.5 percent. The downturn would see the decline of automobile and truck production, as well as steel production. Housing starts eased as well. The recession would mark the first year in which plastics production declined. The unemployment rate would rise from 3.5 percent in 1969 to 4.9 percent during 1970. The unemployment rate would peak at 6.1 percent in December 1970, one month after the recession officially ended. The Nixon administration launched a series of policies that would temporarily put a stop to the downswing. However, inflation hardly moved, and continued its upward push, rising from the average 5.5 percent rate during 1969 to 5.9 percent during 1970. Thus, a recession without falling inflation led to the birth of modern stagflation, and with it, the death knell for Keynesian economics. During 1970, postal workers went on strike, further exacerbating the downturn.

Cycle 41: Wage and Price Controls, the Decoupling from Gold, Inflation, Oil Price Shock, and Recession of 1973-75

The downswing of Cycle 40 came to an end in November 1970, and a different type of upswing would emerge. It would last 36 months, to November 1973, and real gross output would gain 26.3 percent over these three years. However, Cycle 41 would feature higher inflation than that experienced in the prior decade and also slower growth. This is the definition of stagflation. The Nixon Administration was confronted with something entirely new, and the policy responses were total misjudgments.

During the 1970 recession, Penn Central, then the largest railroad, failed and defaulted on its commercial paper. Commercial paper was deemed low risk, and the default jolted financial markets and led to a liquidity crisis. The Fed intervened, and a larger crisis did not emerge.

Inflation remained at a stubbornly high level, at least compared with the two prior decades, as the recovery was quick enough that measures of full employment were soon reached. Unemployment continued to rise into 1971 and would average above 5.0% for 1972 as well. Thus, began stagflation.

In August 1971, the Administration announced a stimulus plan, a "new economic policy" consisting of wage and price controls, a 10% import surcharge, and other measures. The wage and price controls were to occur in four phases, beginning with a 90-day freeze on all wages and prices. This would be followed by gradual exception of covered items, until wage and prices controls were to be emulated in early 1974. The intent was to reduce the inflation rate by slowing the economy. Remember that Keynesian thought still held sway, and this was a typical remedy.

Wage and price controls never work, as they cause market distortions. For a while, they mask inflation, but not for long. The advice of most economists was ignored. It's likely that the wage and price controls had no effect on the inflation rate and with the distortions that controls create, they soon became unpopular.

The United States had seen balance of payment deficits during the 1960s with signs of an overvalued dollar. A number of nations were concerned about a devaluation of the dollar and began exchanging dollars for gold and thus prompted an outflow of capital. This accelerated in 1971, leading to heightened fears of devaluation. In August 1971, President Nixon also announced the decision to take the United States off the gold exchange standard, a relic of the Bretton Woods agreement that had been in place since the end of World War II. This suspended the most fundamental rules of the international monetary system, affecting the prices of commodities and all products and services in world trade and commerce. Uncoupling the dollar from gold was consistent with a larger U.S. retrenchment. The nation was trying to wrest itself from Vietnam and was focusing on domestic policy. The Bretton Woods agreement effectively ended in December 1973, when the major nations agreed to let their currencies float. The floating exchange rate system is still in place in the 2020s, although many nations have actively managed the value of their currency.

A fixed exchange rate might have fostered more cautious policy responses, moderating the 1972 boom. After falling in 1970, real gross output would rise 3.3 percent in 1971, 7.5 percent in 1972 (an election year), and 7.3 percent in 1973, one of the strongest periods of growth in the United States. The year 1973 was one associated with widespread signs of capacity pressures amid new records for production of automobiles. Sales of the latter were pushed forward due to impending safety and pollution regulations that would boost vehicle costs. The boom would foster numerous speculative developments, which their nature must inevitably unwind. Monetary growth during the time exceeded 13 percent in both 1971 and 1972. This was highly expansionary.

Housing starts exceeded two million units per year during 1971-73, with an all-time high of 2.36 million units in 1972. This boom was led by the multi-family segments, fostered by the rise of the baby boom generation and also by construction of public housing, a legacy of Great Society programs.

Even though inflation was becoming more of a problem in the 1960s, it wasn't until this cycle that it threatened to interrupt continuous growth and plunge the economy into major recession. After 1972, inflation would become different in degree to anything experienced before, as strong world economic growth led to a boom in commodity prices and accelerated inflation even further.

Monetary policy was highly expansionary. Some questioned the independence of the Fed during 1972, a year in which President Nixon ran for re-election. Fed Chair Arthur Burns would be criticized about this. The wage and price controls partially hid inflation. A series of external events would soon sustain and accelerate inflation.

First, was a series of weather events, which reduced crop yields in the Midwest, the Soviet Union, and elsewhere. A crop failure was so large in the Soviet Union, that the nation began buying large quantities of grain from the United States. This drove up grain and food prices worldwide. In combination with loose monetary policy, it would push up prices for farmland and farmers' debt. Federal Reserve policy encouraged banks to extend riskier loans. Eventually, the boom in farmland prices would crest and collapse, as prices converged toward underlying value. This would present difficulties for banks in the Midwest.

Second, was the energy situation. With inflation continuing to rise and even accelerate in the United States, in combination with the devaluation of the dollar, the Organization of Petroleum Exporting Countries (OPEC) thought again about its strategy and became determined to modify the Tehran Agreement of 1971, which had negotiated higher prices. The Arab-Israeli War of 1973 (also known as the Yom Kippur War) created a new urgency among the Arab members of OPEC. They later announced a unilateral increase in oil excise and related taxes, put production cuts in place, and with new strength as a producers' cartel, placed embargoes on oil exports to the United States and the Netherlands. As a result, the world price of oil rose fourfold between 1972 and 1974 (to $11.58 per barrel) and would further feed inflation. Facing higher energy costs, households cut back on purchases of other goods and services. For business, oil was a prime input for virtually all goods and services, and the energy price gains rendered much capital stock obsolete. As a supply shock, it also helped to foster a recession, affecting many manufacturing and transportation industries' output. Still, inflation remained stubbornly high.

By early-1973, the Fed realized that inflation was pervasive and started slowing the growth of the money supply. This put upward pressure on short-term interest rates, which hammered the housing industry and housing financing. At the time, Federal regulations placed ceilings on interest rates that banks and savings and loan associations could pay depositors. As a result, depositors pulled their funds for investment in Treasuries and money market mutual funds, a process termed disintermediation. This withdrew funds available for new housing loans, and combined with higher interest rates, led to a collapse of housing. Housing starts would fall from 2.36 million units in 1972 to 1.16 million in 1975.

In general, policymakers responded to the environment of high inflation and unemployment by tightening fiscal and monetary policy. Monetary policy, for example, would steadily tighten in the course of 1973. By late-1973, all of these forces (monetary, fiscal, energy, inflation, etc.) began to have adverse effects on the economy. The stock market collapsed in 1973-74, leading to falling business and consumer confidence, and reduced business investment and consumer spending. The downturn emerged in November 1973. Production fell, especially in the automobile industry, as foreign vehicles were deemed to be more fuel efficient. Supplier and associated industries declined, as did those related to housing construction. Disposable income fell, as rising inflation eroded real wages. Furthermore, in a progressive income tax regime, inflation pushed earners into higher tax brackets, further eroding real incomes. As a result, consumer spending fell further. Firms cut back further on business investment, impacting the production of capital goods.

In the early-1970s, REITs borrowed heavily from banks, in the bond market, and in the commercial paper market. With the 1973-75 recession, real estate developers soon encountered credit problems, many fell behind on their debts, and many filed for bankruptcy.

The uncoupling of the dollar in 1971 is a classic example of the unintended consequences of policy. A system of fiat currencies emerged with freely floating exchange rates, and it continues today. Despite the benefits of floating exchange rates, fluctuating currencies can be volatile and complex, fostering uncertainty. In the post-war years until the early-1970s, there were hardly any global banking crises. With the era of floating exchange rates, there would be many, from the Latin American debt explosion of the late 1970s to the market crash of the Great Financial Crisis. New financial instruments would arise to deal with risks associated with fluctuating exchange rates, which would add to instability in banking.

The downturn that emerged in November 1973 would last 16 months, with real gross output falling 9.9 percent, making it a severe (or major) recession. Unemployment would average 8.5 percent in 1975. Inflation nearly doubled from 6.2 percent in 1973 to 11.0 percent in 1974 and would "moderate" to 9.1 percent in 1975. Stagflation apparently was here to stay, and it was this recession that put an end to the Phillips Curve thinking that suggested a trade-off between inflation and unemployment. It also marked the decline of Keynesian demand policy. As a result of this recession, more emphasis was placed on aggregate supply rather than aggregate demand. Supply-side influences were incorporated into what would be called the new- or neo-Keynesian models and thinking. In addition, real business cycle theory would emerge.

Figure 5.8
Cycles 41 and 42: The 1970s
Index of Real Gross Output where 2017 = 100

The downswing (or recession) was worldwide in nature, with nearly all advanced economies affected, as well as many emerging markets. World trade fell in 1975 for the first time since the 1930s. The downswing would see a number of large failures, the most notable being the collapse of Franklin National. At the time, it was the largest bank failure in history.

As the increases in food, energy, and other prices eased; as inventories were depleted; and as monetary policy turned expansionary, the recession ended in March 1975. Comparisons at the time marked it as the worst recession since the 1930s, yet inflation remained elevated.

In the background, President Nixon faced increased scrutiny in wake of the Watergate scandal. He resigned in August 1974 and was succeeded by Vice President Gerald R. Ford, a Republican Congressman, who only 10 months before was confirmed Vice President when Vice President Spiro Agnew resigned, amid charges of tax evasion and money laundering.

With the scandal in the background, the Budget and Impoundment Control Act was passed and signed in 1974. This ended the president's power to impound appropriated funds and left Congress in full control of spending. Federal government spending would spiral out of control. With high inflation and "bracket creep," tax revenues would fund much of this, but budget deficits would be the norm for the 1970s into the late-1990s.

Cycle 42: Stagflation, Second Oil Price Shock and 1980 Recession

The mid-1970s recession fostered challenges for policymakers used to a post-war consensus and a Keynesian approach to demand management. The recession ended in March 1975. The Tax Reduction Act of 1975 supported spending and investment, and the economy grew for the remainder of 1975. After the official end of the recession, the unemployment rate reached 9.0 percent in May 1975. The upswing would be one of the longest in business cycle history to date but would feature consumer discontent. The so-called Misery Index, the addition of the inflation rate and the unemployment rate, would reach an all-time high of 20.6 in 1980, nearly double the 1970 index reading. It was an economy distressed by inflation, relatively high unemployment, slow productivity, and slow gains in real incomes.

In 1976, the Misery Index eased to 13.5, still a high level compared to earlier in the decade and the 1960s. Confidence among consumers and business was low amid concern over inflation and the economy. As a result, in the 1976 presidential election, President Ford was defeated by Georgia Governor James E. Carter, also known as Jimmy Carter, a Democrat.

The upswing would last 58 months, ending in January 1980. The end of Cycle 42 was brought about by many of the same forces in the previous cycle. During these nearly five years, real gross output would rise 26.3 percent. This period would be characterized by a Federal Reserve (under some influence from the administration) fostering higher inflation by boosting monetary growth and stimulating an economy operating at full employment output. It's likely that the Fed didn't truly understand how its monetary policy in the 1970s was stoking inflation and affecting the productive economy, a theme that would echo in later decades.

This was particularly the case by 1978. The natural rate of unemployment had been rising since the 1960s due to the entry of women and baby-boomers into the labor force. The higher unemployment rates were falsely taken as a sign of weakness, and policymakers strove to ratchet unemployment down. Monetary growth was explosive, and fiscal policy reflected this bias as well. In 1976 through 1978, Congress enacted a series of tax cuts — the Tax Reform Act of 1976, Tax Reduction and Simplification Act of 1977, and Revenue Act of 1978 — but most were temporary and thus had no effect on the real economy.

By the 1970s, American steel companies had begun to falter. The year 1973 would be the high-water mark — at 150.8 million tons — for American steel production. Finally, in 1975, the world steel market crashed, and foreign steel imports surged. In 1975, American consumption of foreign steel had risen to 13.3 percent from 2.5 percent in 1958. By 1978, imports would reach 17.8 percent, and layoffs and plant closings would be the norm. Although the steel industry had built new furnaces and finishing mills since the 1940s, the older facilities became obsolete. The Mahoning Valley, Buffalo, and Pittsburgh districts were particularly affected, and many integrated steel mills were shut down. By 1980, steel production fell to 111.8 million tons. Chart 5.4 illustrates the long-term structural decline of the American steel industry. It is emblematic of the rise of the Rust belt amid deindustrialization.

In the automobile industry, domestic producers' model offerings were based on inexpensive energy and were caught flat-footed by import competition. Plants in in Michigan and elsewhere in the Midwest were shuttered. Many cities suffered, and structural unemployment became a serious issue. Many industrial firms became reluctant to rehire idled workers.

A feature of the upswing was that inflation, while moderating from 1974 levels, remained high. In addition to negative demographic trends, the minimum wage was gradually increased in 1978 and beyond. This coincided with a productivity slowdown. By 1978, full employment was reached, although fiscal and monetary stimulus continued. The latter showed up in inflation rather than the real economy. Annual inflation would rise from 5.8 percent in 1976, to 6.5 percent in 1977, and 7.6 percent in 1978. Accelerating inflation would lead the Administration to establish voluntary wage and price guidelines that would be monitored by a Council on Wage and Price Stability. These were ineffective.

G. William Miller, the CEO of Textron (an industrial conglomerate) and prominent Democrat, was appointed chair of the Federal

Reserve in March 1978. Many challenged his qualifications, and his short tenure was unremarkable. In August 1979, he would be replaced by Paul Volcker, who would be widely credited with ending the high levels of inflation during the 1970s and early 1980s.

Strong world economic growth led to a boom in commodity prices and reaccelerated inflation. This would lead to a second oil price shock, a repeat of events in 1973-74. After strikes in Iranian oilfields, the Shah of Iran fell, and with the outbreak of war between Iran and Iraq, OPEC again doubled oil prices, which averaged $31.61 per barrel in 1979 and $36.83 in 1980. Inflation would rise further, hitting 11.3 percent in 1979 and 13.5 percent in 1980. Oil was a significant input to many industries, and as before, the higher prices served as a shock to these industries. Business activity fell across a large number of industries.

Amid the high interest rates of the time, housing starts plunged from 2.00 million in 1978 to 1.72 million in 1979. Consumer purchases for big ticket items (automobiles, appliances, etc.) declined as well. This further affected supplier industries and set the stage for economic weakness.

Monetary policy focused on eliminating inflation. In late-1979, the Fed's Board of Governors announced that the Fed would target monetary aggregates and would restrain monetary growth. A monetarist experiment was underway. Real money growth slowed, and nominal interest rates rose to their highest levels in American history.

The Depository Institutions Deregulation and Monetary Control Act of 1980 provided deregulation of banking by phasing out deposit rate ceilings and also by extending the Fed's member bank services to non-member banks. However, it also gave the Federal Reserve greater control over these non-member banks, forcing all banks to abide by the same reserve requirements and other Fed rules. It enhanced the Fed's ability to control monetary growth. In addition, the Administration authorized the Federal Reserve to impose targeted credit controls.

These controls, combined with the higher interest rates increased by the Federal Reserve, fostered a large decline in housing and durable goods. The 1980 recession was the result.

Starting in January 1980, the downswing would last only six months, ending in July 1980. Real gross output fell 5.2 percent from peak to trough. The recession was due in part to the second oil price shock, much as the 1973-75 recession had been partly due to the first. Both recessions were similar, but there were also differences. The recession, like the one before, placed companies under great financial pressure. Stagflation characterized both recessions. Businesses and consumers had adapted to the events of 1973-74 and a subsequent rise in inflation and recession, so both became largely anticipated in 1979 and 1980. Whereas as the mid-decade recession was 16 months in length, this downswing was only six months, the shortest on record at that point.

In early 1980, an attempt by the Hunt brothers to corner the silver market failed. This bubble popped and would lead to a steep drop in silver prices that would foster panic on commodity and futures exchanges.

Credit controls were lifted in June, and a trough was reached in July. An upswing emerged, one that would be characterized by continuing high inflation and persistent high unemployment. Annual inflation eased to only 10.3. percent in 1981, and unemployment would average 7.6 percent. The Misery Index at 17.9 in 1981, was at its second highest level. Confidence was weak.

The Misery Index had reached an all-time high in 1980, an election year. The American public wanted relief and change, and President Carter was defeated by former California Governor Ronald W. Reagan, a Republican who promised to reduce inflation, and who also ran a more positive campaign.

The economy experienced a temporary recovery from the recession beginning in the summer of 1980, although the continued efforts to combat inflation would spur another recession the following year.

Under the Carter administration, this cycle saw the start of deregulation of the American economy. Since the 1880s, a number of regulatory agencies (Interstate Commerce Commission, Civil Aeronautics Board, etc.) had been created. This accelerated starting in the 1930s, and by the 1970s, wide expanses of the economy were under strict regulatory control. This stifled economic growth and resulted in higher costs for business and consumers. The year 1977 saw the deregulation of air cargo and passenger air services a year later. In 1980, interstate truck and rail transportation were deregulated. The latter allowed the railroad industry to consolidate and once again flourish. The deregulation trend continued in the 1980s and into the 1990s, when international aviation was opened up. Deregulation would support economic growth and foster the success of such companies as FedEx and Amazon, among others.

Cycle 43: Stagflation, Second Oil Price Shock, the 1980 Recession and Volcker, the Taming of Inflation, and the 1981-82 Recession

It was apparent at the end of Cycle 42 that the short recession had done nothing to reduce the pace of inflation. The upswing from the July 1980 end of the recession would prove short, lasting only 12 months, ending in July 1981. Real business activity would expand only 5.2 percent. The upswing was characterized by persistently high inflation, which eased from 13.5 percent in 1980 to 10.3 percent during 1981. Moreover, unemployment trended up slightly and remained relatively elevated in between recessions.

With sustained inflation, labor strife became widespread. In August 1981, the Professional Air Traffic Controllers Organization went on strike and shut down the nation's airline industry. This exacerbated the downswing. After giving strikers 48 hours to return, President Reagan fired more than 10,000 who refused, breaking the strike, and in combination with rising import competition, labor's grip on power. Work stoppages, numbering 145 in 1981, would drop to a low of five in 2009.

Moreover, the Federal Reserve would play a large role in the pending recession. In response to an acceleration of inflation arising largely from the boom in world commodity and oil prices, monetary policy became restrictive. Under Fed Chair Volcker, interest rates were raised dramatically in an effort to end the inflation of the 1970s and early-1980s. Despite the Fed's claim of targeting monetary aggregates with its enhanced tools, interest rates were raised even further. The prime rate reached its all-time high in 1981 of 20.5 percent. The Fed's higher interest rates fostered a large decline in housing and durable goods.

There were considerable differences of opinion among economists concerning the Fed's role. The monetarists argued that the Fed was primarily responsible, while others debated that the Fed was a victim of exogenous changes in the financial system. The 1981-82 recession was the result. Debates would rage for years over the role of the Fed and the decline of money velocity due to changes in the financial system. Bank deregulation was cited as a cause.

The cost of reducing inflation would prove high, as strict monetary policies aimed at reducing inflation produced the deepest recession since 1937-38. Many sectors of the economy were disrupted, and the downswing caused high unemployment. The downturn was severe, lasting 16 months from July 1981 until November 1982, with real gross output falling 6.0 percent. Unemployment would rise from 7.6 percent in 1981 to an average of 9.7 percent in 1982 and would remain near that level for another year. The downswing would see the collapse of Drysdale Government Securities and Oklahoma-based Penn Square Bank. Many industrial corporations defaulted on loans or entered bankruptcy.

Industries sensitive to the higher interest rates — steel, construction materials, appliances, automobiles, machinery, and equipment, etc. — were severely affected, adding to structural issues that emerged in the 1970s. By 1982, steel import penetration reached 21.1 percent of demand. Capacity utilization in the industry averaged 48.4 percent during the year when steel production fell to 74.6 million tons, one-half of the 1973 level. The concept of the Rust Belt emerged as manufacturing and construction were both hammered. Moreover, high interest rates resulted in a stronger dollar, which further affected exporting industries and industries subject to import competition. Exports declined, and a shift away from tradable goods towards non-tradable goods began to occur in industry.

The long-promised ramp-up (by candidate, now President Reagan) in defense spending was beginning. In addition, the promised tax cuts were being phased in. This recession was thus associated with very large budget deficits.

Figure 5.9
Cycles 42 and 43: Stagflation, Second Oil Price Shock, the 1980 Recession and Volcker, the Taming of Inflation, and the 1981-82 Recession

Index of Real Gross Output where 2017 = 100

The recession, however, was long and deep enough to reduce inflation to its lowest level since 1976. Fed Chair Volcker withstood pressure from Congress to loosen monetary policies, resulting in a drop in inflation by October 1982, and the end of the recession. Falling inflationary expectations, falling economic output, and rising monetary growth lowered short-term interest rates, and thus set the stage for recovery. In addition, the first stage of the paring back of income tax rates took effect during 1982. Housing turned positive, and then motor vehicles and other consumer durable goods followed. The recovery was underway by the end of the year.

Many economists consider the 1980-81 and 1981-82 recessions to be one long extended downturn. I tend to agree with this, as the peak activity in Cycle 43 (January 1980) was not reached until well into the upswing during September 1983, nearly 10 months after the second recession. In this work, I maintain the NBER classification of the cycles since the 1850s. The early 1980s are sometimes referred to as a "double-dip" or "W-shaped" recession. I present both cycles in Figure 5.8 to illustrate these dynamics.

President Reagan's economic policy was aimed at moderating monetary growth to reduce aggregate demand while reducing tax burdens to stimulate growth in aggregate supply. The Administration's thinking was that the latter would more than offset the former. The first couple of years did not go according to plan, but eventually would, and the 1980s would then lead to the longest American business cycle upswing in history.

Cycle 44: The Heyday of Supply-Side Economics, a Long Expansion, the Gulf War, and 1990-91 Recession

Both monetary and fiscal policy became simulative during the second half of 1982 and gave way to recovery. Fed Chair Volcker's experiment in "practical monetarism" gave way to fairly solid credit expansion and economic growth. Inflation would moderate and remain low for the next few decades. The downturn ended in November 1982, and recovery emerged.

The upswing would be one of the longest in American business cycle history, aided by favorable economic policy, falling oil prices, advantageous demographics (Baby Boomers in their prime spending years), and the diffusion of the personal computer. The upswing was fully 92 months, starting in November 1982 and continuing to July 1990. During this upswing, real gross output would expand 36.9 percent. A sustained economic expansion would characterize the rest of the decade.

The recovery in Cycle 44 was initially gradual, but business investment soon grew rapidly. Early on, there were signs of a fall in inflation, and concerned about unemployment, the government made reductions in taxes to promote recovery and boost long-term growth. This is the story of the supply-siders. Supply-side economics emerged in the 1970s in response to the failure of Keynesian economics. Supply-side economists cited high taxes, burdensome regulation, and an extensive welfare state for the economic malaise of the decade. Their policy responses were tax cuts and a broader tax base. President Reagan campaigned on this platform of tax cuts, and in 1981, managed to cut the top rate to 50 percent, and again with the tax reforms of 1986, cut the top rate further to 28 percent. Along with deregulation, these tax cuts, in combination with monetarist-inspired tightening by the Fed, ended stagflation. Those tax cuts and other policy initiatives triggered another decade of solid economic growth. Supply-side economics had its foundations in the older classical economists and would define the rest of the 1980s, and some would argue, the 1990s as well.

A feature of fiscal policy during the Reagan Administration would be boosting defense spending while limiting non-defense spending. The former goal was largely accomplished; the latter wasn't. Supply-motivated tax cuts, along with a build-up of defense spending, boosted economic growth during the 1982-84 period.

During the first few years of the upswing, growth was rapid. Real gross output would expand 3.6 percent in 1983 and then 7.7 percent in 1984. In 1985, the rapid economic expansion eased to a more moderate pace of 3.0 percent in 1985 and 3.3 percent in 1986. Production of light vehicles and other consumer durable goods, along with strong business investment (and the production associated with its supply), were drivers, as was rising defense spending for the rest of the decade.

Economic disruption in the Rust Belt, however, would continue. By the mid-1980s, steel import penetration would exceed 25 percent, and capacity utilization would remain below 70 percent until 1987. The industry was faltering. In 1979, the steel industry employed 453,000; ten years later, only 169,000. Steel production would remain below 100 million tons for 12 years. It has been referred to as the "hollowing out" of American manufacturing, a process that would accelerate in the 1990s and 2000s.

Figure 5.10

Cycle 44: The Heyday of Supply-Side Economics, a Long Expansion, the Gulf War, and 1990-91 Recession

Index of Real Gross Output where 2017 = 100

Inflation waned during this cycle, partly because oil and other commodity prices eased, especially after 1985. Also, as the expansion gathered traction, rising productivity dampened the wage-price spiral of the prior decade. After falling from an average of 6.2 percent in 1982 to 3.2 percent in 1983, inflation rose slightly to 3.2 percent in 1984, but would fall to a low of 1.9 percent in 1986. Unemployment gradually fell from an average of 9.7 percent in 1982 to 7.0 percent in 1986. At that point, inflation began to rise, and many economists at the time felt that the economy had reached full employment.

The overhang of the late-1960s and 1970s and the recessions of the 1980s resulted in many bank and corporate defaults and bankruptcies. In 1984, Continental Illinois became the largest bank failure in American history, when a run on the bank led to its takeover by the Federal Deposit Insurance Corporation (FDIC).

In 1985, depreciation of the dollar fostered boom conditions. This led to a rise in exports, while domestic demand rose at a more moderate pace. In addition, oil prices collapsed in 1986 as the OPEC cartel fell apart when Saudi Arabia boosted production. In addition, many of the energy conservation projects of the previous decade had borne fruit and had dampened demand. Prices collapsed from $27.56 per barrel in 1985 to $14.43 in 1986, prompting a regional recession in Texas and elsewhere and the collapse of real estate prices in the area, fostering troubles for regional banks. The United States was a high-cost producer and unable to compete with the product from the Middle East. Many oil and gas wells were shut in. With rising unemployment in Texas, this prompted instances of "underwater" homeowners literally walking away and handing their house keys to the banks. This was a harbinger of what was to come nationwide two decades later.

Since the United States was more energy efficient than in 1974, the decline in the oil price did not have the positive effect on the economy that one would have expected. Because the nation was still a large producer of oil and gas, the decline did present a modest drag on the economy. Consumers, however, did benefit, and along with Federal Reserve intervention boosting monetary growth, a downturn was averted.

The Tax Reform Act of 1986 raised the effective tax rate on business investment, which fostered softness in structures investment. The other components of business investment, however, continued to expand.

By 1987, activity picked up, and real gross output rose 6.5 percent. The economy appeared to be overheating, as inflation nearly doubled from 1.9 percent in 1986 to 3.6 percent in 1987. The stock market was on a tear, and speculation abounded. In October, the Dow Jones Industrial Average dropped 508 points in one day, by far the largest absolute, and relative daily, decline on record. The stock market crash was known as "Black Monday," and fearing a repeat of the Great Depression that followed the Wall Street Crash of 1929, monetary authorities around the world moved quickly in a coordinated attempt to provide liquidity and loosen monetary policy. The Federal Reserve (at this point headed by Alan Greenspan), flooded the banking system with liquidity by purchasing. bonds and discounting. This prevented the financial contagion from spreading to the real sectors of the economy. This was successful, and after a period of uncertainty, it was apparent that a downturn would not occur, and consumer spending and business investment returned. The economy continued to expand, with real gross output rising 2.2 percent in 1988 and 2.3 percent in 1989. Unemployment would continue to ease, falling from 6.2 percent in 1987 to 5.3 percent in 1989.

The U.S.-Canada Free Trade Agreement was signed by President Reagan and Prime Minister Brian Mulroney in early 1988, with the goal of eliminating all tariffs on trade between the two countries. It would be the harbinger of free trade agreements in the 1990s.

One legacy of the inflation of the 1970s and regulatory changes during that decade and early-1980s is that it pushed lenders into riskier real-estate lending. This came to roost in the form of the savings & loan (S&L) crisis, which was caused by speculation, volatile interest rates, and moral hazard brought about by government guarantees and deregulation. Corruption and fraud played a role as well. Lending standards were weakened and broadened, leading S&L associations and banks to take on too much risk, backed by too little capital. The crisis resulted in the failure of nearly a third of the over 3,200 savings and loan associations in the United States between 1986 and 1995. It would eventually cost over $160 billion, of which over 80 percent was borne by taxpayers. It would be a contributing factor in the next recession. Debt-fueled growth would come home to roost in bank failures. The Federal Reserve's efforts to reduce inflation in the 1980s also provided the backdrop for the downturn.

Oil prices rebounded in the late-1980s in wake of rising demand from a strong global economy, reaching an average $23.73 per barrel in 1990. The pace of growth in borrowing by consumers, businesses, and government was subsiding, and when it stopped growing, lender's margins declined and resulted in a subsequent tightening of lending standards and pull-pack in lending. The phrase "credit crunch" entered the evening news.

A rise in inflation in 1988 and 1989 led the Federal Reserve to raise the discount rate to 8 percent in early 1990, restricting credit into the already slowing economy. In addition, Iraq invaded Kuwait in 1990, and oil prices spiked, as uncertainty was in the air. Manufacturing activity fell. After a business cycle peak was reached in July 1990, a downswing ensued, which would last eight months, ending in March 1991. Real gross output would fall 3.8 percent peak-to-trough. The recession was mild. The unemployment rate would rise from 5.6 percent in 1990 to 6.8 percent in 1991.

Background to the 1980s was the reelection of President Reagan in 1986. In addition, Vice President George H.W. Bush, in 1988, was able to win the White House, while campaigning as a sitting vice president. Prior to that only Martin Van Buren (in 1836) was able to be elected as a sitting vice president. The strong American economy of the 1980s was a key factor in the election outcome.

From a geopolitical viewpoint, the seeds of the fall of the Soviet Union and the end of the Cold War were laid in the 1980s. The United States boosted defense spending and outspent the Soviets. By 1989, the Cold War began to thaw across Eastern Europe and would result in the fall of communism in Eastern and Central Europe. The fall of the Berlin Wall in December 1989 marked the end of the Iron Curtain and the Cold War. Reforms by Soviet President Mikhail Gorbachev proved too little, too late and unleashed internal political, economic, and ethnic forces, leading to the dissolution of the Soviet Union in 1991. This was a pivotal event in world history.

Cycle 45: The Great Moderation and Long Expansion of the 1990s, and the Internet Bubble and Bust

Amidst the recession, the Federal Reserve cut interest rates as an emergency measure, from over five percent to less than three percent by the end of 1992. This marked a new era of easy monetary policy.

The recovery from the 1990-91 recession was slow. For the first time since the 1930s, the economy underwent a "jobless recovery," where business activity and corporate earnings returned to normal levels, while job creation lagged. This contrasted with the basic patterns of the post-World War II recoveries. It was something new, or so it seemed. Unemployment averaged 6.8 percent in 1991 and would rise to 7.5 percent in 1992, and would contribute to President Bush not being reelected, and the election of Arkansas Governor William J. Clinton, a Democrat. The latter campaigned on the weak state of the economy, a jobless recovery, and the uncertainty surrounding it. Thus ended 12 years of Republicans in the White House.

After the Gulf War, oil prices stabilized, which aided economic growth. The recovery was spurred further by the rise of the computer and technology industries. Indeed, the investments in information technology during the 1980s came to fruit in the 1990s, boosting productivity, but also providing for a variety of new services and industries. Economic growth and corporate earnings returned to normal levels while job creation lagged. The financial and service sectors of the economy became more important than manufacturing. The latter is typically volatile because of inventory fluctuations, and the greater importance of these other sectors contributed to less volatility in the economy.

The decade of the 1990s would be remembered as prosperous. It was the decade when the Internet exploded, as did the stock market. Unemployment would eventually reach a low level. It would be marked by a period of a falling ability to conduct fiscal policy and a rising presence of the Fed in conducting monetary policy. Although consumer price inflation would rear its head from time to time, the 1990s and the two decades after would see moderated inflation by this measure. The other measure of inflation, that of asset prices, however, would strengthen during these three decades, the result of low interest rate policies and money creation. It would result in speculation and artificial expansion, and the eventual implosion and recession. Several booms and busts would occur.

Many of the supply-side policies enacted during the Reagan and Bush administrations remained in place, as did momentum for trade agreements. Although this new administration attempted to introduce a new health care program and an energy tax, most changes in fiscal policy were tinkering around the edges. Indeed, these attempts resulted in vast changes in the 1994 mid-term elections. It has been termed the "Republican Revolution" because the Republican Party captured unified control of Congress for the first time since 1952. Republicans picked up eight seats in the Senate and won a net of 54 seats in the House of Representatives. Republicans also picked up a net of ten governorships and took control of many state legislative chambers. This resulted in a balance and check, and thus stability in policy, which reduced business uncertainty.

Figure 5.11

Cycle 45: The Great Moderation and Long Expansion of the 1990s, and the Internet Bubble and Bust

Index of Real Gross Output where 2017 = 100

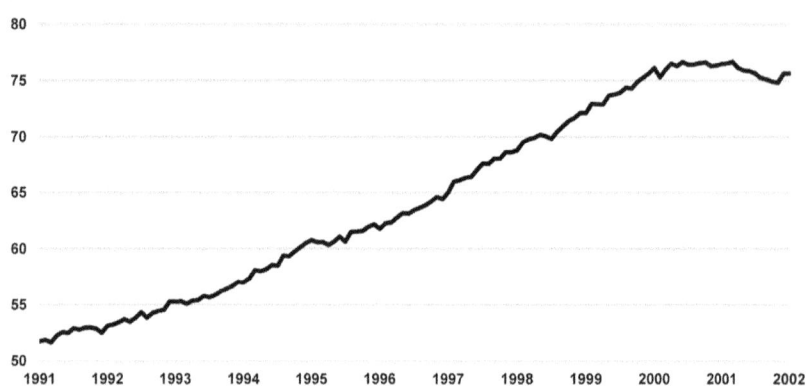

This economic prosperity, combined with several budget reconciliation acts (which restrained spending) allowed the federal government to go from a $290 billion deficit in 1992 to a record $236 billion surplus in 2000. This string of budget surpluses had not been seen since the classical economic policies adopted by Treasury Secretary Andrew Mellon in the 1920s. This reduction in government borrowing alleviated the "crowding out" of private capital and freed up capital in markets for businesses and consumers. This caused interest rates to fall, creating a "virtuous cycle" that reinforced growth.

Unemployment fell, and inflation moderated. Unemployment would fall to 4.0 percent by the end of the decade, and inflation would reach a low of 1.6 percent in 1998. As the recovery progressed, the 1990s would feature a decade of solid economic growth, steady job creation, low inflation, rising productivity, and a surging stock market that resulted from a combination of technological change and favorable monetary policy. The upswing would last 120 months, starting in March 1991 and peaking in March 2001. This was the longest upswing in business cycle history, until it was breached by another in 2019. Real gross output would rise 41.6 percent during these 10 years.

In 1994, real business activity accelerated (to a 5.2 percent gain), but 1995 would bring a slowdown in growth, primarily because the Federal Reserve raised interest rates from 3 percent to 6 percent beginning in late 1994, to prevent inflation from rising. In addition, two government shutdowns temporarily slowed the economy. The pause was short-lived, and a surge of investment in the "dot-com" sectors would lead the economy, beginning in late 1995. Gradually, unemployment began to fall and during 1996 averaged 5.4 percent. This resulted in the reelection of President Clinton. Demand recovered in 1996 and 1997. Growth actually accelerated in 1997, with real gross output rising 6.0 percent. It would average 5.0 percent during the next two years.

The second half of the decade is remembered for a series of global economic financial crises: Mexico in 1994; East Asia in 1997; Russia in 1998, and Argentina in 1999. These slowed growth in their wake. The Federal Reserve supported the economy by lowering interest rates to 4.75 percent by November 1998 to provide liquidity in world financial markets with dollars, and to prevent a global economic crisis. They also sought to restore confidence within the American economy which panicked during the height of the Asian financial crisis in 1997. Long-Term Capital Management (LTCM), a large hedge fund led by Nobel Prize-winning economists and renowned Wall Street traders, blew up in 1998, forcing further intervention to prevent financial markets from collapsing. All of this easing of credit coincided with spectacular stock market run-ups in 1999 and 2000, resulting in the dot-com bubble.

The mid-1990s witnessed the widespread introduction of computers into the home and the rise of the internet. This increased productivity was created by the new information technologies. Other factors behind the long upswing included a healthy dependency ratio, as Baby Boomers were at their peak working and earning years, and a higher savings rate, supporting more credit and investment. Growth of 401Ks as a means of providing retirement benefits fostered prodigious flows into equity markets. Welfare reform mid-decade contributed to an improvement in labor force participation. The decade would see household wealth and home ownership reach all-time highs. Growth was so strong for so long that economists talked of a Great Moderation in the economy and again, the elimination of the business cycle.

The ability to conduct fiscal policy deteriorated slowly in the 1990s and succeeding decades. At the same time, the Fed's ability to conduct monetary policy and experiment would strengthen. The Fed would focus on fighting consumer price inflation rather than asset price inflation during this Great Moderation.

The hollowing out of the Rust Belt continued as manufacturing moved offshore. The North American Free Trade Agreement (NAFTA) was enacted in 1994. Beyond the Rust Belt, however, enactment of NAFTA aided economic growth via improved comparative advantage, which reduced prices for traded goods. With similar effects, the World Trade Organization (WTO) was created in 1995, replacing the General Agreement on Tariffs and Trade (GATT) that had been established in 1948. The WTO is an intergovernmental organization that regulates and facilitates international trade between nations, as well as enforces the rules that govern international trade.

The Y2K scare was the fear that due to programming expediencies, older computers that couldn't cope with dates past 1999 would crash. Fears of bringing down vast networks controlling utilities and payment systems were rampant. The dire warnings about Y2K did spur massive upgrades and replacement of systems. This led to an information technology (IT) capital-spending boom in 1999. After the upgrades were completed by New Year's Day 2000, however, there came a IT bust that helped precipitate the following year's recession. The dot-com bubble peaked in March 2000.

The Federal Reserve's steady tightening of monetary policy in 1999-2000 during the IT boom also had something to do with the downturn. The Federal Reserve hiked rates to 6.5 percent in May 2000. It appeared by late-2000 that the business cycle was not eliminated, but simply peaking. Growth eased, job creation slowed, the stock markets plunged, and the foundations for the 2001 recession were being laid, thus ending the economic boom of the 1990s.

In addition, the 2000 presidential election was contested, fostering uncertainty that lasted until January 2001. Texas Governor George W. Bush, a Republican, was elected 43rd president, having defeated Vice President Albert Gore in the Electoral College. It would mark the beginning of divisive partisan bickering.

The downturn would last eight months, starting in March 2001 and lasting until November 2001. The 9-11 attacks on the World Trade Center and the Pentagon have been cited as a factor behind the recession, but since they were late in the recession, it was likely that the attacks only delayed recovery by a month or two. The downturn was mild, with real gross output falling peak to trough by less than 1.0 percent. This was another instance where a recession occurred but did not feature two consecutive quarters of declining real GDP.

Immediately after the attacks, the Federal Reserve reassured markets that the Fed was operating as normal and that the discount window was available to any bank that needed liquidity. Financial markets calmed down, and a liquidity crunch was avoided. In addition, the Fed immediately started to buy Treasuries in the open market, injecting about $100 billion in liquidity per day in the three days after the attacks. Central banks in Europe, Canada, and Japan coordinated with the Fed to support the U.S. dollar. The Fed enacted several rate cuts (totaling 2.5 percentage points) by the end of the year. In addition, the new Bush Administration authorized $40 billion in emergency funds to help with the relief efforts, and by January 2002, the tax cuts were enacted.

The downturn would lead to a series of bankruptcies. Most notable was Enron. At the time, it was the largest bankruptcy in American history and threatened to destabilize the economy. Investments disappeared; jobs were lost; reputations destroyed; and accounting firm Arthur Andersen collapsed. Several Enron executives went to jail. The failures of Enron's board and executives resulted in the Sarbanes-Oxley Act, and the corporate responsibility movement.

Cycle 46: The Housing Bubble and Bust, and the Great Financial Crisis

The Cycle 45 downswing ended in November 2001, as the Federal Reserve cut interest rates, and President George W. Bush signed extensive tax cuts to aid American families. The Federal Reserve pursued a low interest rate policy and took other emergency measures, which became largely permanent. The resulting upswing would be long, lasting 73 months, coming to an end in December 2007. During the period, real gross output would rise 17.8 percent, a slow recovery.

Early in the upswing in December 2001, China became a member of the WTO. China's reentry into the global market and its strategy of export-led growth would play a large role in shaping the global economy during subsequent decades. Indeed, China would be referred to as the "factory floor to the world" in subsequent years. Free trade extends the division of labor on an international scale and is beneficial. It furthers economic integration and efficiency. That said, during this upswing, American manufacturing didn't fully partake in the improving economy. Much of the incremental new supply for manufactured goods came from China and other nations. Add to import competition, the role of large productivity gains, and the economies of the Rust Belt suffered and never fully recovered. Between 2001 and 2006, for example, manufacturing employment would fall from 16.4 million to 14.2 million. There was talk of the "hollowing out" of American manufacturing.

A recovery did take place, but it was largely outside the industrial sectors, centered in finance and services. Too much of the recovery proved to be the result of an expanding credit bubble, fueled by historically low interest rates. A housing bubble, which had been forming for years, accelerated to an unimaginable level. Monetary policy would overly stimulate the economy in the next several years, resulting in a housing bubble replacing the stock market bubble.

The Federal Reserve would take a lead in stimulating the economy, substituting one asset bubble (dot-com companies) for another bubble (housing). In 2004 and 2005, housing construction and real estate gathered strength, with the price of housing rising sharply across the nation. The Fed kept interest rates at 1.0 percent for too long and would raise them ever so slowly. Fear of rising consumer price inflation would cause the Fed to raise interest rates sharply in 2006 (to about 5.0 percent), setting the stage for the eventual bust in asset prices. When asset prices corrected, it would lead to large scale financial instability.

Figure 5.12
Cycle 46: The Housing Bubble and Bust, and the Great Financial Crisis

Index of Real Gross Output where 2017 = 100

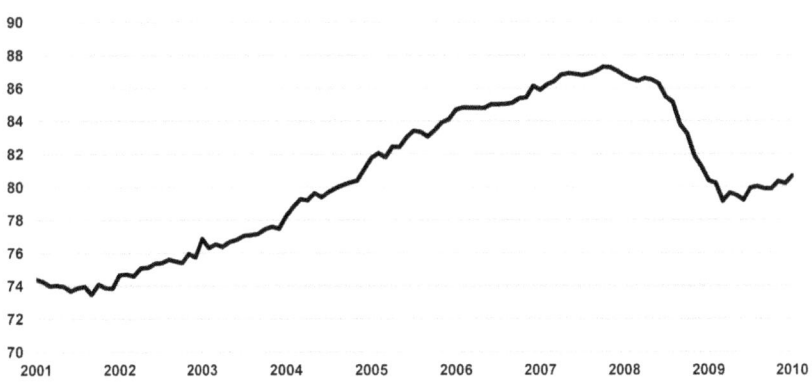

The roots of the housing bubble went back several decades. The Community Reinvestment Act of 1977 (CRA) was a key part of the drive for affordable housing. In 1992, the Federal Housing Enterprises Financial Safety and Soundness Act mandated affordable housing goals for Fannie Mae and Freddie Mac. Both lowered nationwide underwriting standards. In addition, the Clinton and Bush administrations sought to increase the number of low-income homeowners. During the 2000s, banks and mortgage companies relaxed lending standards to borrowers with poor credit-rating histories (so-called subprime borrowers). As banks and mortgage lenders relaxed their lending standards, the subprime sector went from 8 percent of mortgage originations to 24 percent in 2006. By 2008, 27 million mortgages (50 percent of the total) were subprime or Alt-A loans. The median loan-to-value ratio rose from 90 percent in 2005 to nearly 100 percent in 2007.

Other government policies included the 1999 repeal of the Glass-Steagall Act, which since the 1930s had separated commercial and investment banking. All of this was fostered by the lobbying efforts of real estate and financial industries.

Moreover, the Federal Reserve's Fed's low interest rate policy after the 2001 downswing provided fuel to the boom. Loan-to-value ratios approached 100 percent, and interest-only and adjustable-rate mortgages became the norm. Expansion of mortgage credit was supercharged by securitization of mortgages (by investment bankers), in which mortgages were sliced, diced, and packaged into mortgage-backed securities (MBS) with AAA ratings. Unregulated mortgage brokers fed the bubble with increasingly toxic loan instruments and subprime credits. Moreover, the investment-rating firms applied faulty stress tests to justify top ratings for undeserving MBS offerings. These financially engineered securities would fail spectacularly. Moreover, even riskier mortgages were repackaged as Collateralized Debt Obligations (CDOs). The securitization of mortgages created highly marketable instruments, which allowed worldwide speculation, and at one point, over 60 percent of U.S. mortgage funding was foreign.

The originate-to-distribute model meant that mortgage originators were less likely to screen borrowers carefully and any potential consequences were passed on.

Securitization, by allowing banks to lower their lending standards and thus issue more mortgages, amplified, and pyramided leverage. Securitization also allowed investors to participate in the housing boom without having to buy or sell houses, or lend to homeowners. As a result, easy mortgage credit (and predatory lending) resulted in the poorest members of society being swept up in the Subprime Bubble. The Federal Reserve and other financial regulators failed to apprehend the systemic threat these instruments and development created.

Low mortgage interest rates prompted consumers to buy houses in an unprecedented fashion. Mortgage debt increased from $5.3 trillion in 2001 to $10.5 trillion in 2007, almost as much in six years as in the entire period from 1776 to 2000. Between 2000 and 2008, nearly 15 million new homes were completed in the United States, of which perhaps as many 3.5 million were not needed. Housing completions peaked, just as the number of new household formations (the prime driver of housing demand) collapsed.

Most of America got caught up in this boom. Homes became marketable objects of speculation with banks providing unlimited amounts of leverage. Consumers began to see houses as an investment, not for rental income but for capital appreciation. Television played a role with *House Hunters*, *Flip That House*, and similar popular shows. Unlike other bubbles, however, housing is nearly impossible to short sell.

During the first half of the decade, housing prices soared. This boosted household wealth, and through mortgage equity withdrawals (MEW), was a large factor in sustaining consumer spending. Indeed, the savings rate actually turned negative during this period.

Continuous gains in housing values supported this. Another trend was the growth of lending secured on property. As with all bubbles, the price of the asset would eventually converge towards the actual value of the asset.

In 2006, Fed Chair Greenspan retired, and Ben S. Bernanke was appointed Fed Chair in February 2006. His first term would be marked by the Great Financial Crisis (GFC), the result of the bursting of the housing bubble.

The housing bubble could not last and mortgage delinquencies started rising in 2006 and accelerated in 2007, as housing values peaked and then declined. Several lenders failed, leading to the clogging of securitization, and freezing of the interbank market in the summer of 2007. Housing prices slumped sharply. Although the recession began in December 2007, it was not widely recognized. Many business economists thought the emerging housing crisis was solvable and temporary. The author remembers being in a meeting of about 20 business economists in July 2008 and being one of only two who viewed the economy to be in recession. The consensus of forecasters also reflected a non-recession scenario.

Mortgage delinquencies continued to soar in 2008, and MBSs continued to default. The eventual fall in housing prices disproportionally affected lower income homeowners, wiping out most of their wealth. In September 2008 the U.S. Treasury placed government-sponsored entities (GSEs), Fannie Mae and Freddie Mac, into receivership. September also saw the failure of Lehman Brothers and the bailout of AIG.

The collapse of the housing bubble and resulting record foreclosures and financial crises threw markets worldwide into a tailspin. The housing (or property) boom of the 2000s was global in nature. Ireland, Spain, the United Kingdom, and the United States had simultaneous major property bubbles (and eventually busts). Housing bubbles are a perfect example of an economically and socially destructive bubble. In its wake, the housing bust left behind ghost developments, shells of homes, and dampened expectations. The downswing resulted in very high unemployment.

Falling housing values contributed to a global financial crisis, even as oil and food prices soared. The crisis led to the failure or collapse of many of the United States' largest financial institutions: Bear Stearns, Fannie Mae, Freddie Mac, Lehman Brothers, and AIG, as well as a crisis in the light vehicle industry.

Equity markets were adversely affected. The Dow Jones Industrial Average, for example, fell by half from over 14,000 in October 2007, reducing average household wealth by 20 percent.

Fearing a repeat of the Great Depression that followed the Wall Street Crash of 1929, monetary authorities around the world moved quickly in a coordinated attempt to provide liquidity and loosen monetary policy. In response, the Federal Reserve lowered interest rates to zero in an effort to spur investment. The Fed used extraordinary measures, including quantitative easing (QE) and zero interest rate policy (ZIRP), resulting in interest rates close to zero for 10 years. This was a key difference compared to prior recessions. The increases in credit spreads arising from the shock to credit supply were allayed by lower risk-free rates and lending rates that fell in absolute and real terms. Central banks around the world resorted to QE and other methods to preclude potential deflation. Emergency lending programs in wake of the crisis would include the Term Auction Facility (TAF), Term Securities Lending Facility (TSLF), and the Primary Dealer Credit Facility (PDCF).

In 2008, Congress passed the Troubled Asset Relief Plan (TARP), a $700 billion financial support and stimulus package. President Bush was not eligible for re-election, and Arizona Senator John McCain ran on the Republican ticket against junior Illinois Senator Barack Obama. The public was so unnerved about the GFC and recession that Senator Obama handily won. Early in his administration, the American Recovery and Reinvestment Act of 2009 (ARRA) was passed. This was a $787 billion stimulus package. These stimulus packages aimed to help citizens, while the light vehicle and finance industries were given bailouts to prevent their collapse.

From its peak in October 2007 to its trough in March 2009, the S&P 500 declined 56 percent. The cyclical downswing in the real economy started in December 2007 and was sharp and prolonged. It lasted 18 months, ending in June 2009. The recession was one of the worst in the U.S. economy since the Great Depression, with real gross output falling 9.0 percent from peak to trough.

The speed and severity of the downturn was rapid compared to the Great Moderation that had come before. The downswing was severe. Nearly 8.7 million jobs were lost, and 2.5 million businesses closed. Virtually all sectors of the economy were affected. Manufacturing employment would fall from 14.2 million during 2006 to 11.8 million in 2009. The recession was worldwide, affecting virtually all nations. The GFC led to collapse in world trade and would result in the Euro Area crisis of 2011 and 2012.

In 2005, Hurricane Katrina devastated Louisiana and left Gulf Coast offshore oil and gas operations off-line for an extended period. Natural gas prices, in particular jumped, rising four-fold. This sent a price signal, and along with technological developments in horizontal drilling, hydraulic factoring (aka fracking) and computational modeling would foster the shale revolution in unconventional oil and gas. This revolution would lower energy prices in the United States and foster new investment by energy-consuming industries. The revolution in the oil and gas industries would help pull the economy out of recession, and these were also a factor in the long recovery of the 2010s.

The Great Financial Crisis was global in scope. It would lead to anemic growth in much of the world. In Europe, the crisis never really ended. The debt overhang among many nations was just too high, and actions by the European Central Bank (ECB) would hamper economic growth. A secondary recession in Europe would occur in 2011.

Cycle 47: Slow, Long Economic Recovery and the COVID Recession

President Obama's January 2009 inauguration was held in the depths of a deep recession. The new administration continued the banking bailout and auto industry rescue begun by the previous administration and immediately enacted a near $800 billion stimulus program, the American Recovery and Reinvestment Act of 2009 (ARRA). The ARRA increased spending for infrastructure, health care, education, and social benefits, with targeted tax cuts.

The Administration intervened in the troubled light vehicle industry in March, renewing loans for General Motors and Chrysler to continue operations while they reorganized. Over the following months, the Administration set terms for both firms' bankruptcies, including the sale of Chrysler to Italian automaker Fiat and a reorganization of General Motors, giving the U.S. government a temporary equity stake in the company. The president also signed into law the Car Allowance Rebate System program, also known as "Cash for Clunkers." The latter was largely ineffective, merely pulling demand forward slightly, with sales soon returning to trend. By late 2013, the federal government had disposed of all of its investments in Chrysler and GM.

President Obama followed with the 2010 Patient Protection and Affordable Care Act (ACA), commonly referred to as "Obamacare." After a wobbly start, by 2016, the law covered approximately 24 million people with health insurance via a combination of state healthcare exchanges and an extension of Medicaid. The Dodd-Frank law would lead to more complex regulation of banking. With the high cost of regulatory compliance, the United States would see a wave of bank consolidation, losing one-third of independent banks after Dodd-Frank. A new regulatory agency, the Consumer Financial Protection Bureau (CFPB), would affect banking in subsequent years. An international banking standard, known as the Basel III accord, would also add to bank oversight.

In the 2010 mid-term elections, the reaction against the administration's policies was large. The Republicans retook the House of Representatives. The rise of the Tea Party movement would limit the ability of a Democrat administration and Senate to enact additional progressive policies.

By March 2010, the private sector began creating jobs consistently each month, a trend which continued through the end of the decade. Public sector employment was slower to recover. The recovery and expansion from the Great Financial Crisis (GFC) were slow. With a large debt overhang, a long period of anemic economic growth would arise. The unemployment rate remained stubbornly high. Non-farm employment took until May 2014 to return to its previous peak. After an initial 3.6 percent gain in 2010, real gross output would average only 2.6 percent growth per year through 2014.

Fed Chair Bernanke was nominated by President Obama for a second term. The president referred to him as "the epitome of calm" and in early 2010 he was confirmed for a second term. His leadership in managing the GFC (along with Treasury Secretary Geitner and others) is widely acknowledged although the verdict is out on monetary policy during the recovery and expansion. In 2014, he was succeeded by Janet Yellen.

As the financial system recovered, leveraged loans and the CLO (collateralized loan obligation) would gain in popularity. This would create a new opportunity for banks. The large banks, the ones too big to fail, would become even larger. The number of community banks, for example, would continue to fall, as mergers and acquisitions in the banking industry rose, resulting in consolidation. In addition, a "shadow" banking system would emerge as hedge funds and private equity firms took on many bank-like functions.

In wake of the Cycle 46 downturn, and for long afterwards, the Federal Reserve embarked on a program of unprecedented activism, aggressively intervening with ZIRP and with QE. Zero interest rates were the first in history and would continue long after they were needed. In 2013, signs emerged that the Federal Reserve would reduce the pace of its purchases of Treasury bonds. This change in quantitative easing resulted in a rise in bond yields and the so-called Taper Tantrum, a reaction by equity markets. The Fed didn't actually slow its QE purchasing, but instead launched into a third round of massive bond purchases, totaling another $1.5 trillion by 2015. Increasingly, the Fed (and other central banks) through quantitative easing and other tools, simply overwhelmed bond markets, distorting price signals and credit markets. No single policy would do more to reshape American economic life and foster inequality, the gap between rich and poor. QE would flood the financial system and would push banks (and investors) to make riskier loans in search of yield. The search for yield would push monies into corporate debt and stocks, commercial real estate, developing nations, and also into the oil and gas industry. High and increasing leverage, lax financial supervision, and adding money to the monetary base only added to this experimentation. Near permanent intervention would be the norm and would lead to further bubbles. One of the strangest outcomes of QE and ZIRP policies would be the emergence of negative-interest-rate-bonds, especially in Europe.

The Federal Reserve for decades, had its hawks, those that hated inflation, and its doves, those less afraid of inflation. The terms would change to mean, respectively, those seeking to limit the Fed's reach and those arguing for more aggressive intervention. In addition to QE, the Fed would introduce "forward guidance" as well as Operation Twist, a bond buying experiment attempting to push down long-term interest rates.

The Federal Reserve under Fed Chair Yellen eventually committed to raising — or "normalizing" — interest rates. She spent considerable time attempting to unwind some of the earlier Fed interventions. In December 2015, the Federal Reserve raised interest rates above the zero lower bound for the first time in seven years. Over the next two-and-half years, six more hikes occurred, bringing the target range of the federal funds rate to 1.75 to 2.00 percent range by June 2018. The European Central Bank would follow the Fed's lead and end its own QE program. Monetary policy around the world became less accommodative and turned toward tightening.

Due to the shale revolution, production of oil would rise from 5.1 million barrels per day in 2005 to 9.4 million barrels per day in 2015. Similarly, natural gas production would rise from 51.9 billion BCF per day to 78.8 BCF in 2015. This created an enormous competitive advantage to energy consuming industries such as chemicals. It resulted in a wave of new investment and expansion of basic petrochemical capacity of nearly 40 percent during the decade. The shale revolution provided a lifeline to the steel industry in the form of increasing demand for pipe, resulting in investment in new mills and re-starts of others. A number of industries (tires & rubber products, plastic products, aluminum, etc.) also benefited.

In 2014, OPEC and Russia would work together to maintain market share and restrict production, aiming to lower prices and force the new shale gas companies in America out of the market. In 2013, oil prices averaged nearly $109 per barrel. By 2016, prices averaged less than $44 per barrel. Although lower prices benefited the consumer, it had the effect of moderating oil and gas production. Supplying industries were also affected. Gains in real gross output slowed from a 3.0 percent pace in 2014, to 2.3 percent in 2015, and 2.2 percent in 2016. By 2015, steel import penetration reached an all-time high of 29.1 percent of demand. However, oil and gas production would continue to expand. By 2019, oil production would average 12.2 million barrels per day, and natural gas production would average 100 BCF per day.

The 2016 presidential election was another contested election. It featured former Secretary of State Hillary Clinton (and wife of former President Clinton) as the Democratic candidate and businessman Donald J. Trump, a populist running under the Republican banner. The former won the popular vote while the latter won the vote in the Electoral College. Partisan acrimony would intensify.

President Trump did not reappoint Fed Chair Yellen to a second term. Instead, he nominated Jerome Powell as chair in November 2017, and Powell became Fed Chair in early 2018. One of Powell's first actions was to continue to raise interest rates, as a response to the increasing strength of the economy and as an attempt to further normalize Fed policy.

Figure 5.13

Cycle 47: Slow, Long Economic Recovery, the COVID Recession, and post-COVID Recovery

Index of Real Gross Output where 2017 = 100

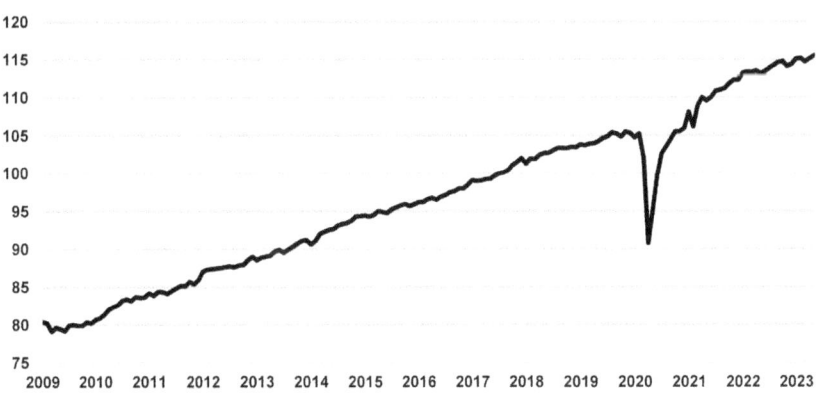

The new Administration's economic policy would be known for two major developments. Although elected as an economic populist, President Trump would pass significant corporate tax reform. Since the Reagan Revolution of the 1980s, most OECD nations followed the suit of the United States and lowered their corporate income tax rates. By the 2010s, the United States was no longer competitive, as its corporate tax rates were among the highest internationally.

The Tax Cuts and Jobs Act (TCJA) was the largest overhaul of the tax code in three decades. It created a single corporate tax rate of 21 percent and changed deductions, depreciation, expensing, tax credits, and other tax items that affect businesses. By lowering the cost of capital, it led to renewed business investment and an improvement in growth. Real gross output would expand 2.8 percent in 2017 and would accelerate to a 3.4 percent gain in 2018. However, the Administration's other major economic policy development would mute this.

Trade policy was strictly populist. The Trump tariffs were a series of U.S. tariffs imposed as part of his "America First" economic policy to reduce the United States trade deficit by shifting American trade policy from multilateral free trade agreements to bilateral trade deals. Tariffs were imposed on solar panels, washing machines, steel, and aluminum from most countries. The administration separately set and escalated tariffs on goods imported from China, leading to a trade war. The tariffs angered trading partners, who implemented retaliatory tariffs on U.S. goods. This "trade war" had an effect of slowing business activity and the economy going into 2019. Real gross output slowed from a 3.4 percent gain in 2018, to a 2.1 percent gain in 2019, leaving the economy more exposed to a shock.

Some analysts criticized the Fed's December 2018 rate hike as a "policy mistake" and with the "Powell Pivot" in 2019, the Fed had to reverse its normalizing policy when a trade war and inventory build-up led to global economic weakness. In 2019, the Fed reacted too much to market volatility, and in the last quarter of 2019, expanded its balance sheet again, in the absence of any economic crisis. The Fed also cut interest rates, even though the economy was growing. The stock market rose to new highs with that expansion. Essentially, the Fed underwrote a massive upward move in equity markets. Warning signs of the financial fragility would soon occur with the disturbances in the "repo" market. To stem failure, the Fed reacted with a $400 billion bailout. The Fed closed 2019 with Chairman Powell and the Board of Governors insisting they had cut enough and were confident that rates would hold steady for the foreseeable future. The "Fed Put" was extended and more deeply entrenched in financial markets. Bailouts were now becoming the policy tool of choice.

The upswing in Cycle 46 would be the longest on record, fully 128 months, beginning in June 2009 and lasting until February 2020, although signs of weakness had been present for nearly a year prior to the latter. During the upswing, real gross output would rise 32.8 percent. A major reason for its longevity was that the initial recovery through 2016 was so slow that few imbalances and distortions arose. In addition, favorable tax policies enacted in 2017 provided the nation with a competitive corporate tax system. This fostered greater business investment, although this has to be placed within context of a major trade war and trade distortions, which fostered uncertainty.

In September 2019 weakness was apparent when the Federal Reserve had to begin interventions in the repo market after the overnight lending rate spiked above the Fed's target rate, in an attempt to keep the economy afloat due to a liquidity issue. However, an unforeseen shock would arise to end the upswing and push the nation into recession.

The first documented case of COVID-19 emerged in Wuhan, China, in November 2019. China's government first instituted travel restrictions, quarantines, and stay-at-home orders. When efforts to contain the coronavirus in China were unsuccessful, other countries in Asia and Europe instituted similar measures in an attempt to contain and slow the spread of the virus. The initial outbreak expanded into a global pandemic and would quickly reach America.

The World Health Organization officially declared a pandemic in March 2020. Actions were taken by the United States and other nations around the world — restricting travel, shuttering nonessential businesses, and implementing social distancing policies — to curb the spread of the coronavirus. These led to severe economic (and social) consequences.

Business conditions were already weak going into 2020. The index of real gross output peaked in November, the result of a long trade war with China and a slowdown in global manufacturing and inventory imbalance. The COVID-19 coronavirus pandemic spread to the United States, Europe, and other nations during January, thus setting the stage for an adverse supply-side shock. The policy response in the United States led to recession, as governors — with stay-at-home orders and mandated business closings — deliberately sought to shut their respective state economies down in an effort to slow the spread of the pandemic. The recession was a government-led supply-side crisis, not an accidental demand-side recession. Consumers were not suddenly prohibited from buying many goods and services because they had no income. Rather, they had no income because they were barred from producing goods and services by working in some "non-essential" jobs or opening "non-essential" businesses. Thus, a severe lockdown recession, imposed by governors to slow the spread of the virus, was the hallmark of this downturn.

The "COVID recession" was a shock, brought about on purpose by policymakers as a means of dealing with a health pandemic. Most governors did not want to "stimulate" the private economy. Rather, they wanted to shut it down, to reduce or eliminate social and economic exchange all together. The economic effects of the pandemic were severe. It was the most severe disruption of the American economy since the Great Depression. A series, of at times, mis-informed public health policies led to business shutdowns, school closures, and mask mandates that achieved, at best, only minor slowdowns in the disease's spread. The cost, however, was tremendous economic destruction and social disruption. The suppression of the economy primarily hurt individuals at the lower end of the income scale.

The COVID recession was literally a switching off of economic exchange, which could not be detected by the usual indicators or large-scale macroeconomic models. Some of the leading barometers of the business cycle did show enough weakness in the economy, suggesting higher probabilities of recession before COVID struck. However, literally no credible business economists in late-2019 had an inkling of what was to come.

To their credit, the NBER quickly identified the February business cycle peak. Most measures of business activity bottomed in April. The downturn was the shortest in business cycle history. I know some economists who feel this was not an actual recession, but rather a severe supply-shock that lasted two months but had lingering effects. I believe it was an actual recession, one fostered by this public health threat and the government response, a supply-side shock.

The recession was short but deep, lasting only two months (beginning in February 2020 and ending in April 2020) and the shortest on record; real gross output would fall 13.7 percent in those months. In the space of two months (February to April), over 22.1 million jobs were lost. New unemployment claims peaked at 6.62 million in the week ending on March 28th, 2020. Many professionals and white-collar workers were able to work from home, leading to a surge in purchases of computers and related equipment and furniture. The demand for personal protection equipment (PPE) was a major factor behind plastics being one of the only industries to expand in 2020. Most service jobs, however, are not amenable to remote work, and since these positions were most affected by the lockdowns, the government response to the pandemic exacerbated inequality. Large sections of the economy were closed for months. This had never happened before, even during the pandemic of 1918-19. The cost was beyond calculation. It resulted in destruction of new kinds of unemployment, bankruptcy, and lost output, but would include multiplying unprecedented public debt, broken supply chains, rising depression, suicide, and other serious health problems.

The COVID recession was the first in history in which incomes actually rose, the result of massive transfer payments. Also unique to this recession, government tax revenues rose as a share of economic output in 2020, as job losses were concentrated in low-wage employment and high-income jobs were hit less hard. In absolute terms, tax revenues fell as the economy contracted sharply. However, federal government tax revenues fell only slightly in nominal dollar terms to $5.3 trillion in 2020.

The economy was in a free fall with widespread state and local lockdowns of activity starting in March, adversely affecting food service, leisure and hospitality, education, and other sectors. Sporting events, conferences, and other economic exchange where human interaction was present resulted in cancellations and lockdowns. A number of fiscal responses were quickly made. First, the $8.3 billion Coronavirus Preparedness and Response Supplemental Appropriations Act of 2020 was passed in early March 2020. Then, two weeks later, the Families First Coronavirus Response Act injected $225 billion into the economy. Two weeks after that, the Coronavirus, Aid, Relief and Economic Security (CARES) Act would inject $2.2 trillion. It created the Paycheck Protection Program (PPP). In April, the Paycheck Protection Program and Health Care Enhancement Act provided $483 billion in funding for PPP and other initiatives. In December, the Consolidated Appropriations Act of 2021 provided $920 billion in spending, and included $600 stimulus checks, renewed the Paycheck Protection Program, provided billions for vaccines, and permitted a renewal of a federal boost to unemployment benefits at $300 per week.

Going into the recession, corporate debt levels were at high levels, giving companies little room to maneuver. Equity markets collapsed, and several automatic shutdowns in trading would be triggered. The Fed responded with unprecedented and rapid-fire emergency measures, a show of overwhelming force. The Fed would create three special purpose vehicles (SPVs) to get around limits placed on its lending authority. New programs included the Main Street Lending Program, as well as purchases of corporate and even riskier bonds, the so-called Secondary Market Corporate Credit facility. The latter included the purchase of ETFs (electronically trade funds) that had invested in junk debt. In a way, the Fed became the lender of last resort for everyone. The Fed kept interest rates near zero and provided $120 billion per month in QE for more than a year-and-a-half.

The Federal Reserve quickly provided liquidity to the banking system, extending QE and ZIRP. Most economists, financial professionals, and historians would say that it worked. The Fed's pledges to backstop an array of lending would unleash a torrent of private borrowing, based on the promise of central bank action. This was reinforced by the massive assistance by Congress, which authorized unprecedented monies that would cover any losses. The pandemic forced rate cuts to zero and started another program on quantitative easing. Consisting of large open-ended purchases of bonds, this expansive monetary policy would eventually see the Fed more than double its balance sheet (by more than $4 trillion) to an $8.9 trillion portfolio of Treasury and mortgage securities. It was QE on steroids. The Fed would soon own about one-third of both the Treasury and mortgage markets, and its balance sheet would double from the start of the pandemic to 40 percent of gross domestic product. During this cycle, the Fed placed a heightened focus on achieving its full-employment goals, a goal of broad-based, inclusive, and maximized employment. The emphasis was on employment rather than inflation. That latter, however, would soon become heated.

The economic downturn was worldwide, with only one major economy, that of China, where the coronavirus originated, experiencing growth during 2020. The economic downturn was more severe in Europe, where stricter lockdowns were in place. Within the United States, the economic damage was more severe in states with stricter lockdowns, although the latter may have had better health outcomes.

Cycle 48: From the Pandemic: The Start of a New Cycle

The downturn was unforeseen at the start of 2020. By March, various cities and states imposed lockdowns on economic activity. So did the national government.

The "COVID recession" was a shock, brought about on purpose, by policymakers as a means of dealing with a health pandemic. The downturn was sharp and deep, but short, lasting only two months. Unlike the prior recession, the recovery in jobs was fairly quick. It was V-shaped.

The political response to the pandemic and the recession resulted in high unemployment and consumer uncertainty. President Trump had poor favorability ratings and lost reelection to former Vice President Joseph Biden. The election outcome was contested in several states and added to the partisan acrimony.

The development of COVID-19 vaccines for use in the country occurred fairly quickly. By December, the roll-out of vaccinations began, and many states started reopening, starting first in the South and Midwest, and spreading to other states.

Well after the end of the recession, Federal Reserve policy was still extremely loose. Interest rates were anchored at zero, and the central bank was buying $120 billion-worth of assets each month — $80 billion of Treasuries and $40 billion of mortgage-backed securities (MBS) — in order to depress long-term interest rates. This continued into the 1st quarter of 2022, even though housing activity had fully rebounded and was experiencing all sorts of material and labor shortages. One consequence of Fed monetary policy was sending the stock market to new record highs. This exacerbated inequality. Federal Reserve officials are examining how and when they could shrink their $8.9 trillion portfolio of Treasury and mortgage securities.

By August 2020, the Federal Reserve was impatient with the low inflation rate of the Bernanke and Yellen years. Chairman

Powell called low inflation the pre-eminent economic challenge. So, the Fed initiated a new policy regime to boost inflation. Along with aggressive (and unnecessary) fiscal policy, it worked. By early 2022, consumer prices were up 8.5 percent year-over-year. In a break with precedent, the Fed also explicitly endorsed the large boost in federal spending. Fed policy also contributed to financial and other asset inflation.

The new Biden Administration was able to pass the American Rescue Plan (ARP) in 2021, which provided $1.9 trillion in funding for $1,400 stimulus checks, money for schools to reopen, and billions for vaccine distribution and development. The ARP was entirely deficit-financed. Federal spending increased from an average of about 21 percent of gross domestic product in the prior decade to more than 30 percent in fiscal 2020 and 2021. National debt would increase to over 100 percent of GDP. The year would feature passage of a $1.1 trillion infrastructure bill in November and continuing debates over the Administration's "Build Back Better" social spending bill. Economists and historians are only beginning to grasp the implications of the aggressive fiscal policy response.

Consumer spending recovered quickly from the COVID pandemic. The pandemic and the policy responses (i.e., lockdowns) changed buying plans. Consumers shifted from dining out and entertainment (i.e., services) to purchasing goods. COVID stimulus payments to consumers encouraged additional purchases. The pandemic pulled forward spending by consumers, such as a rush to buy light vehicles by those fleeing locked-down cities and states for homes in the suburbs and states with less strict lockdowns. This fostered strong demand for appliances and furniture, as well as computers for work (and education) from home. The lockdowns led to a surge in the demand for building supplies for DIY projects.

The stimulus monies, combined with few opportunities to spend, also resulted in abnormally high savings rates and savings. Household balances sheets in the aggregate did not suffer and were actually boosted. The lockdowns and working from home resulted in high demand for consumer goods at a time when supply was constrained. The combined stimulus packages with high consumer savings fostered a demand shock once the lockdowns ended, which overwhelmed supply and disrupted global supply chains. There were many similarities with the bout of inflation during 1946-48. Fiscal policy was a major reason for the 2021 and 2022 surge in inflation, which would peak at 8.9 percent year-over-year in June 2022. The rise in household balances sheets would support consumer spending when inflation began to erode real incomes during 2022, and as the economy slowed.

Unlike previous recessions, the COVID recession was actually very short, lasting only two months. Many forms of economic activity, such as retail spending and home building fully recovered within months. After the 2007-09 recession, for example, it took four years. With demand quickly recovering, supply was unable to keep up.

This would lead to supply-chain bottlenecks: a queue of ships waiting off LA/Long Beach with shipping containers stacked high on those docks, waiting to be picked up by truckers, also in short supply. By some estimates, the shortage of drivers numbered 80,000. The media reported on potential empty shelves ahead of the holidays, and this resulted in some demand being pulled ahead in late-2021. The supply chain bottlenecks were widespread across industries. Most notable were semiconductors. Virtually all industries were affected. Adding to this were weather events such as the 2021 winter storm in Texas and Hurricane Ida.

The recovery introduced a number of labor issues. The pandemic-induced stimulus packages provided overly generous support. This provided incentives to askew work in favor of not-working and fostered extended unemployment. This held back labor force participation. A number of states recognized this, and they withdrew the added unemployment benefits in the summer of 2021, and their record on employment improved relative to those states that maintained the benefits. Added to this was a rising equity market, which allowed Baby Boomers to retire. Along with mothers pursuing childcare instead of a career and the ability of workers to leave a job and seek another better one, these changes evolved into what has been called the Great Resignation. At the same time, the number of young people who would typically enter the labor market declined sharply, the result of lower births after the mid-1990s. By 2021, job openings outnumbered the unemployed, resulting in a tight labor market and rising wages. The widespread labor shortages are also attributable to demographic trends and are structural in nature.

Union representation steadily declined during the post-World War II period, especially after 1981, and at the end of the 2010s, accounted for only 11 percent of the total labor force and just six percent of the private sector. The COVID pandemic brought about many changes, one of which was a new restlessness among workers, many of whom left the workforce or changed careers. Coupled with demographic trends, labor shortages and challenges affected virtually every industry. In early 2022, there were nearly two job openings for every unemployed worker, and the unemployment rate fell to near pre-pandemic levels. The resulting tight labor supply and mismatch of skills led to higher wages and emboldened workers to seek a better deal. Turnover and the quits rate were high, and in 2021, work stoppages rose. This could be the start of rising power for labor at the expense of capital.

Combined with QE and other monetary stimulus, the higher demand with constrained supply resulted in rising prices for consumer durable goods which spread to consumer non-durable goods and consumer services, as the economy reopened. Inflation was the result, and it soon reached levels last seen in the early-1980s. QE also discouraged investments in real assets like capital equipment, relative to financial assets such as stocks. It's a reason why business investment lagged behind pre-pandemic trend, and for that matter, lagged below trend since the advent of QE in the 2010s. Inflation began to heat-up in 2021, and by late-2021 and into 2022, the Fed recognized that inflation was not "transitory" and began to accelerate its tapering of its asset purchases. It is possible that the Fed simply doesn't know much about the situation it has created. In March 2022, the Fed would reverse course and embark on a program of quantitative tightening (QT) and rate hikes. The hikes during the following 12 months would be very aggressive. The ramifications of this unprecedented tightening are beginning to be felt in the economy.

Unlike previous post-war recession, there was record fiscal and monetary support for state and local governments. The nature of this recession was different, in that high-income earners were less affected. As a result, income- and sales-tax revenues held up better than in a typical recession. In addition, an increase in housing prices typified the recovery. That's important for local bonds, which depend primarily on property-tax collections, which reflect housing prices.

Epilogue

The history of business cycles in the United States for two and a half centuries has been an irregular progression through the phases of recovery, expansion, peak, downswing, trough, and then back to recovery. At the time of this writing, the United States has emerged into expansion from a sharp recovery from the COVID recession. The record of business cycles supports the hope of further expansion of business activity in the years to come. Indeed, *The Economist, MoneyWeek,* and *Bloomberg Businessweek* have all run issues with covers addressing the "Roaring Twenties" theme. Only time will tell. The same magazines have run issues addressing the return of inflation. The current recovery is marked by labor shortages, the result of government-contrived scarcity induced by generous unemployment benefits, which reduced incentives to work but also improved household balance sheets. It is also marked by a resurgence of inflation.

It is clear, in hindsight, that the nature of work has changed. Many professionals and white-collar workers continue to work remotely, often in other states. The author is one. Companies are having a hard time recruiting employees and are experimenting with remote work, part-time work, four-day weeks, and other means of recruiting and retaining employees. The nature of education has also changed.

Debt-laden companies withstood the COVID recession far better than many had feared, but the downturn was a unique shock to the economy, more like a natural disaster than a typical recession. A more typical downturn that raises borrowing costs for a longer period and presents more serious damage to household finances would have been more severe.

More than three years after the outbreak of COVID, most agree that the Fed's actions to provide liquidity helped to save the economy from going into a severe depression. The question now is what will the long-term costs and implications of those emergency actions will be, not only for the financial markets and the real economy, but also for the Fed itself as many question the independence of the institution. Only time will tell.

The nation experienced a boom in housing values, in part spurred on by this loose monetary policy. The housing market was already heated up by demographic change, and the Fed has "added fuel to the fire" by buying MBS and suppressing mortgage rates. This is at a time when the housing recovery is solid. This stimulus was clearly not needed. Economists, financial professionals, and historians are only beginning to grasp the implications of the aggressive monetary policy response. Another "boom-and-bust cycle" in the housing market — as we have seen so often in history — may be in the making.

The monetary policies of the Federal Reserve (and other major central banks) during the pandemic were ultra-loose, causing investors to chase returns by taking on greater risks. Some of the best-rewarded risks were in emerging markets. Capital flooded into South America, Africa, and Asia. Governments and the private sector in many emerging markets took on increased borrowing, but with rising interest rates in 2022 and into 2023, the risks for crisis and default are rising. The recent turmoil in banking is the result of loose monetary policy. The result will be tighter credit, which will serve to slow economic exchange.

Monetary policy led to another boom that will likely end in a bust. This is the stock market. The two years after COVID saw rising valuations for technology (or growth) stocks. A handful of companies have accounted for a disproportionate share of the gain in the overall capitalization of equity markets. The stimulus checks provided the funds for many new investors. Prior bubbles in equities (canals and railroads, 1929, dot-com, etc.) have not ended well, and loose monetary policy has contributed to this boom as well. There was a large correction in tech valuations in late-2022, as well as in early-2023 with the collapse of Silicon Valley Bank, whose customer base was the tech industry. The banking turmoil will result in credit tightening.

A final boom that has burst is that for crypto-currencies, the value of which rose six-fold during 2021. The stimulus checks provided the funds for many new investors, but the Federal Reserve (and other central banks) made credit essentially free, which encouraged speculation. Labor shortages resulted in strong wage and salary gains and, along with monies left from the COVID fiscal stimulus, supported consumer spending.

Russia's invasion of the Ukraine has certainly exacerbated supply chain constraints and fostered a rise in energy prices, another potential supply shock. Inflation was running well over 8 percent per year, and the Federal Reserve has entered a tightening cycle. This raised borrowing costs and is resulting in banking sector turmoil. Lending standards tightened. At the time of this writing there were already signs of a weakening economy and talk of recession.

The history of the business cycle indicates alternating periods of expansion (upswings) and contraction (downswings) that have proceeded with a certain irregular but notable rhythm. Business cycles have varied in length, spread, and depth. Upswings have been weak and strong, while downswings have been mild and severe. Some are long, and some are short. They've occurred in an American economy that, during different times in history, could be characterized as pre-industrial agrarian, industrial, and post-industrial in nature. They've occurred in times of market freedom and in times of large government presence. They've occurred in the absence of a central bank and under a central bank. In its long 110-year history, the Federal Reserve has presided over 20 recessions, seven over the last 50 years alone when it has had full policy decision-making in wake of the abandoning of the gold exchange standard in 1971.

Business cycles differ as the patterns of the various cycles vary in their duration and in their ebbs and flows. However, human nature and other forces do not change. As a result, there are many similarities. Throughout our history, business cycles have existed, and they will continue to influence our economy because the same underlying fundamentals that caused previous cycles still exist. One lesson of this history, however, is that we do not learn from history. Understanding the past, however, is essential to forecasting and decision making.

Business leaders who don't pay attention to business cycles are likely to be swept along with the tide. Movements in the business cycle can be foretold if one is willing to spend the needed time studying the fundamental conditions. Edward Yardeni (2018) provides an excellent foundation for "current analysis" of the economy. History shows that there is a certain sequence of events in business cycles. Sometimes one stage runs longer, but the sequence is usually the same.

The story of the American business cycles has been a story of missteps. When every business cycle ends, it reveals problems that seem obvious in hindsight. Over 20 years ago, it was the poor business models of Internet companies as well as accounting frauds. After the Great Financial Crisis, it was Wall Street, where problems have been recurrent throughout history. Understanding where tomorrow's problems may lie is not easy. Business leaders and investors seeking to avoid blow-ups should pay particular attention to the industries, companies, leaders, and securities that encapsulate the boom.

What do all these very different downswings (or recessions) have in common? Unsustainable booms are often concentrated in one major sector of the economy, but also extend to supplying industries. In many cases, the most important single factor is a period of expansionary monetary policy in the years prior to the downswing, sometimes to help fund government war spending, or sometimes in an attempt to re-inflate the economy after the previous recession. Rapid expansion of credit and speculation are important factors leading to inflation and tend to feed themselves for a time, until they don't.

Once the resulting debt bubbles burst, several years' worth of overextended, debt-based ill-advised decisions and investments tend to be wiped out in a process of debt deflation in a relatively short period. This drags down economic exchange and fosters unemployment.

Beyond the underlying monetary trends, real economic shocks also trigger a turning point in the cycle, from expansion into recession. For example, oil price swings appear to be consistent and frequent historical precursors to U.S. downturns, especially in the post-WWII years. In the 19th century, there were often poor harvests. The only thing we can be sure of is that there will be more cycles to come, each different (as with families) in its own way, but also having some similarities with the past.

Business performance depends primarily upon the ability of leaders to anticipate the future. Leaders who have been able to foresee developments have long been leaders, not only in business but also in world affairs. A perusal of the biographies of many of the entrepreneurs and empire builders of the 19th, 20th, and 21st centuries confirm this. In world affairs, Churchill's ability to anticipate the threats from the rise of Nazism is just one example.

While at work, the business leader lives in the future. This is always the case as today's commerce, finance, and industry are in anticipation of tomorrow's requirements. As a result, leaders succeed in business in direct proportion to their ability to forecast the future, whether in trends in society, technology, industry/market dynamics, or in the ebbs and flows of the economy. The leader able to foresee developments has a decided advantage over less fortunate rivals.

In the preface, I cited two quotations, one ancient and one modern. I find both inspiring. I end on another quotation, one from Henry Wadsworth Longfellow, from *The Building of the Ship*:

> "Humanity with all its fears,
> With all the hopes of future years,
> Is hanging breathless on thy fate!"

Bibliography

There is a vast number of books published on business cycle theory and American economic history. This bibliography lists all the books used in this text and some others of interest to anyone wanting to explore the subject later.

Anderson, Benjamin M., *Economics and the Public Welfare: A Financial and Economic History of the United States, 1914-1946.* Indianapolis: Liberty Press, 1979

Anderson, Benjamin M., *Chase Economic Bulletin.* New York: Chase National Bank of the City of New York, various issues

Ayres, Leonard P., *The Chief Cause of This and Other Depressions.* Cleveland: The Cleveland Trust Company, 1935

Ayres, Leonard P., *Turning Points in Business Cycles.* New York: The Macmillan Company, 1939

Ayres, Leonard P., *Diagrams Relating to Turning Points in Business Cycles.* Cleveland: The Cleveland Trust Company, 1949

Babson, Roger W., *Business Barometers for Anticipating Conditions.* Wellesley Hill, MA: Babson Park Company, 1926

Bruner, Robert F. and Carr, Sean D., *The Panic of 1907: Lessons Learned from the Market's Perfect Storm.* Hoboken, NJ: John Wiley & Sons, 2007

Burns, Arthur F., *The Business Cycle in a Changing World.* New York: National Bureau of Economic Research, 1969

Burns, Arthur F. and Mitchell, Wesley C., *Measuring Business Cycles*. New York: National Bureau of Economic Research, 1946

Burton, Theodore E., *Financial Crises and Periods of Industrial and Commercial Depressions*. New York: D. Appleton & Co., 1902

Calverley, John P., *Bubbles and How to Survive Them*. London: Nicholas Brealey Publishing, 2004

Chamberlin. John. *The Enterprising Americans: A Business History of the United States*. New York: Harper & Row Publishers, 1961

Chancellor, Edward, *Devil Take the Hindmost: A History of Financial Speculation*. New York: Penguin Group, 2000

Chancellor, Edward, ed., *Capital Returns: Investing Through the Capital Cycle: A Money Manager's Reports 2002-15*. London: Palgrave, 2016

Clay, Henry, *Economics - An Introduction for the General Reader*. London: MacMillian and Co., 1927

The Cleveland Trust Company, *Business Bulletin*. Cleveland: The Cleveland Trust Company, various issues

Dewey, Davis R., *Financial History of the United States*. New York: Longmans, Green, and Co., 1902

DiLorenzo, Thomas J., *How Capitalism Saved America – The Untold History of our Country, from the Pilgrims to the Present*. New York: Crown Forum, 2004

Dorfman, Joseph, *The Economic Mind in American Civilization – 1606-1865*. New York: The Viking Press, 1946

Dow, Christopher, *Major Recessions – Britain and the World, 1920-1995*. Oxford: Oxford University Press, 1998

Edwards, George W., *The Evolution of Finance Capitalism*. New York: Longmans, Green and Co., 1938

Fels, Rendigs, *American Business Cycles, 1865-1897*. Chapel Hill: The University of North Carolina Press, 1959

Fischer, David H., *The Great Wave: Price Revolutions and the Rhythm of History*. New York: Oxford University Press, 1996

Frickey, Edwin, *Economic Fluctuations in the United States: A Systematic Analysis of Long-Run Trends and Business Cycles, 1866-1914*. Cambridge: Harvard University Press, 1942

Frickey, Edwin, *Production in the United States, 1860-1914*. Cambridge: Harvard University Press, 1947

Friedman, Milton and Schwartz, Anna Jacobson, *A Monetary History of the United States 1867-1960*. Princeton: Princeton University Press, 1963

Friedman, Milton and Schwartz, Anna Jacobson, *The Great Contraction*. Princeton: Princeton University Press, 1965

Gailbraith, John K., *The Great Crash, 1929*. New York: Pelican, 1961

Glasner, David, ed., *Business Cycles and Depressions: An Encyclopedia*. New York: Garland Publishing, 1997

Gordon, John S., *An Empire of Wealth*. New York: HarperCollins, 2004

Gordon, Robert J., ed., *The American Business Cycle*. Chicago: University of Chicago Press, 1986

Gordon, Robert J., *The Rise and Fall of American Growth*. Princeton: Princeton University Press, 2016

Gorton, Gary B., *Misunderstanding Financial Crisis*. Oxford: Oxford University Press, 2012

Grant, James, *Money of the Mind – Borrowing and Lending in America from the Civil War to Michael Milken*. New York: Farrar Straus Giroux, 1992

Grant, James, *The Forgotten Depression: 1921, the Crash that Cured Itself*. New York: Simon & Schuster, 2014

Greenspan, Alan and Wooldridge, Adrian, *Capitalism in America – A History*. New York: Penguin Press, 2018

Guerard, John B., *The Leading Economic Indicators and Business Cycles in the United States*. Cham, Switzerland: Springer, 2022

Haberler, Gottfried, *Prosperity and Depression*. Cambridge, MA: Harvard University Press, 1937

Hall, Thomas E., *Business Cycles: The Nature and Causes of Economic Fluctuations*. New York: Praeger Publishers, 1990

Harvard Economic Service, *Weekly Letter*. Cambridge: Harvard University Committee on Economic Research, various issues

Harwood, E.C., *Cause and Control of the Business Cycle*. Cambridge, MA: The Hampshire Press, 1939

Higgs, Robert, *Depression, War, and Cold War*. Oxford: Oxford University Press, 2006

Homer, Sidney and Sylla, Richard, *A History of Interest Rates*, 4th ed. Hoboken, NJ: John Wiley & Sons, 2005

Howe, Daniel W., *What Hath God Wrought: The Transformation of America*, 1815-1848. New York: Oxford University Press, 2009

Hull, George H., *Industrial Depressions*. Norwood, MA: The Plimpton Press, 1926

Hultgren, Thor, *Cost, Prices, and Profits: Their Cyclical Relations*. New York:National Bureau of Economic Research, 1965

Juglar, Clement, *A Brief History of Panics in the United States*. New York: G.P. Putnam's Sons, 1916

Karabell, Zachary, *Inside Money, Brown Brothers Harriman and the American Wasy of Power*. New York: Penguin Press, 2021

Kates, Steven, *Classical Economic Theory and the Modern Economy*. Cheltenham, UK: Edward Elgar Publishing, 2020

Keynes, John Maynard, *The General Theory of Employment, Interest and Money*. London: Macmillan, 1936.

Krug, J.A., *Production: Wartime achievements and the Reconversion Outlook*. Washington, D.C.: U.S. War Production Board and Government Printing Office, 1945

Lightner, Otto C., *The History of Business Depressions*. New York: The Northeaster Press, 1922

McClay, Wilfred M., *Land of Hope: An Invitation to the Great American Story*. New York: Encounter Books, 2019

Meltzer, Allan H., *A History of the Federal Reserve*. Chicago: University of Chicago Press, 2014

Middlekauff, Robert, *The Glorious Cause: The American Revolution 1763-1789*. New York: Oxford University Press, 2005

Mirowski, Philip, *The Birth of the Business Cycle*. New York: Routledge, 2015

Mitchell, Wesley C., *A History of Greenbacks*. Chicago: University of Chicago Press, 1903

Mitchell, Wesley C., *Business Cycles*. Berkeley: University of California Press, 1913

Mitchell, Wesley C., *Business Cycles: The Problem and Its Setting*. New York, National Bureau of Economic Research, 1927

Mitchell, Wesley C., *What Happens during Business Cycles: A Progress Report*. New York: National Bureau of Economic Research, 1951

Morris, Charles R., *A Rabble of Dead Money – The Great Crash and the Global Depression: 1929-1939*. New York: Public Affairs, 2017

Nettles, Curtis P., *The Emergence of a National Economy, 1775-1815*. New York: Harper & Row, 1969

North, Douglas C., *The Economic Growth of the United States 1790-1860*. Englewood Cliffs: Prentice Hall, 1961

Perkins, Edwin J., *The Economy of Colonial America*. New York: Columbia University Press, 1988

Powell, Jim, *FDR's Folly*. New York: Three Rivers Press, 2003

Quinn, William and Turner, John D., *Boom and Bust – A Global History of Financial Bubbles*. Cambridge: Cambridge University Press, 2020

Reinhart, Carmen M. and Rogoff, Kenneth S., *This time is different: eight centuries of financial folly*. Princeton: Princeton University Press, 2009

Roberts, Alasdair, America's *First Great Depression"; Economic Crisis and Political Disorder after the Panic of 1837*. Ithaca: Cornell University Press, 2012

Say, Jean-Baptiste, *A Treatise on Political Economy*. New Brunswick, NJ: Transaction Publisher, 2001

Schumpeter, Joseph A., *Business Cycles*. New York: McGraw-Hill Book, 1939

Shlaes, Amity. *The Forgotten Man – A New History of the Great Depression*. New York: HarperCollins Publishers, 2007

Silberling, Norman J., *The Dynamics of Business*. New York: McGraw-Hill Book, 1943

Silvia, John E., *Dynamic Economic Decision Making*. Hoboken: John Wiley & Sons, 2011

Skousen, Mark, *The Structure of Production*. New York: New York University Press, 2007

Smiley, Gene, *Rethinking the Great Depression*. Chicago: Ivan R. Dee, 2002

Snyder, Carl, *Business Cycles and Business Measurements*. New York: The MacMillan Company, 1927

Snyder, Carl, *Capitalism the Creator – The Economic Foundations of Modern Industrial Society*. New York: The MacMillan Company, 1940

Sprague, Oliver M., *History of Crises under the National Banking System*. Washington: Government Printing Office, 1910

Strauss, William and Howe, Neil, *The Fourth Turning: An American Prophecy*. New York: Broadway Books, 1997

Temin, Peter, *The Jacksonian Economy*. New York: Norton & Company, 1969

Thorp, William L., *The Annals of the United States of America*. New York: National Bureau of Economic Research, 1926

Wells, David A., *Recent Economic Changes – And their Effect on the Production and Distribution of Wealth and the Well-Being of Society*. New York: D. Appleton and Company, 1889

Wood, Gordon S., *Empire of Liberty – A History of the Early Republic, 1789-1815*. New York: Oxford University Press, 2009

Wright, Robert E., *The Wealth of Nations Rediscovered: Integration and Expansion in American Financial Markets, 1780-1850*. Cambridge: Cambridge University Press, 2002

Yardeni, Edward, *Predicting the Markets*. Brookville, NY: YRI Press, 2018

Yardeni, Edward, *In Praise of Profits*. Brookville, NY: YRI Books, 2021

Zarnowitz, Victor, *Business Cycles, Theory, History, Indicators, and Forecasting*. Chicago: University of Chicago Press, 1992

Zeihan, Peter, *The Accidental Superpower*. NY: Hachette Book Group, 2014

About the Author

With an extensive career as a business economist, Dr. Swift is senior economist for global chemicals at ICIS (Independent Commodity Intelligence Services), where he is responsible for quarterly thought pieces addressing key market dynamics and is demand advisor for long-term supply demand balances. He joined ICIS after retiring as chief economist at the American Chemistry Council (ACC). Prior to joining ACC, Dr. Swift was vice president of research at The Freedonia Group and director of research at Predicasts, where he started as an economist. He is also managing director of Swift Economics LLC, a consultancy providing high quality micro and macroeconomic advice to companies, trade associations, and government.

A long-standing member of the National Association for Business Economics (NABE), for his service as a professional economist and contributions to the profession, he was elected a NABE Fellow. He would later serve as NABE president. Dr. Swift is a member of the Harvard Discussion Group of Industrial Economists and National Business Economics Issues Council. He is a member of *The Wall Street Journal* Forecasters' Survey panel and other forecast survey panels.

Dr. Swift is a graduate of Ashland College with a B.A. in History and Case Western Reserve University with an M.A. in Economics.

He holds a D.B.A. (doctorate in business administration) from Anglia Polytechnic University and has studied at Harvard and Oxford. Dr. Swift is an instructor of economics at Catawba College and previously taught at the University of Mary Washington. He was also a member of the Heritage Council of the Science History Institute.

In addition to his extensive knowledge of industry, his research interests are in business economics and the interaction of strategy, management, and economic developments, especially as they relate to the business cycle and classical economic thought. A specialty is the integration of economic theory with business practice to facilitate decision-making, problem-solving, and planning by management.

Dr. Swift and his wife of 45+ years, Sherry, live near Charlotte, NC where they enjoy spending time with their children and grandchildren near Lake Norman. Other interests include rowing, swimming, reading, stone carving, and dry-stone masonry.

www.ingramcontent.com/pod-product-compliance
Lightning Source LLC
Chambersburg PA
CBHW051607120626
46551CB00014B/1708

* 9 7 9 8 9 8 8 1 8 5 7 1 0 *